D1545126

Early Prehistoric Agriculture

The publication of this book was made possible by generous support from Marianne and J. Michael O'Shaughnessy.

To Emil Haury, Herbert W. Dick,
and all the other pioneering students
of southwestern agriculture.

Early Prehistoric Agriculture

in the American Southwest

W. H. Wills

A School of American Research Resident Scholar Book

School of American Research Press : Santa Fe, New Mexico

SCHOOL OF AMERICAN RESEARCH PRESS
Post Office Box 2188
Santa Fe, New Mexico 87504-2188
Phone   (505) 984-0741

DIRECTOR OF PUBLICATIONS: Jane Kepp
EDITOR: Tom Ireland
DESIGNER: Deborah Flynn Post
TYPOGRAPHER: Casa Sin Nombre
PRINTER: BookCrafters

DISTRIBUTED BY UNIVERSITY OF WASHINGTON PRESS

Library of Congress Cataloging-in-Publication Data
Wills, W. H. (Wirt Henry)
Early prehistoric agriculture in the American Southwest /
    W. H. Wills—1st ed.
    p.   c.m.
"A School of American Research resident scholar book."
Revision of the author's thesis.
Bibliography: p.   Includes index.
ISBN   0-933452-25-X :$27.50

1. Indians of North America—Southwest, New—Agriculture.
2. Indians of North America—Southwest, New—Antiquities.
3. Agriculture—Southwest, New—Origin. 4. Southwest, New—
Antiquities I. School of American Research (Santa Fe, N.M.)
II. Title.
E78.S7W56 1988   630'.979—dc19   88-23591   CIP

Contents

Illustrations

Tables

Preface

This book is a revised version of my dissertation, which I wrote in 1984–85 as a Weatherhead resident scholar at the School of American Research. Thereafter, I had the wonderful opportunity to work at the Smithsonian Institution under a postdoctoral fellowship, and I was able to think more widely about a number of issues related to agricultural origins. Consequently I have modified some of my original conclusions and refined the basic arguments for this book. In addition, a number of important studies of prehistoric southwestern agriculture have been published since then, and I have tried to incorporate these as much as possible.

Other southwestern archaeologists may see this book as a reevaluation of the important early agricultural site of Bat Cave. In many respects it is. New interpretations of the Bat Cave stratigraphy based on fieldwork by the University of Michigan in 1981 and 1983 are summarized here for the first time. I must emphasize, however, that my object in this study is not to produce a Bat Cave site report but to gain perspective on the adoption of domesticated plants by hunter-gatherers. There will be a new site report published in the near future, and the information in this book is only a small portion of what has been obtained by recent investigations.

In the same respect, this book is not about the culture history of the preceramic period in the Southwest, although I have spent considerable effort discussing the empirical basis of the cultural models that are currently in use. I am concerned that we often confuse our arbitrary classifications of artifacts with biological or cultural entities such as populations or ethnic groups, and in doing so we make it difficult to fully appreciate economic developments such as the shift to food production. I have been critical of certain models of culture change because they do not seem appropriate to the question of agricultural adoption, not because I am proposing new models.

This presentation is more concise than the dissertation. The reader can find more detailed discussion of some subjects in the original study, particularly paleoenvironmental change. I should point out that the argumentative structure of the book often involves interpretations based on other interpretations. For example, I suggest that patterning in regional radiocarbon chronologies can be understood in terms of changing vegetation patterns, which are themselves interpretations. The result is what I consider a plausible argument, supported with available empirical observations. Nevertheless, the reader should watch out for the various articles of faith as they slip past.

Finally, I want to emphasize that this book is very much a child of cooperation. The pleasure of reworking a dissertation (if there is any pleasure in it) is that it brings together a new group of people, including editors, reviewers, and illustrators. I have been immensely fortunate to find friendship and support in this group. My thanks begin and end with the School of American Research and Douglas Schwartz, who provided the time to write the dissertation through a Weatherhead fellowship and the impetus to publish it. Jane Kepp and Tom Ireland were thoughtful and patient editors who made a difficult process actually pleasant. Many of the illustrations were drawn by Katrina Lasko, and Douglas Easton prepared the index. Jeff Dean and an anonymous reviewer taught me lessons about clarity, logic, and humility that I hope never to forget. Dick Ford and John Speth continue to be stimulating and helpful friends, as they were as members of my dissertation committee at the University of Michigan, and Steve Plog, Mindy Zeder, Bruce Smith, and Bill Merrill have added greatly to the further development of ideas that appear in this book. Herb Dick made much of my research possible through his generous sharing of information and experience. In many ways, this book should be seen as a continuation of efforts that he began forty years ago. I thank them all, and I hope they always share themselves with other young archaeologists as much as they have with me.

Introduction

The cultivation of domesticated plants by prehistoric hunter-gatherers profoundly changed the relationship between these societies and their environment. Farming is an economic strategy predicated on the manipulation of plant biogeography and productivity. In contrast to foraging strategies, which respond largely to natural resource availability, the use of domesticates signals an investment in actually managing the availability of future resources by controlling plant ecology and physiology.

The active participation by humans in structuring future resource availability through agriculture has long been considered a major development in human evolution, in large part because domesticate husbandry entails significant economic correlates, such as land tenure and surplus production, that underwrite complex forms of social structure (Bender 1978, 1981). The conditions leading to the decision by hunter-gatherers to develop or adopt modes of production based on domesticated plants are therefore immensely important to understanding the development of different socioeconomic forms.

My objective in this book is to present a general economic explanation for the decision-making process that resulted in the adoption of fully domesticated plants by prehistoric hunter-gatherers in the American Southwest. My immediate concern is thus with the dispersal of food production strategies based on domesticated plants, rather than with the hunting-gathering strategies which produced domesticates (see Flannery 1973, 1986; Reynolds 1981; Lowe 1985). I assess this construct by considering as a case study the initial introduction of domesticated plants into the area of west-central New Mexico and east-central Arizona known as the Mogollon Highlands (Haury 1962).

I will argue that the decision to adopt fully domesticated plants can be understood as a product of selective advantage for enhanced resource predictability. I view domesticated plants as sources of information as well as food, and their value to a population should be examined from both perspectives.

Throughout this study, the cultivation of domesticates by human groups will be termed "agriculture." This is primarily a matter of convenience, for there are analytical problems in the study of food production that do not accommodate so general a definition (see Green 1980). As used in this study, agriculture carries no implications for field sizes, crop variety, or dietary dependence; it is only the cultivation of domesticates.

PREVIOUS INVESTIGATIONS
OF EARLY SOUTHWESTERN AGRICULTURE

The study of the introduction of domesticated plants into the southwestern United States has been, until quite recently, almost exclusively an interest in plant geography. Maize, squash, and beans are tropical plants domesticated in Mesoamerica, and their presence in prehistoric North America has, with few exceptions (e.g., Edmonson 1961), been viewed as an example of diffusion from the south.

Carter's (1945) seminal study of prehistoric agriculture, *Plant Geography and Culture History in the American Southwest*, set a tone that continues to influence prehistorians in the region today. He established an analytic framework emphasizing the current distribution of domesticates as the key to their origin and cultural affiliation. Carter also posited a series of limiting relationships between specific cultigens and climate regimes and presented the agricultural practices of modern Indian tribes as analogs for various prehistoric agricultural strategies.

For many years after Carter's study, early agricultural research in the Southwest fell largely to botanists working with ethnographic or archaeological material. Their interests were, understandably, oriented toward explaining morphological variability in the plants (e.g., Sauer 1952; Weatherwax 1950; Anderson 1947; Cutler 1968; Mangelsdorf 1950, 1958, 1974; Mangelsdorf and Smith 1949; Mangelsdorf and Lister 1956; Galinat 1979; Galinat and Campbell 1967; Gentry 1969; Kaplan 1956, 1965, 1981). Although archaeology provided the data for these studies (Ford 1981:1), the questions being addressed were largely issues of botany, not archaeology.

The first significant attempt by an archaeologist to synthesize the botanical information on early agriculture in terms of cultural development was

Haury's (1962). He proposed a model for the initial introduction of cultivars into the Southwest that relied implicitly on the concepts of climatic limits and "useful areas" suggested earlier by Carter (1945:84–85). Specifically, Haury assumed that domesticated plants entered the Southwest through a "highland corridor" in the Sierra Madre Occidental of Mexico. He believed that higher elevations offered climatic conditions more favorable to the tropical domesticates, especially maize, than did lower, hotter desert regions.

Carter did not have the archaeological evidence to support such a route (1945:106), but Haury did. Preceramic maize found in rockshelters along the eastern edge of the Sierra Madre in Chihuahua, Mexico (Mangelsdorf and Lister 1956; Lister 1958), and in rockshelters of the mountains in west-central New Mexico appeared to confirm the Sierra Madre corridor hypothesis. Haury (1962:116) argued that maize had entered the Southwest through this corridor by 4500 B.P. but was then confined to the Mogollon Highlands until about 2500 B.P., at which point it dispersed rapidly to other parts of the Southwest (fig. 1). The ecological restriction of maize to upland locations in Haury's model continues to be the current general archaeological position on initial agriculture in the region (Ford 1981; Minnis 1985; Hunter-Anderson 1986).

Haury's model was founded on the observation that preceramic maize discovered in 1948 at Bat Cave in west-central New Mexico was associated with radiocarbon dates of approximately 6000 and 5600 B.P. (Mangelsdorf and Smith 1949; Mangelsdorf 1950; Dick 1954; see also Dick 1965). The next oldest dates, however, were at 2400 B.P. from Tularosa Cave, only 30 km from Bat Cave (Martin et al. 1952). Haury interpreted this pattern to mean that maize, and perhaps squash and beans, reached the area around Bat Cave quite early, was maintained within the local economy as an unimportant dietary supplement, and did not become widely utilized until nearly two thousand years later.

Haury's interpretation has been extremely influential, and it is still commonly assumed that maize had little economic value to indigenous populations when it was first introduced to the Southwest (e.g., Woodbury and Zubrow 1979; LeBlanc 1982). It is important to remember, however, that Haury's perception of economic unimportance derived from the need to explain the singular presence of agriculture at Bat Cave for two thousand years before it appeared elsewhere.

Despite the general acceptance of Haury's model, there has been dissatisfaction with the early Bat Cave dates nearly from the moment of their publication. Simply because the samples from Bat Cave were among the first archaeological samples submitted for radiocarbon assay, they are suspect due to the unreliable solid carbon processing of the times. But the real concern has always been whether the association between dates and maize was accurate, since the maize itself was not dated (F. Johnson 1955:154; Eggan 1961:87; Jennings 1967:123).

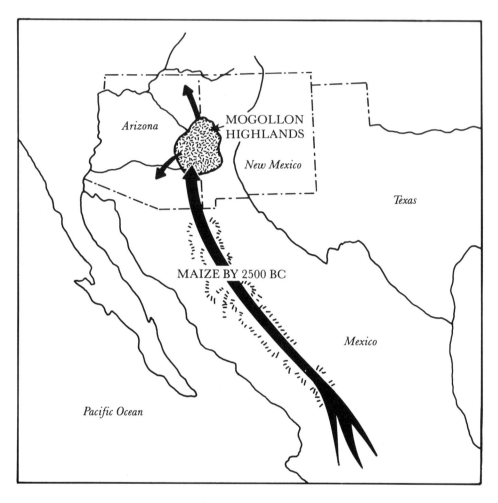

Figure 1. Haury's corridor model for the introduction of maize agriculture into the American Southwest (after Haury 1962).

Publication of the Bat Cave site report (Dick 1965) did not help substantiate the reliability of that association, and discussion about the acceptable age for the earliest maize from the site has continued (Ford 1981; Berry 1982; Minnis 1985). Nevertheless, the central feature of Haury's model—the temporal priority of the Mogollon Highlands for the acceptance of maize—remains intact (Schroeder 1965; Woodbury and Zubrow 1979; Ford 1981, 1984; Berry 1982; Minnis 1985). Along with it persists the assumption that ecologically favorable conditions for cultivation are a likely explanation for the pattern.

Recently, several proposals have been offered for understanding the cultural process of introduction which move away from certain aspects of the traditional model. Berry (1982), for example, has suggested that agriculture came to the Southwest with migrating farmers. In Berry's view, maize and squash appeared rapidly in highland areas in contexts where the artifacts and site architecture show little continuity with those of preceding time periods. He sees the first agriculture as a form of "colonization" (1982:33), with farmers expanding into areas appropriate for cultivation. Berry's model maintains the presumption of more favorable growing conditions in highland areas than at lower elevations.

A second proposal has been outlined by Ford (1984), who argues that the potential productivity of maize and squash was much greater than that of the relatively unreliable wild resources in pinyon-juniper woodlands. The acceptance of maize and squash thus is explicable as a means of enhancing resource security or predictability (see also Cordell 1984:184). Ford's argument is similar to a suggestion by Irwin-Williams (1973:9–10), who considered early southwestern maize to have been a minor dietary component, but one which "presented a relatively concentrated, relatively reliable and seasonally abundant resource, which could for the first time provide a source of localized temporary seasonal surplus."

In a recent overview of early Southwest agriculture, Minnis (1985) proposed two competing but possibly reconcilable models for cultigen acceptance, his "Model of Necessity" and "Model of Opportunity." In the first model, some form of stress leads to a need to intensify food supply. The second model is seen as a sort of insurance strategy that enhanced resource security without requiring any great labor investment. Minnis (1985:310) appears to favor the opportunistic model, for he describes the acceptance of cultigens by southwestern hunter-gatherers as a "monumental nonevent"—a perception shared by Irwin-Williams (1973), Ford (1981), and Cordell (1984). The stress-induced model is more consistent with the views of Whalen (1973), Glassow (1980), and perhaps Berry (1982; Berry and Berry 1986) and LeBlanc (1982). But as Minnis notes, the differences between stress and opportunistic processes or motives are not so distinct in reality or in theory as their assignment to separate models would imply. Indeed, I believe that these two processes are not so much different as complementary, and Minnis's broadly drawn models serve to emphasize the value in integrating them rather than contrasting them.

Hunter-Anderson (1986) has recently offered an ambitious attempt to explain the emergence of agriculture in the Southwest as a process of resource intensification resulting from increasing population. Her focus on density-dependent influences on hunter-gatherer mobility is very similar to mine, but her analytical approach has the curious quality of not addressing the issue of adoption of domesticates by hunter-gatherers.

Hunter-Anderson apparently views the beginnings of agriculture in the Southwest as an indigenous process of domestication (1986:33) and as an inevitable product of increasing population. Whatever the theoretical merits of this position, it allows Hunter-Anderson to ignore the timing of the appearance of domesticated plants in the Southwest after diffusion from Mesoamerica. This timing is immensely important because the date of acceptance reveals the environmental and social contexts of adoption. Despite the heavy emphasis Hunter-Anderson places on environment and demography as causal variables, she relies on twentieth-century environmental patterns in formulating her model. She treats demographic change as a given, and the shift to cultivation as a marker of relatively high density. But because significant environmental changes have occurred in the Southwest over the last several millenia, Hunter-Anderson's study appears limited by not attending to them.

Lack of concern for the specifics of when and where agricultural development actually took place may account for Hunter-Anderson's selection of data derived from archaeological sites postdating 500 A.D. Since she accepts a 3000 B.C. date for maize at Bat Cave (1986:103), nearly thirty-five hundred years earlier than the sites she examines, their relevance for understanding the shift to cultivation seems strained. In fact, Hunter-Anderson's interesting study appears aimed more at understanding these sites than the emergence of agricultural economies.

These departures from the traditional concern with geography and culture history are difficult to evaluate because almost all the primary data for early agriculture were collected between 1948 and 1955 and are generally not suited to the complex issues raised by recent modelling efforts (see Ford 1981). Moreover, since understanding the initial introduction process requires reliable dating of the earliest appearance of cultigens, the early dates from Bat Cave present an empirical problem which remains unresolved. Attempts such as Berry's (1982) to settle the issue on the basis of published data only accent the ambiguities, because the reliability cannot be proved or disproved.

In the following chapters I will offer a series of theoretical positions and empirical studies designed to consider the probable chronological and geographical dimensions of initial agricultural production in the Southwest. Existing data will be reevaluated in conjunction with new information obtained from excavations at Bat Cave and survey in the San Augustine Plains. In summarizing these data, I will suggest that current models of the transition to agriculture in the Southwest have misidentified both the temporal and geographical characteristics of this transformation and have inadvertently conceptualized the process as being far less complex than now seems likely. In turn, I attempt to reconcile the results of recent studies with an evolutionary perspective on the adoption of domesticates by hunter-gatherers that focuses on density-dependent behavioral changes.

1

Culture-Historical Perspectives
on Early Southwestern Agriculture

Most archaeologists working in the Southwest today would not hesitate to acknowledge that culture-historical frameworks provide descriptions of change, rather than explanations. That recognition follows a general perception within archaeology that culture history and explanation are somehow fundamentally dissimilar, often expressed as the difference between empirical pattern recognition and theory building. Culture history is, however, anything but independent of theory, since what is "empirical" depends on assumptions about what is important to recognize and record. In this chapter I consider the significance of culture-historical models for the introduction of agriculture into the Southwest. I have elected to present this discussion before providing a theoretical position on the adoption process because it helps point out how culture-historical thinking can affect theoretical interpretations.

BACKGROUND

Accurately dating the first introduction of domesticated plants into the Southwest is critical in establishing the social context for the process. Although the earliest dates for prehistoric southwestern domesticates have been the subject of ongoing discussion (e.g., Ford 1981; Berry 1982; Simmons 1984, 1986), there is firm evidence that maize and squash arrived in the Southwest prior to ceramic manufacture, sometime before two thousand years ago.

This places the transmission process at least at the end of the preceramic period, usually referred to as the Late Archaic. The Archaic in the Southwest is an extensive period (ca. 10,000 to 2000 B.P.) of indigenous hunter-gatherer adaptation and development. For decades, southwestern prehistorians have used the Desert Culture concept proposed by Jennings (1978) to describe the Archaic as a culturally conservative, stable adaptation based on group mobility and the utilization of numerous plant resources and small game (e.g., Taylor 1956; Longacre 1962; Irwin-Williams 1967). In many ways, the Archaic has been portrayed as much in contrast to a preceding Paleo-Indian "big-game" adaptation as in terms of its own cultural integrity (see Irwin-Williams and Haynes 1970; Bayham 1979; Sayles 1983).

The Southwest Archaic is usually seen as diverging gradually from the basic Desert Culture pattern under the influence of local historical processes associated with adaptations to varying environmental niches. This differentiation culminates in the inception of the ceramic period (Kidder 1954; Jennings 1955; Schroeder 1965; Irwin-Williams 1967; Cordell 1984; Wendorf and Thomas 1951).

The history of divergence and evolution through the Archaic to the ceramic period in the Southwest has been described by two models of cultural change (fig. 2). The first is called the Cochise Culture and refers to the preceramic period in the Sonoran desert areas of the southern Southwest (Sayles and Antevs 1941; Sayles 1983). The second is the Oshara Tradition, which outlines the preceramic for the central Rio Grande Valley and the northern Southwest (Irwin-Williams 1973, 1979).

The Cochise Culture was proposed as an interpretive device for organizing a series of geologically superimposed aceramic sites in southeastern Arizona. The superimposition indicated the relative ages of the sites, which provided a basis for comparing technology and site structure between time periods. Since the differences between noncontemporaneous sites were not very great, it was assumed that a "genetic" relationship existed between sites of each time period, with each successive period representing an evolution from the preceding one. For this reason, the time periods were labelled "stages"; each was a step forward in the indigenous development of a local culture. With the exception, perhaps, of the Big Bend sequence in southwest Texas (Kelley, Campbell, and Lehmer 1940), the Cochise Culture was the first regional developmental outline in the Southwest which covered the entire Archaic period.

By contrast, the Oshara Tradition is based on a local sequence in northern New Mexico, coupled with a synthesis of published preceramic studies from other regions. The primary data upon which the Oshara Tradition is constructed have not been published, making it difficult to assess differences between the temporal phases which constitute it (Cordell 1979; Judge 1981;

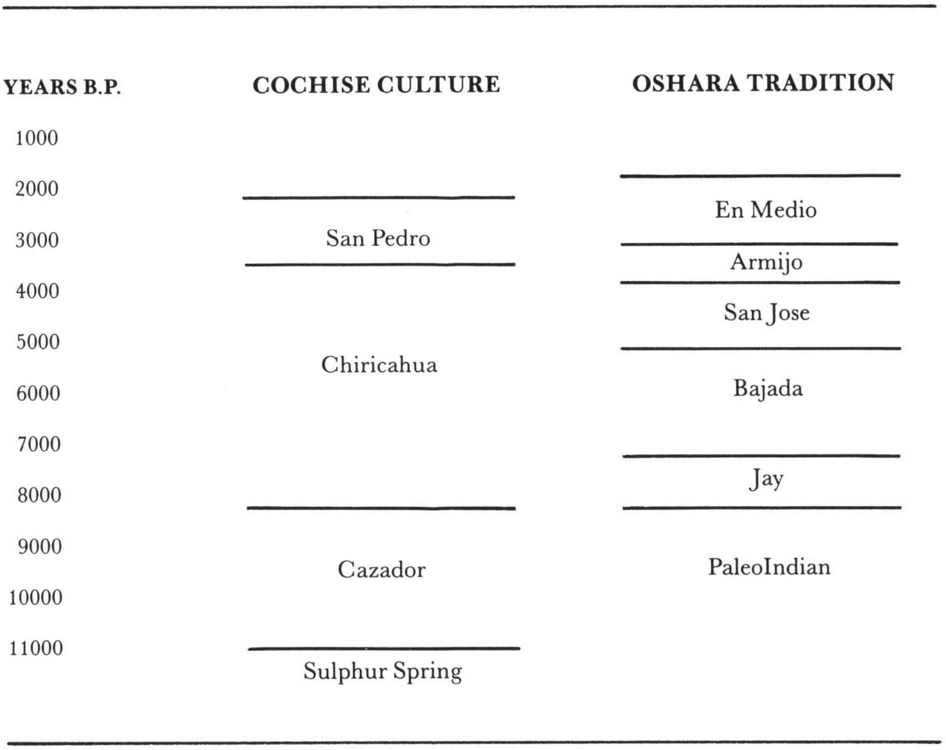

YEARS B.P.	COCHISE CULTURE	OSHARA TRADITION
1000		
2000	————————	————————
3000	San Pedro	En Medio
		————————
4000	————————	Armijo
		————————
5000		San Jose
	Chiricahua	————————
6000		Bajada
7000		————————
8000	————————	Jay
		————————
9000	Cazador	PaleoIndian
10000		
11000	————————	
	Sulphur Spring	

Figure 2. Comparison of stages in two models of cultural change in the Southwest: the Cochise Culture and the Oshara Tradition. Data from Sayles (1983) and Irwin-Williams (1973, 1979).

Simmons 1984; Berry 1982; Berry and Berry 1986). Nevertheless, the Oshara sequence appears to be very much like the Cochise in differentiating time periods on the basis of technological variability in lithic assemblages. The Oshara model, however, places more emphasis than the Cochise on interpreting changing site composition and structure in terms of subsistence change and population growth. And unlike the Cochise, the Oshara construct was originally proposed to explain widespread variability in preceramic materials in terms of cultural evolution (Irwin-Williams 1973:2).

The geographical distinction between the Cochise Culture and the Oshara Tradition has become equated with a distinction between actual biological populations, in the sense that a boundary is thought to have existed between the two proposed cultural entities (see especially Beckett 1973). Recently, archaeologists working with Archaic materials in northern New Mexico have identified Cochise or Cochise-like "intrusions" into the Oshara area (Beckett 1973; Lang 1977, 1980; Baker 1981; Waber, Hubbell, and Wood 1982; Beal 1984; see also Irwin-Williams 1968:52).

Underlying this belief in preceramic cultural boundaries is a series of unstated assumptions about hunter-gatherer organization and about the role of style in egalitarian societies. The fundamental tenet is that material culture varies spatially with social or cultural corporateness. Specifically, the geographical boundaries of the Cochise Culture and the Oshara Tradition—as prehistoric cultural entities—are assumed to covary with the distribution of artifact types considered diagnostic of each. Similarly, the different phases within each culture-historical outline—also seen as cultural entities—are given spatial limits based on the occurrence of diagnostic artifacts (e.g. Irwin-Williams and Haynes 1970).

The perception of preceramic cultural boundaries in the Archaic has strongly influenced discussions of the introduction of cultigens into the Southwest. The first cultigens to reach the Southwest are generally, if not universally, believed to have been transmitted through the Cochise cultural system (Martin et al. 1952; Kidder 1954; Haury 1962; Dick 1965; Irwin-Williams 1967; Whalen 1973; Martin and Plog 1973; Woodbury and Zubrow 1979). The reason for this belief is that the earliest agricultural sites have been assigned to the Cochise Culture on the basis of their associated artifact assemblages.

The assignment of early agriculture to the Cochise Culture implies that there was something about the Cochise which was receptive to cultivation, while other, contemporaneous preceramic cultures were not (cf. Woodbury and Zubrow 1979). Because the dates for the early sites (especially Bat Cave) were so much earlier than dates for the first evidence of agriculture in non-Cochise sites, it has been assumed that for a long time the Cochise practiced a casual form of cultivation that later diffused to other cultural groups (F. Johnson 1955:150; Haury 1962; Woodbury and Zubrow 1979).

If the early involvement of Cochise groups with cultivation is correct, then the nature of the Cochise Culture ought to be of fundamental significance in understanding the process of acceptance. In the remainder of this chapter, however, I will argue that there is actually very little evidence for considering the traditional earliest agricultural sites in the Southwest to be Cochise, and that the processes of acceptance have been obscured by the geographical and cultural implications that are part of the Cochise Culture construct.

COCHISE CULTURE SITES AND EARLY AGRICULTURE

The early agricultural sites in the Southwest traditionally assigned to the Cochise Culture include Bat Cave (Dick 1965; Mangelsdorf 1974), Tularosa Cave (Martin et al. 1952), Cordova Cave (Martin et al. 1952; Kaplan 1963), and Cienega Creek (Haury 1957; Martin and Schoenwetter 1960). Their associated dates are given in table 1; discussions of the sites can be found in Martin and Plog (1973), Woodbury and Zubrow (1979), Berry (1982), Ford (1981), and Minnis (1985).

All of these sites lie in the Mogollon Highlands (fig. 3), a pattern which led to Haury's highland corridor hypothesis (1962). Each site was assigned to the Cochise Culture on the basis of perceived similarities in artifacts, and thus the cultigens in this montane region were seen as having passed through southeastern Arizona first (Whalen 1973; Haury 1962). Since the process of transmission is considered a function of the Cochise Culture, it is important to consider how each of these early sites was given a Cochise label.

TABLE 1. *Radiocarbon Dates Obtained before 1981 from Preceramic Sites in the Mogollon Highlands*

Site	Material	Date (B.P.)[a]	Lab No.[b]	Reference
Tularosa Cave	maize cobs	2223 ± 200	C-584	Libby 1955
Tularosa Cave	maize cobs	2112 ± 230	C-585	Libby 1955
Tularosa Cave	bark	2177 ± 225	C-585	Libby 1955
Tularosa Cave	cobs, plants	3200 ± 200	C-612	Libby 1955
Tularosa Cave	maize cobs	1810 ± 100	M-716	Crane and Griffin 1960
Tularosa Cave	charcoal	2080 ± 100	M-715	Crane and Griffin 1960
O Block Cave	charcoal	2780 ± 100	M-717	Crane and Griffin 1960
O Block Cave	charcoal	2600 ± 100	M-718	Crane and Griffin 1960
Wet Legget	charcoal	4508 ± 680	C-556	Libby 1955
Bat Cave	wood	2239 ± 250	C-172	Libby 1955
Bat Cave	cobs, wood	2249 ± 250	C-164, C-171	Libby 1955
Bat Cave	wood	2862 ± 250	C-170	Libby 1955
Bat Cave	charcoal	2048 ± 170	C-570	Libby 1955
Bat Cave	charcoal	2816 ± 200	C-569	Libby 1955
Bat Cave	charcoal	5605 ± 290	C-571	Libby 1955
Bat Cave	charcoal	5931 ± 310	C-573	Libby 1955

NOTE: Some dates from Bat Cave are not shown, nor are any of the dates from the Cienega Creek site.
[a]Original dates. No corrections have been made.
[b]Laboratory number. C = Chicago; M = Michigan. Sample C-585 was originally presented as an average of the two determinations given here (see Libby 1955).

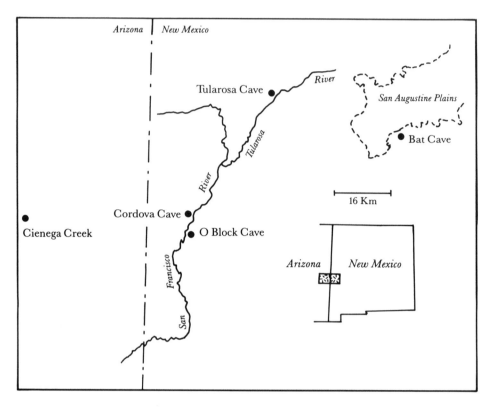

Figure 3. Early agricultural sites in the Mogollon Highlands.

The Cochise Sequence

The Cochise Culture is divided into four stages, each representing an outgrowth of the previous stage (fig. 2). Agriculture purportedly appears in the Chiricahua stage, based on the occurrence of maize at Bat Cave and maize pollen at Cienega Creek in levels assigned to the Chiricahua stage. Maize and squash are also present in the subsequent San Pedro stage, represented at all the preceramic sites in the Mogollon Highlands.

The Chiricahua stage lasted about five thousand years, from 8000 to 3000 B.P., a period Sayles (1983) recognized as one of continuity in the artifactual record. Chiricahua assemblages are discernible more by lack of consistency than by regularity; as described by Sayles (1983:114), the "assemblage is characterized by a wide range of traits occurring in varied association." Part of the pattern was an increase in the diversity and frequency of chipped stone artifacts over the previous stage. Ground stone artifacts exhibited continuity in size and shape with those of earlier stages, with the exception that basin metates were deeper in the Chiricahua.

The San Pedro stage (3000 to 2000 B.P.) is defined primarily from eleven alluvial sites in the San Pedro River Valley (Sayles 1983:125). Five of the eleven sites had shallow pits which have been cautiously interpreted as house structures (Sayles 1945; 1983:125). Bell-shaped pits were associated with these sites, and at least four sites produced burials. The San Pedro stage immediately precedes the introduction of fully developed ceramic manufacturing to southern Arizona and is therefore considered the direct progenitor of the early Mogollon occupation in the region (Haury 1950).

San Pedro sites are fairly common in southeastern Arizona (e.g., Cattanach 1966; Whalen 1973; Windmiller 1973; Huckell 1973a, 1973b). Their diagnostic characteristic is the San Pedro projectile point, a side-notched form with a relatively long blade (Sayles and Antevs 1941:24; Haury 1950). The general form occurs widely throughout the Southwest during the late Archaic, from north-central Mexico (Fay 1955, 1956, 1967, 1968) to southern Colorado (Morris and Burgh 1954).

Radiocarbon dates from type sites of the San Pedro stage, published by Sayles (1983), are relatively limited, and while numerous dates from the San Pedro time span are known (Haynes and Haas 1974), only a few have been reported with diagnostic cultural material. The original description of the San Pedro stage, and the Cochise Culture in general, was elaborated by Haury's work at Ventana Cave in south-central Arizona (1950; see also Bayham 1982). Ventana Cave is one of the major Archaic sites in the Southwest, and its stratigraphic sequence was described in terms of Sayles and Antevs's Cochise-stage classification.

A great deal of new artifactual information, especially in the area of projectile point variability, was added to the Cochise outline by the Ventana Cave research. In Sayles's (1983) final summation of the Cochise sequence, many diagnostic artifact types were, in fact, illustrated with Ventana Cave specimens.

The assignment of Ventana Cave levels to different Cochise stages has been criticized, primarily because the stratigraphic distribution of diagnostic projectile points did not conform perfectly to the sequence proposed by Sayles and Antevs (Chapman 1980; Duncan 1971). Haury was aware of the problem, and designated the lower portion of the Ventana Cave sequence as Chiricahua-Amargosa II, as a way of attributing some of the stratigraphic ambiguity to cultural influences from the west (1950:535). Haury also noted the problem of stratigraphic mixing in the rockshelter, an issue which critics of the sequence have apparently not accepted as valid. Nevertheless, the issue here is not whether the different stages actually exist, but simply whether the early agricultural sites assigned to those stages fit the classificatory criteria.

The Wet Legget Arroyo Site

The Wet Legget site yielded no remains of domesticated plants, but it is relevant to the question of cultural context for early agriculture because it was the first site in the Mogollon Highlands assigned to the Cochise Culture. It therefore established the precedent whereby other preceramic sites were considered to be Cochise.

The Wet Legget site is located in Pine Lawn Valley, a small tributary to the San Francisco River between the San Francisco and Saliz mountains (fig. 3). The site consisted of artifacts eroding out of an arroyo wall and exposed on the nearby ground surface (Quimby 1949). Lithic material was found over a 1-km stretch of the arroyo, but at least eight distinct surface concentrations were noted. Antevs (1949:57), who described the alluvial geology, estimated that some of the geologic beds dated between 5000 and 3500 B.P., an age later confirmed by a radiocarbon date of 4508 ± 680 B.P. (C-556) from charcoal in the arroyo wall (Libby 1955:113).

Although the Wet Legget artifacts were described as Archaic in age, it should be noted that most of the material was on the surface (labelled "bed c"), a geological stratum interpreted as postdating the Archaic (Antevs 1949:56–59). Moreover, the artifacts found in the sides of the arroyo were described as in situ with some circumspection; the site report refers to them as "probably" in place. Excavation in the arroyo walls failed to locate any artifacts (Antevs 1949:56–59).

The Wet Legget artifacts were considered Chiricahua Cochise on the basis of two criteria: the proportion of chipped stone to ground stone, and the morphology of the ground stone artifacts. The proportion of chipped stone to ground stone was mistakenly reported as 4:1 instead of the correct 3:1 (see Martin, Rinaldo, and Antevs 1949:60), but the investigators felt that the ratio was more in line with the Chiricahua stage (5:1) than any other known preceramic cultural period.

However, it was the Wet Legget ground stone that was central to the perception that the site belonged to the Cochise Culture. Six of the seven metates found at the site were shallow-basin or slab types "like those most frequent in the sites of the Chiricahua Stage" (Martin, Rinaldo, and Antevs 1949:62). Three manos were "smaller, thinner and lighter than the large, heavy, round typical San Pedro types." The simple act of comparing these manos to San Pedro artifacts implied that they were Cochise, and Chiricahua stage by default.

The excavators summarized the Wet Legget site, and its Cochise affiliation, as follows:

> In summary, then, it might be said that the proportion of ground stone implements to chipped stone implements at the Wet Legget site is more

> like that of the Cochise culture than like that of any of the other known
> Southwestern non-pottery horizons of equal age. Typologically, the Wet
> Legget complex is most like that of the Chiricahua stage of the Cochise
> culture both in ground stone implements and in the majority of the
> chipped stone implements, although in the chipped stone artifact types
> there are deviations which would establish the Wet Legget complex as a
> variant of the Cochise culture. (Martin, Rinaldo, and Antevs 1949:63)

The importance of the Wet Legget material is that it provided the basis for
subsequent preceramic studies in the region. It gave evidence for the presence
of humans in the area between 5000 and 3500 B.P., and its excavators labelled
those people Cochise. The Cochise assignment was made because of visually
perceived similarities in small samples of lithic artifacts, and neither the
proportions of different tool classes nor the precise shapes of the tools had to
duplicate the diagnostic Cochise material in southern Arizona to which it was
putatively related.

The flexibility of the classificatory criteria employed at the Wet Legget site
was partially the product of the primary research focus among the investigators. Their main goal was to explain why the Mogollon ceramic tradition was
different from other southwestern ceramic traditions (Martin, Rinaldo, and
Antevs 1949:17). Consequently, variation in the preceramic record was interpreted as the first indication of a developmental shift away from the Desert
Culture pattern and toward the distinctiveness of the Mogollon.

However, the classificatory procedures were not founded so much on objective assessment of similarities in lithic artifacts as on the lack of comparative
bases. Consider the following descriptions of the original Chiricahua-stage
ground stone. Sayles and Antevs (1941) divided the ground stone into two categories, handstones and milling stones.

> The majority of the handstones are small, one-hand types; the dis-
> tinctive ones are pitted, wedge-shaped, multiface, or concave. Many
> of them are symmetrical, mostly ovoid, although some are quad-
> rilateral in outline. The others range from asymmetrical stones,
> showing but little use, to those on which the surface shows a great
> deal of use. The latter are normally flat along the surface of the long
> axis, but convex with that [sic] of the short axis. A few of the larger
> types are convex over the entire grinding surface. (Sayles and Antevs
> 1941:17–18)

Contrast that description with the following for the San Pedro stage:

> The handstones, without exception, are of larger size than those
> found in earlier stages, though many of them are nothing more than
> an evolutionary step from earlier models. The least distinctive are

asymmetrical stones, showing little use, ranging to those with well-worn surfaces. There are also pitted, multi-face, and wedge-shaped types. Characteristic of this stage and paralleling the development of the deep basin milling stone, are large handstones with a convex grinding surface. (Sayles and Antevs 1941:24)

A careful reading of these two sets of classificatory criteria finds little differentiation beyond size. Milling stones exhibited a similar lack of variation between the Chiricahua and San Pedro stages. Chiricahua milling stones were described as follows:

Several variations in milling stones are represented by hand-size flat pebbles with worn surfaces showing that they had been used as some sort of abrading stone. All of this type show only slight use. The basin milling stones are more distinctive. These have either a small, shallow oval basin near the center of the stone with the adjacent surface unused; or a deep, large basin sometimes covering the greater part of the stone's surface. (Sayles and Antevs 1941:18)

In the San Pedro stage, however, "the typical milling stone is a large type with a deep oval basin" (1941:24). As with handstones, the criteria for distinguishing Chiricahua from San Pedro milling stones are not especially distinctive, and unlike handstones, milling stones from different stages cannot be discriminated by size.

Thus there is considerable ambiguity in the published descriptions of "typical" stage diagnostics. The criteria even suggest that some variability might be accounted for by factors such as use-life and curation (see Schiffer 1976). Consequently, limited numbers of specimens are probably not a very good means of defining stage affiliation, and any cultural implications associated with such correlations need to be carefully evaluated.

To illustrate this point, I compare the sizes of oval manos from three sites representing three different time periods in the Mogollon Highlands (table 2), using data obtained from catalog records at the Field Museum of Natural History. Estimated volume, which should furnish a rough equivalent to the size criteria employed by Martin, Rinaldo, and Antevs (1949) for distinguishing Cochise stages, is compared using the Kruskal-Wallis median test. The size differences between the three sites are significant only at $p = 0.20$, suggesting a long-term consistency in ground stone technology that is independent of cultural change. Oval manos are not good cultural markers in this region.

Oval or one-hand manos are commonly considered Archaic indicators in the Southwest, despite their frequent occurrence in Pueblo sites; often they are more common in Pueblo sites (e.g., Chapman and Biella 1977:264–66). Clearly, oval manos are characteristic of the Archaic but not exclusive to it. If

TABLE 2. *Comparison of Oval Mano Volume (cm³) from Mogollon Sites*

	N	Min.	Max.	Mean	S.D.
Wet Legget preceramic	7	219.82	593.36	480.90	128.34
SU site, A.D. 500[a]	12	341.88	1233.40	672.27	304.15
Turkey Foot Ridge, A.D. 750[b]	5	306.60	1595.00	935.33	490.87

Kruskall-Walllis Statistic = 3.1697	Significance = 0.2050	
Median = 2.9571	Significance = 0.2280	

[a]Radiocarbon dated at 1520 ± 140 B.P. (lab number Beta-24309).
[b]Radiocarbon dated at 1220 ± 70 B.P. (lab number Beta-13901).

it is difficult to separate the preceramic from the ceramic period according to this class of artifact, it may be even harder to identify cultural periods within the preceramic period alone, using one-hand manos as the criterion.

It is also possible that if one aspect of ground stone technology changed little through time, then other aspects may have been equally conservative. One reason oval manos are identified with the Archaic is their occurrence on nonceramic sites. If they are functionally specialized tools that are not temporally diagnostic, they may be associated with other such time-insensitive tools. Hence many nonceramic sites may have no relationship to the preceramic period. Moreover, if the resource associated with ground stone processing did not shift its spatial distribution as people adopted ceramic manufacture, a single site might exhibit the same range of ground and chipped stone during its ceramic occupation as during its preceramic period of use (cf. Vierra, cited in Binford 1978:496).

Given these problems, the identification of early agricultural sites in the Mogollon Highlands as belonging to the Cochise Culture on the basis of ground stone seems questionable.

Bat Cave

Bat Cave is widely considered the earliest known agricultural site in the Southwest, and according to Dick (1965:16), the earliest levels in the rockshelter represented the Cochise Chiricahua stage. Dick (1965:56) found no significant variability in the ground stone from different levels of the site; instead, he assigned levels to the Chiricahua stage on the basis of projectile points. Apparently he was wary of a "genetic" relationship between projectile points from Bat Cave and those of the Cochise stages (Dick 1951:161), so he described the Bat Cave specimens as variants of the Cochise Culture—a position similar to that taken by other prehistorians working with preceramic materials in the Southwest at the time (e.g., Campbell and Ellis 1952; Hibben 1951). Nevertheless, Dick coined type names for some of his specimens that explicitly indicated a cultural and temporal connection between the Cochise Culture and Bat Cave.

Outstanding among these is the "Chiricahua" point, which has become synonymous with the Chiricahua stage (Beckett 1973). As described by Dick (1965:26–27), the Chiricahua point is "triangular in outline; deep concave base; flaring rounded ears in contrast to pointed ears on type 10A [a similar form]; base usually larger than body; notches and shoulders more prominent than on type 10A. Might be considered a variant of type 10A."

The general form or shape represented by Dick's Chiricahua point (fig. 4) has a clear preceramic distribution in areas peripheral to the central Rio Grande drainage. Lister (1951a, 1951b) found similar preceramic point forms at Hells Midden in northwestern Colorado. Frison (1976) described concave-based, eared points from the Late Archaic on the High Plains, and Kelley, Campbell, and Lehmer (1940) recovered such specimens in preceramic alluvial sites near Big Bend, Texas. However, the chronological position of this form in the central Southwest, and especially in the Mogollon Highlands, is more ambiguous.

At Ventana Cave, points fitting Dick's classification did occur in Chiricahua levels, but the majority came from ceramic Hohokam deposits (fig. 5). In the various rockshelters near Bat Cave excavated by the Field Muscum of Natural History, the Chiricahua form was rare (N = 11), and only two specimens were found in preceramic levels, both postdating 2800 B.P. (Field Museum of Natural History catalog records). The Moquino site in north-central New Mexico (Beckett 1973) is cited as a Chiricahua campsite on the basis of Chiricahua projectile points (Beckett 1973:142–44; Irwin-Williams 1968:52), but all the specimens stratigraphically postdated radiocarbon dates of 3920 ± 155 B.P. and 2235 ± 95 B.P., and most were in disturbed dune deposits. A point found at Ojala Rockshelter in northern New Mexico and associated with a date of 3700 B.P. (Waber, Hubbell, and Wood 1982:335) was labelled a Cochise Chiricahua point, but it bears only slight resemblance to the type description.

At Bat Cave, all the specimens found by Dick came from levels that postdated 2800 B.P. or were recovered from undated and disturbed deposits on the talus slope (Peabody Museum records). Consequently, there is some question about the correct temporal placement of this form; most of the existing data for the Rio Grande area indicate a Late Archaic age rather than the Middle Archaic time associated with the Cochise Chiricahua.

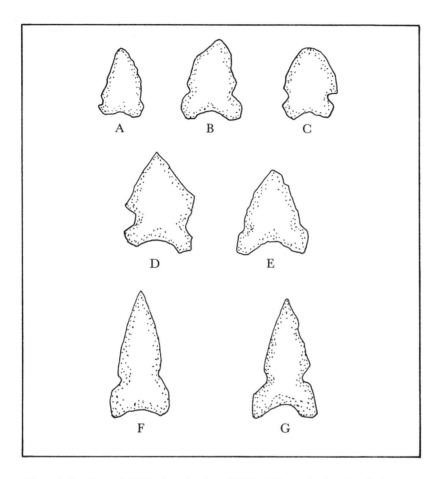

Figure 4. Outlines of Chiricahua (*a–e*) and White Mountain Apache (*f–g*) projectile points. *a–c*, Bat Cave (Dick 1965: fig. 21k–m). *d–e*, Chiricahua:3:16, southeastern Arizona (Sayles and Antevs 1941: plate XIc–d). *f–g*, Drawn to scale at Field Museum of Natural History, catalog numbers 68813-3, 63561-16.

An example of the ambiguity associated with the Chiricahua form can be seen by examining historic Western Apache arrow points, which are very similar in form to Chiricahua points and have a similar geographic distribution. Collections of stone-tipped Apache arrows obtained from the White Mountain Apache reservation, about 160 km west of Bat Cave, are curated at the Field Museum of Natural History and the American Museum of Natural History. The points at the Field Museum were collected in 1906 and include several specimens made of amber bottle glass. The Apache points have the same broad "ears," or tangs, and side notches as the "classic" Chiricahua point (fig. 4).

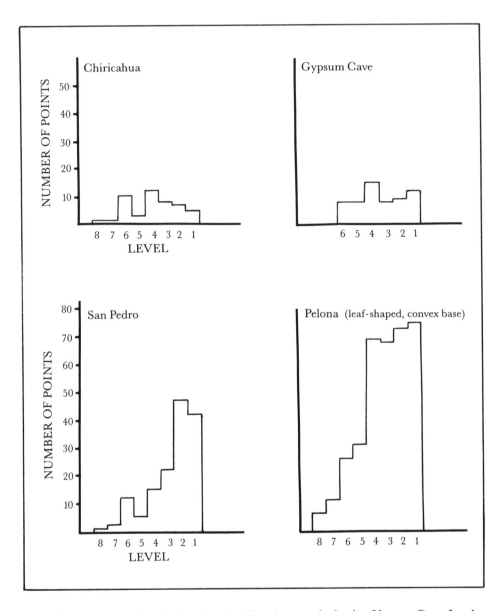

Figure 5. Distribution of selected projectile point types by level at Ventana Cave. Levels 1–3 are ceramic Hohokam deposits (Haury 1950:356).

In figure 6, the neck width and maximum width measurements for a series of White Mountain Apache stone arrowheads (Thomas 1978) are plotted against measurements for two samples of identified prehistoric Chiricahua points, one from the San Augustine Plains (Peabody Museum collections) and the other from the Moquino site (Beckett 1973:173–74). The Apache arrowheads and the San Augustine Plains points form distinct groups, with the

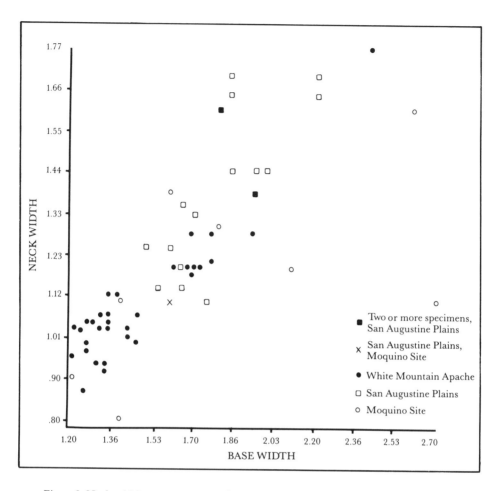

Figure 6. Neck width measurements plotted against base (maximum) width measurements for two samples of prehistoric Chiricahua projectile points and one of historic White Mountain Apache arrowheads.

Moquino sample dispersed around the Apache arrowheads. The San Augustine Plains points had wider necks than the other two samples, probably corresponding to thicker foreshafts (table 3). Interestingly, the two measurements are highly correlated in the Apache group, moderately so in the San Augustine Plains sample, and weakly correlated in the Moquino set (table 4). In other words, the least consistent relationship between neck width and base width came from a single site assemblage, and the most distinctive from a known social group.

The Apaches were well known for utilizing prehistoric artifacts (e.g., Opler 1941:384; Goodwin 1971:231), even camping on ruins to be close to a source of ready-made tools (Hough 1907; see also Vivian 1970; Asch 1960). Yet some of the Field Museum points are of bottle glass, and at least one historic account

TABLE 3. *Measurements (cm) of Chiricahua and Apache Projectile Points*

	N	Min.	Max.	Mean	S.D.
Neck Width					
Apache	35	0.87	1.77	1.11	0.166
Moquino site[a]	10	0.80	1.60	1.21	0.268
San Augustine Plains	17	1.10	1.70	1.38	0.215
Base Width					
Apache	35	1.20	2.41	1.49	0.265
Moquino site[a]	10	1.20	2.70	1.82	0.505
San Augustine Plains	17	1.50	2.20	1.80	0.211

[a]Measurements taken from photographs in Beckett (1973).

TABLE 4. *Least Squares Regression for Chiricahua Projectile Point Neck and Base Width*

	N	r	R
Apache	35	0.928	0.861
Moquino site	10	0.482	0.232
San Augustine Plains	17	0.761	0.580

describes collecting chert from sites as material for manufacturing tools (Goodwin 1971:231). Schaafsma (1979) describes a number of projectile points from northern New Mexico that clearly fit the Chiricahua form but are considered Navajo (see also Thoms 1977). Consequently, the "heirloom effect" often attributed to prehistoric artifacts in historic contexts cannot be the only explanation for the similarity between Apache points and prehistoric Chiricahua points.

These data (tables 3 and 4, fig. 6) reveal the complexity of equating point types with presumed prehistoric cultural entities or time periods. The scatterplot in figure 6 does not mean that Moquino points are Apache points, or vice versa; it means that point form alone may not always be a reliable way to assess the sources of variation in this particular tool class. More specifically, it can at least be argued that the Chiricahua point, as commonly recognized in the Rio Grande drainage, is not a good temporal indicator and therefore not a reliable cultural marker. It might be appropriate at this juncture to emphasize that archaeologists working with classic Cochise material in southern Arizona have never designated a single "Chiricahua" projectile point type; this classification originated at Bat Cave, not in southeastern Arizona.

Dick (1965:27) named another projectile point type when he referred to distinctive contracting stem points found frequently in the San Augustine Plains as "Augustin" points.

> Diamond-like in outline; stem usually triangular; base pointed to slightly rounded; flat in several examples; edges commonly serrated; shoulders are slight projections or knobs on serrated specimens; on some, shoulder on one side is smaller and lower than on the opposite side.

He saw the Augustin point (fig. 7) as part of the tradition of contracting stem points represented by Gypsum Cave points (Harrington 1933) and Manzano

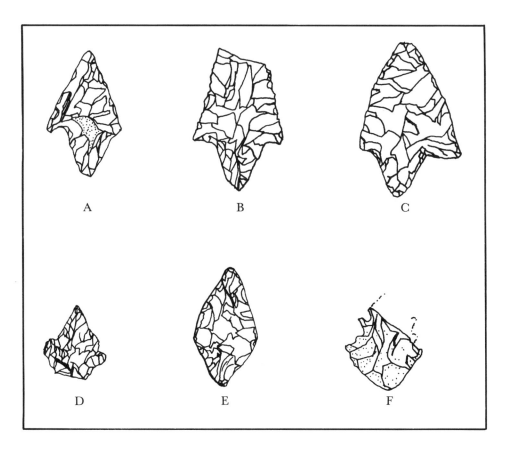

Figure 7. Augustin (*a–c*) and Pelona (*d–f*) projectile points from LA 50827, an open-air lithic site located on the San Augustine Plains near Bat Cave. To scale. *a*, Specimen BN13, basalt. *b*, BN52, basalt. *c*, BN62, rhyolite. *d*, BN3350, obsidian. *e*, BN5075, obsidian. *f*, BN5058, basalt.

Cave points (Hibben 1941). In the early 1960s, the Gypsum Cave series was estimated to date between 10,500 and 8500 B.P., but subsequent radiocarbon dates suggest a placement of 3000 to 2500 B.P. (Thomas 1981:35). Dick felt that, stratigraphically, the Augustin fell along a hypothetical line separating the Chiricahua and San Pedro stages of the Cochise sequence (1965:32). Because Haury (1950:295) saw similarities to Gypsum Cave points in specimens from Ventana Cave, the Ventana sequence was interpreted as a hybrid of Great Basin and southern Arizona material culture, which in turn allowed Dick to consider his Augustin points as part of the Cochise sequence.

Nevertheless, the stratigraphic distribution of Gypsum Cave-like points from Ventana Cave does not give weight to an *exclusive* Cochise designation. Figure 5 shows the distribution of these points by level; clearly the bulk of their occurrence is in ceramic levels (cf. Chapman 1980). Moreover, contracting stem points are not common on open-air Cochise sites in southeastern Arizona (e.g., Huckell 1973a, 1973b; Windmiller 1973).

Contracting stem points with triangular blades are common, however, in preceramic contexts in the lower Rio Grande Valley, especially south from the junction of the Pecos River. Two types fitting the basic Augustin characteristics have been defined, the Langtry and the Almagre (Suhm and Jelks 1962). The Langtry differs from the Almagre principally in size and flaking characteristics; Langtrys are smaller and more precisely made. Joel Shiner (1984, personal communication) suggested that Almagres are blanks or preforms for the Langtry.

Marmaduke (1978) compiled a chronological outline for the lower Rio Grande in which Langtry and Almagre points indicate the Langtry horizon, lasting from 4500 to 3200 B.P. Many sites along the lower Rio Grande have produced both types, including Centipede and Damp caves (Epstein 1960), the Shumla caves (Schuetz 1956), Roark Cave (Kelly 1963), Reagan Canyon (Kelly and Smith 1963), and Devil's Mouth (Johnson 1964).

The distribution of the Langtry-Almagre series can be traced into Mexico. MacNeish (1958:156–57, 151) described an Almagre phase from excavations in rockshelters in Tamaulipas, dating between 4300 and 3500 B.P. and interpreted as a period of increasing agricultural dependence.

The contracting stem form north of El Paso is concentrated in the San Augustine Plains, where hundreds of such points have been collected (Hurt and McKnight 1949; Dick 1965; Beckett 1980; Fromby 1986). Robert Weber (personal communication) found Augustin specimens from Socorro south into the Jornada del Muerto, and specimens have been reported throughout the White Sands area (e.g., Beckett 1983). Three specimens were found at Manzano Cave (Hibben 1941), and Reinhart (1967) excavated seven specimens from a preceramic site west of Albuquerque. None of the specimens recovered from Bat Cave was found in ceramic levels; some occurred in deposits dated between 6000 and 3000 B.P. and some in later contexts. Table 5 summarizes the dimensions of twenty-six complete specimens from the San Augustine Plains, which are consistent with the dimensions reported for Langtry and Almagre points. On the basis of these data it seems unnecessary to assign the Augustin points in the San Augustine Plains to the Cochise Culture of southern Arizona. Rather than give the Augustin point a specific cultural tag, it might be better to say that there appears to be greater temporal and morphological affinity between the Augustin series and point forms found in the Rio Grande Valley than with Cochise forms of southern Arizona.

Dick named a third point type, the Pelona. Pelona points are oval to triangular bifaces with a convex base and no side indentation (fig. 7). In the San Augustine Plains, the general form often exhibits complex serration, sometimes with the denticulation oriented upward, oblique to the blade edge rather than perpendicular to it. Pelonas often occur with Augustins on open-air sites, suggesting that they might be contemporaneous forms.

Dick felt that Pelonas were similar to Cochise bifaces:

> Similar points have been found in the Chiricahua Stage of the Cochise Culture (Sayles and Antevs 1941), in the Ventana-Amargosa Stage in Ventana Cave (Haury 1950) and in the Amargosa I and II stages in southeastern California (Rogers 1939). In Bat Cave these points are stratigraphically comparable to similar points found in the above sites. (1965:30–32)

An examination of the distribution of Pelona-like points from Ventana Cave, however, suggests that like Augustins, most occur in ceramic contexts (fig. 5). A single Pelona-like point was recovered from Chiricahua 3:16, one of the original Chiricahua stage sites, although it was considered intrusive (Sayles and Antevs 1941:plate XI).

TABLE 5. *Measurements (cm) of Augustin Points from the San Augustine Plains*

	N	Min.	Max.	Mean	S.D.
Length	26	1.85	5.20	3.24	0.91
Blade length	26	1.41	3.75	2.35	0.63
Stem length	26	0.65	1.45	1.20	0.78
Shoulder width	26	1.35	2.95	2.03	0.40
Neck width	25	0.75	1.65	1.23	0.22
Base width	26	0.28	1.40	0.61	0.29
Blade thickness	26	0.40	0.80	0.58	0.12
Base thickness	26	0.20	0.55	0.33	0.08

Leaf-shaped and oval bifaces are common in many time periods in the Southwest as blanks or preforms for the manufacture of projectile points (e.g., Worman 1953) and as the product of small nodules requiring a bipolar reduction strategy. This technology has no necessary relationship to any particular cultural or temporal period. Interestingly, of the sixteen Pelonas collected by Dick on the San Augustine Plains, twelve were obsidian, which occurs locally in small nodules. None was greater than 5.3 cm long, with a mean of 3.5 cm — very much at the short end of the range of Archaic projectile points in the region.

Consequently, there seems to be little substantive reason for assuming that the diagnostic points used to assign Bat Cave to the Chiricahua stage are reliable for that purpose. The geographical similarities implied by the Bat Cave projectile points are to the Rio Grande Valley to the southeast, and not to the Cochise Culture area of southern Arizona.

Cienega Creek

Cienega Creek (Haury 1957) is a stratified alluvial site in the White Mountains of eastern Arizona, important especially for the presence of *Zea mays* pollen assigned to the Chiricahua stage. This assignment was made cautiously, as Haury (1957:24) felt that artifact typology might not be reliable as a stage marker in this case. Nevertheless, Cienega Creek is regularly placed in the Cochise Culture (Sayles 1983; Woodbury and Zubrow 1979).

The entire artifact assemblage for the Chiricahua bed at the site consisted of two complete grinding slabs, two fragmentary grinding slabs, two manos, one projectile point, at least two scrapers, and thirty pieces of debitage. The grinding slabs were indistinguishable from grinding slabs in younger beds, and the manos fell "within the range of handstone types usually associated with the Chiricahua stage of the Cochise Culture" (Haury 1957:20). The projectile point had an indented base and deep side notches, similar to those of points recorded by Haury in the Chiricahua-Amargosa II levels at Ventana Cave.

The artifactual evidence assigning the Cienega Creek site to the Chiricahua stage is therefore not substantial. Moreover, reanalysis of the original radiocarbon samples indicates that bed D-1, the Chiricahua bed, dates between 2700 and 2400 B.P. (Damon and Long 1962), within the San Pedro stage.

Tularosa and Cordova Caves

The Tularosa and Cordova caves, excavated by the Field Museum of Natural History in 1950–51, contained large quantities of maize and squash in preceramic deposits radiocarbon dated to about 2500 B.P. and considered San Pedro Cochise (Martin et al. 1952). That conclusion was largely based on the explicit assumption that the Mogollon ceramic tradition evolved from the Cochise.

The excavators of the caves also saw similarities to the lithic assemblage at the Wet Legget Arroyo site (Martin et al. 1952:500) and to lithic assemblages in southern Arizona:

> Rinaldo has likewise made a comparative study of the mano, metate, and projectile point types from the Southern Basin culture—Pinto Basin, Ventana Cave, Chiricahua 3:16 (Southern Arizona Cochise culture)—Tularosa and Cordova caves, and has found a relationship between those tool types on a Pinto-Amargosa II-Chiricahua Stage time level; that is, the manos, metates, scrapers, and projectile points are similar and clearly related typologically: all have sub-rectangular one hand manos, shallow basin metates, keeled scrapers, uniface choppers, and narrow-shouldered points with concave bases. (Martin et al. 1952:501)

The issue here is whether or not typological similarity represents cultural unity. It has already been shown that neither ground stone nor projectile points are good temporal markers, and therefore, as with the other early agricultural sites in the Mogollon Highlands, the assumption that Tularosa Cave and Cordova Cave were Cochise Culture sites rests on doubtful or vaguely intuitive typological arguments.

CONCEPTUAL BASIS OF THE COCHISE CULTURE MODEL

Preceramic sites in the Mogollon Highlands were, and still are, considered Cochise manifestations because the Cochise Culture model offered the only chronological sequence for the Archaic when these sites were excavated. As one of the first attempts in the Southwest to synthesize preceramic cultural development within a region, this model logically became the basis for assessing new Archaic discoveries. Only a few people were actually involved in this research, all colleagues of one another. For example, Antevs was in some way involved with every early agricultural site in the Mogollon Highlands, and he was a key figure in the development of the Cochise sequence (see Martin, Rinaldo, and Antevs 1949; Dick 1965; cf. Campbell et al. 1937).

Not until the late 1960s did an interpretive framework for Archaic development elsewhere in the Southwest become available—the Oshara Tradition. The Oshara model incorporated the Cochise Culture as a contemporaneous but geographically separate "ethnic" group, assuming that the early agricultural sites in the Mogollon area were Cochise (Irwin-Williams 1967:443; 1968:52; 1979:41).

Placing these early agricultural sites in the Cochise Culture has had the effect of framing subsequent analytical studies with the presumption that the route of agricultural diffusion was through hunter-gatherer populations in the lower Sonoran region and the northwest Sierra Madre Oriental. It has also defined the Mogollon Highlands as the northern extent of Cochise development, so that the early appearance of maize, squash, and beans in the mountains is viewed as a product of cultural factors and favorable ecological conditions unique to the Cochise "way of life." The original use of Cochise Culture as a classificatory model for describing stone tools has apparently been lost in the study of early southwestern agriculture. The Cochise Culture model was designed to describe variation in lithic technology and settlement organization, which could be ascribed to local economic adaptations to a gradually changing environment. The model is an ordering of data based on the perception of artifact variation and the logical assumption that such variation was economically significant. Cultural boundaries and regional "ethnicity" were applied later on the basis of widespread similarity in some artifact classes.

It is critically important for the study of early agricultural adaptations in the Southwest to appreciate that the extension of the Cochise Culture to areas other than southeastern Arizona resulted from shared perceptions among prehistorians about the nature of the archaeological record. Archaeologists were working from the assumption that a panwestern socioeconomic adaptation based on food gathering and hunting small game had taken place during the Archaic. Regional environmental differences gave rise, over time, to "variants" on this basic pattern, which in turn evolved into the different ceramic traditions recognized in the Southwest. The evolutionary logic of this argument fit neatly with the strong sense of historical continuity to which archaeologists working in the Puebloan area were accustomed.

The concept of a widespread hunter-gatherer adaptation in the American West encompassing many local variations is undoubtedly correct. What requires scrutiny is the unilineal evolutionary argument equating social boundaries with subjectively perceived differences in limited classes of technology. This brief overview of the Cochise Culture in west-central New Mexico indicates that research *before* the discovery of early agricultural sites had a significant and perhaps primary role in underwriting the expansion of presumed prehistoric cultural boundaries to include those sites. The assignment of Bat Cave to the Cochise Culture was based on a need to give the site a cultural tag, to establish its cultural affinity. The Cochise Culture was the only existing "culture" for the Southwest preceramic period, and the Mogollon was believed to have emerged from the Cochise. To have considered Bat Cave as something other than Cochise would likely have been seen as a denial of a perfectly obvious connection.

Or at least it would have to archaeologists. The Cochise Culture, the Oshara Tradition, and other culture-historical constructs are simply tools archaeologists have used to describe perceived similarities in stone implements. The notion that these models actually reflect bounded, coherent, prehistoric groups or populations is a post hoc assumption, and a careful review of the criteria for distinguishing different ethnic groups or cultural phases suggests that this is an unwarranted assumption. Thus, when initial agriculture in the Southwest is attributed to the Cochise Culture, a certain culture-historical model (which its authors probably never intended) is being reified on the basis of a shared paradigm among archaeologists, not an actual demonstration that such a relationship existed.

The Cochise Culture continues to be extremely influential among archaeologists studying the perceramic period in the Southwest (Berry and Berry 1986). To the extent that early agriculture is seen as characteristic of the Cochise Culture, the appreciation of agricultural adoption as a process involving the structure and organization of cultural systems will be needlessly impaired. Those systems will have been defined by convention rather than by observation.

I want it to be clear that I am not criticizing the pioneering research that underlies the Cochise construct. Indeed, the careful attention to assumptions and interpretations in that work makes it possible to understand the model's development and importance. And it may well be that the Cochise model is a perfectly adequate representation of the Archaic in the Sonoran desert region. What concerns me here is that the evidence for the early transition to agriculture in the Southwest may be unnecessarily embroiled in attribute typology, to the detriment of perceiving that change as an evolutionary process.

Even if the early agricultural sites in west-central New Mexico were part of a cultural entity that could be described by Cochise criteria, we would not know why agriculture was adopted by that social system. Culture-historical frameworks acknowledge that certain kinds of changes have taken place, but they do not explain the process of change. In the next chapter I will provide an outline of the conditions which may have been responsible for the initial adoption of domesticated plants by prehistoric southwestern peoples. These conditions have no necessary relationship to any of the classificatory features considered representative of the Cochise Culture.

2

The Adoption of Domesticated Plants

by Hunter-Gatherers

in the American Southwest

I believe the adoption of domesticated plants by hunter-gatherers can be understood as the result of an intentional decision to enhance resource security within the context of long-term evolutionary selection for increasing environmental predictability.[1] It is unnecessary to model the acceptance process as a cultural response to perceived economic or demographic stress, but it is impossible to account for adoption without considering the deliberate decision to incorporate a dependent resource into an economic system predicated on the collection of wild resources. In addressing the issue of initial agriculture in the Southwest, I take the position that the development of socioeconomic conditions favoring the adoption of domesticated plants can be explained as natural selection for strategies that reduce environmental uncertainty and thus increase population fitness, but the timing and location of acceptance were the result of a conscious decision to control annual variation in resource availability and are thus related to local historical variables.

---

1. Domestication is a process that transforms a wild species to one dependent upon human cultivation for survival. Adoption is an act that does not necessarily produce a transformation in the domesticated species, but that does require a commitment to cultivation.

Botanists do not always agree on the precise morphological characteristics distinguishing domesticates from nondomesticates, but I assume that a plant's inability to reproduce efficiently without human assistance is an adequate definition of full domestication (cf. B. Smith 1985:54). Rindos (1980, 1984) pointed out that there is a continuum between domesticated species and their wild progenitors, and a cultivated plant is not necessarily one that has been domesticated. Domestication results when cultivation effectively isolates a plant species from competitors and begins to select for features desirable to the cultivators (Heiser 1973).

Regardless of whether or not domesticates are involved, cultivation is a deliberate effort to control the future availability of a resource. Assuming cultivation to be any attempt to manipulate the environment to enhance the survival, reproductive success, or location of a resource, a variety of practices conducted by hunter-gatherers would qualify, including burning grasses to encourage pioneer vegetation, diverting surface water to wild plants, or even broadcasting their seeds (Steward 1938:32–33; Lourandos 1980).

An important distinction I want to make between cultivation and domestication is not so much that the latter stems from the former, but that cultivation in general is a strategy of control. The goal of cultivation is clearly to increase the predictability that a specific resource or set of resources will be available at some point in the future; the cultivators intend to influence plant survival (Flannery 1986; B. Smith 1985). Domesticated plants are an outcome of that concern, and the evolution of a domesticate represents a dramatic increase in the ability of the cultivator to control the future temporal and spatial distribution of the species.

The control which a cultivator is able to exert over a domesticate has a price. Because of their obligate relationship to humans, domesticates must be planted, harvested, and, in temperate environments, stored for the next season's planting. Since domesticates are ill equipped to contend with wild competitors, they often require substantial human attention during their growth, and unless the cultivators have the wherewithal and inclination to transport the harvested plant, they will either have to set up residence near the stored crop or return to the storage location seasonally (Flannery 1973; cf. Binford 1980).

Thus when we ask why hunter-gatherers would elect to adopt domesticated plants, we have to consider the obligatory constraints which such a decision implies. While plant domestication under cultivation may have been a long-term process (but see Iltis 1983 and Galinat 1985), the acceptance of fully domesticated plants by erstwhile hunter-gatherers must have been relatively rapid. The requirements of domesticates for mere survival would prohibit any adoption strategy which did not immediately meet plant needs through planting, harvesting, and storage. With anything less than a commitment to the minimal requirements of the specific domesticates, there could have been no sustained involvement with these species.

As we turn to a consideration of these issues and their relevance to the introduction of agriculture into the Southwest, there are two major points around which I want to explain adoption: the obvious advantage of predictability in a domesticated plant, and the required commitment to strategies ensuring propagation in the decision to adopt a domesticated resource. The first point suggests that selective pressures for reducing risk and uncertainty favored adoption, while the second indicates that specific historical factors probably controlled the time and place that it occurred. In this approach I follow a position taken by Flannery (1986:4), who argues that the "origins of agriculture involved both human intentionality and a set of underlying ecological and evolutionary principles." I hope to show that intentional decision-making is even more prominent in the adoption of domesticated plants than in the processes which led to their domestication.

EVOLUTION AND UNCERTAINTY:
ULTIMATE AND PROXIMATE CAUSALITY

Slobodkin (1968:192) described evolution as coping with environmental unpredictability through change. The long-term persistence of a population depends on its ability to respond to unpredictability, a capacity commonly called "adaptability" (Bennet 1976; Slobodkin 1977; Kirch 1980; Dunnell 1980). Many evolutionary biologists conceptualize adaptability as arising from selective pressures favoring the minimization of risk or loss (Riechart and Hammerstein 1983:379). Slobodkin (1968:191) saw it as selection for homeostasis, the ability to counteract the effects of variance introduced by the environment.

Homeostasis is maintained by behavioral flexibility and accurate anticipation of future environmental change (Harrison 1979). It is a dynamic process of adjustment that attempts to avoid intolerable fluctuations between a population and its resource base. Biologists find it convenient to address this relationship in terms of population density or size; the function of homeostasis is to keep population in balance with available resources through reproduction (see Pianka 1978).

Anthropologists have taken a similar position on homeostasis, casting it as the process of establishing population equilibrium below the carrying capacity of an environment, primarily through cultural adaptations (Athens 1977; Hayden 1981; Hassan 1981). Anthropologists are, however, notably disconsonant on the issue of whether humans do or do not regulate population density homeostatically (Hassan 1981).

This ambiguity is not particularly important to this study. What I want to consider is the possibility that a systematic relationship exists between the need for homeostatic capacity and the investment a population makes in the attempt to obtain it—not that they actually achieve homesostatic states, but that they are under some pressure to do so (cf. Slobodkin 1977).

Conrad (1976) argued that evolutionary selection tends to retain the minimum amount of adaptability necessary to ensure high probabilities of persistence. Over time, the range of behavioral or physical strategies employed by a population should decline or rise to the level of uncertainty in the environment, meaning that excess or unnecessary variation will be selected against. Thus there should be a close correlation between the amount of uncertainty a population experiences and the amount of energy it invests in adaptability.

This correspondence is the basis of a theoretically attractive relationship between population density and environmental uncertainty. Recent studies in biology and anthropology have employed a model of selection processes derived from the logistic equation for population growth (fig. 8). At low density, a population generates little competition for resources and expends a great deal of effort in reproduction. Resource scarcity is solved by emigrating to new areas, and reproduction is critical to raising population size above the level at which random environmental catastrophes could affect significant reproductive portions of that population. As density increases, however, competition becomes increasingly prevalent because the success of simply moving to new resource patches declines with higher relative population. The result is that selection pressures shift from reproduction to efficiency and maintenance, or in other words, to behaviors that contribute to successful competition among foragers. Selection for reproduction is designated by r, the coefficient of the intrinsic rate of growth, and selection for efficiency is denoted by K, the coeffcient for carrying capacity. For biologists, selection is a genetic process (Pianka 1978), but anthropologists seem inclined to view selection in terms of the cultural transmission of learned behavior and experience (cf. Osborn 1977; Christenson 1980; Schacht 1980).

The point to be made by introducing r- and K-selection is that competition becomes an important factor as population density increases. Competition can be avoided at low density because people have adequate space in which to seek resources, and inefficient foraging strategies can therefore be tolerated. In fact, unstructured or random foraging might be beneficial in maintaining maximum contact between potential mates, consistent with r- selection. But population growth, the hallmark of successful adaptation and population fitness, reduces the leeway in unstructured foraging. The selection emphasis therefore shifts toward behaviors providing greater efficiency and hence success in foraging, and which are essentially means for alleviating environmental uncertainty.

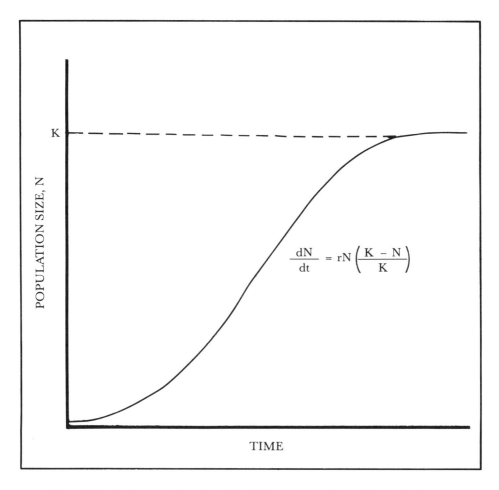

$$\frac{dN}{dt} = rN\left(\frac{K - N}{K}\right)$$

Figure 8. Population growth under the logistic equation, where *d* is the death rate, *r* is the intrinsic rate of natural increase, and *K* is carrying capacity.

I am reluctant to view human economic strategies as either *r*- or *K*-selected, a method that implies far too much inflexibility and simplicity for cultural (and hence nongenetic) adaptations. Nevertheless, I believe that the development of human behavioral strategies for increasing efficiency and reducing uncertainty is an entirely reasonable expectation of competition resulting from increased density.

Archaeologists have not overlooked the implications of density-dependent selection for homeostatic behavior. Hayden (1981) and Binford (1983a, 1983b), among many, argued that increasing density leads to increased use of low-return resources, especially immobile ones such as plants. This intensification eventually involves attempts to increase productivity, leading to domestication and agriculture. This scenario is consistent with recent models of unintentional, symbiotic domestication processes (Reynolds and Ziegler 1979; Rindos

1980, 1984; Flannery 1986; Reynolds 1986; Lowe 1985), although these models emphasize that only the deliberate manipulation of a plant's environment is required to initiate the process, not increases in population density.

This is a crucial point for understanding the adoption of fully domesticated plants by hunter-gatherers because the selective advantage for homeostatic behaviors varies. Enhancing environmental predictability will always represent an economic advantage. The issue is whether or not the cost of maintaining that advantage is justified. At low density, such an advantage might be relatively superfluous, but at high density it is exceptionally valuable. In other words, we can be certain that increasing population density creates conditions favoring the adoption of behaviors that reduce uncertainty, but this tells us little about when specific resources are acquired. It is not until we combine selection for predictability with two additional evolutionary principles that I think we achieve a reasonable approach for assessing agricultural diffusion.

The first is the observation that evolution is essentially a conservative process. Although rates of change may vary (see Eldridge and Gould 1972), change itself tends to occur where there is least resistance or where it is least disruptive (Hockett and Ascher 1964; Dobzhansky 1972; Slobodkin 1977). This principle, sometimes called "Rohmer's Rule," states that evolutionary change establishes adaptability while maintaining the status quo; change can be seen as small adjustments which actually prevent major change.

The rule implies that incorporation of domesticated plants into hunter-gatherer economies sustains the ongoing system instead of changing it. It is reasonable to argue that placing this kind of economic decision-making within a framework of evolutionary selection leads to the position that hunter-gatherers adopting agricultural strategies were concerned with the success of hunting and gathering strategies, not with developing a dependence on cultivars. In this view, domesticates were first adopted not for food production itself, as some anthropologists have suggested (e.g., Cohen 1977), but rather for their contribution to the success of existing foraging strategies. Stated more simply, foragers adopt domesticated plants not to become farmers but to remain effective foragers.

The second principle is that change is usually nondisruptive. If change takes place in minor or nonresistant aspects of a socioeconomic system and serves to maintain the essential structure of that system, then such change should logically involve little or no overall alterations. Selection for new means to ensure persistence of the system should not modify its fundamental characteristics.

If change is initially nondisruptive, then the adoption of domesticates by hunter-gatherers implies a congruence between the socioeconomic system and the organizational requirements entailed by the cultivation of domesticates. In other words, the domesticates should have fit into the system rather easily. Adoption, as opposed to domestication, must have involved a recognition of the organizational requirements and potential risks associated with domesticates (Green 1980) because the decision to accept had to rest with an assessment of the existing economic organization and the place domesticates were to assume within it.

Thus it is possible to address the question of adoption—or diffusion—in terms of ultimate and proximate causality. The selective advantages of domesticated plants are control and predictability, and because it increases with competition, selective pressure for reducing uncertainty is density dependent. At that level we have an ultimate cause. However, the decision to adopt food production as a procurement strategy also depends on the development of a socioeconomic system consistent with the demands of a culturally dependent resource. At this level we find the proximate cause of adoption, the relationship between a particular economic organization and specific resources (cf. Flannery 1986:5). It appears that organizational consistency or congruence between economy and resource is a necessary but not sufficient condition for adoption, while density increase is sufficient but not exclusive.

If the adoption of domesticated plants by hunter-gatherers is predicated on the existence of an economy into which these new resources can be incorporated without major adjustment, then the archaeological record of this process will probably not exhibit any change beyond the addition of the plants. We can, however, expect to see the development of economic organization consistent with the cultivation of domesticates preceding adoption. Moreover, we can use the physiological and ecological characteristics of these plants to establish the kinds of economic strategies that must have been present to ensure their propagation.

SOUTHWESTERN HUNTER-GATHERER ORGANIZATION

Four domesticated plants were introduced into the prehistoric American Southwest from Mesoamerica in the preceramic period: maize (*Zea mays*), squash (*Cucurbita pepo*), beans (*Phaseolus vulgaris*), and bottle gourd (*Lagenaria siceraria*). Ford (1981) has labelled them the "Upper Sonoran Agricultural Complex" to indicate their common geographic distribution within vegetative zones generally found between elevations of 1500 and 2000 m.

All four species are annuals, but they have somewhat different ecologies. *Zea mays* is the hardiest or most adaptable of the four, and consequently I will use it as a general model for initial food production. Maize was apparently domesticated from wild teosinte (*Zea mexicana*) in the semiarid highlands of Mexico around 7000 B.P. (Flannery 1986). As with most domesticated grains, the cultivation of teosinte led to changes that increased seed size at the expense of seed dispersal, producing a large cob containing many densely packed kernels enclosed in husks (Galinat 1985).

It is not clear if modern maize physiology is completely analogous to that of prehistoric varieties, although the anatomical differences are not considered great (Weatherwax 1950; Anderson 1947; Galinat 1985). All early maize in Mesoamerica and the Southwest was a pod-popcorn variety named chapalote.[2] It is possible that chapalote was a generalist species, that is, one adapted to a wide range of environmental situations and competition with wild plants, and not especially productive. The development of several varieties of maize in the later prehistory of the Southwest may indicate deliberate selection for productivity in conjunction with intensive cultivation and thus a shift from generalist to specialist characteristics as competition with wild plants was buffered (cf. Ford 1981). Nevertheless, because we do not know the specific requirements and tolerances of chapalote, except that it appears to have adapted to the short-day environment of Mesoamerica (Galinat 1985:276), and because it differs from modern corn primarily in size (Galinat 1985; cf. Smith 1985), I will use modern corn as an analog for prehistoric southwestern maize.

Maize has a number of important physiological requirements, but two are particularly critical to survival: the length of maturation, normally requiring about 120 days, and the necessity of soil moisture at planting for seed germination (Classen and Shaw 1970). Planting should take place after the last frost; cold inhibits seed germination and can kill newly germinated seeds. Planting must also occur when there is enough seed moisture for germination (see also Cutler and Whitaker 1961). In the Southwest the combination of these two requirements can pose a tricky problem, since maize must be planted while there is still enough soil moisture from winter precipitation and before it is lost to evaporation as the climate becomes warmer. Local climatic conditions therefore play a fundamental role in where and when planting takes place.

Maize cultivation also necessitates several minimum strategic commitments from cultivators. Because the domestication of corn has selected for seeds that adhere to the rachis and thus cannot propagate without human assistance, cultivators must plant seeds in spring and harvest plants in fall. At some point between harvest and planting, the kernels must be removed from the cob, dried or parched, and a seed crop must be selected for the next season.

The storage of domesticates is not as simple as caching the seeds. In the evolution of annual domesticated plants, humans have selected species that tend to germinate when planted or, in other words, that do not remain dormant for unpredictable lengths of time (Harlan et al. 1973:319). Wild plants

---

2. Recent excavations in south-central New Mexico (Upham et al. 1987) have reported eight-row maize, or *maiz de ocho*, directly radiocarbon dated at 3125 B.P. I consider this date ambiguous with respect to the maize variety, however, because the radiocarbon determination was made by pooling four specimens of eight-row maize and four specimens of some other (unreported) maize variety. A direct reading on a single specimen of eight-row maize would help determine the age of this important variety.

use dormancy as a means of preventing premature germination and subsequent loss to unfavorable climatic conditions; dormancy counters random environmental variation with stochastic maturation in individual seeds (Galinat 1985:249). The thick seed coat (epiderm) of wild plants enhances resistance to moisture or insects (Smith 1985:59). Human selection for large seeds is accompanied by a reduction in the thickness of the epiderm and an increase in the thickness of the perisperm, which contains the seed nutrients—often the focus of human consumption. In selecting for larger seeds, the thinner epiderm and enhanced nutritional source also contribute to greater susceptibility to germination, and thus to more predictable maturation at the time of planting (cf. Smith 1985:60).

Increasing the predictability of germination at planting has obvious advantages, but at least one disadvantage. Increased susceptibility to moisture and temperature allows seeds to germinate while in storage if those variables are not adequately controlled. Smith (1985:60) suggests that this increased need for seed maintenance may have been a factor in the construction of subsurface storage pits in the prehistoric midwestern United States.

Storage of corn in above-ground facilities is well known, especially in the Southwest, but maintaining cool and dry conditions seems to be a common goal in all regions where corn is grown. Where below-ground storage of maize is documented, it apparently covaries with a need to hide stored resources or with periodic abandonment of the storage location. For example, the Pawnees dug large, grass-lined pits for storing cultigens when settlements were left during the bison hunting season (Weltfish 1965). Where mobility is important, subsurface storage may be required because of an inability to monitor the stored resource.

The behaviors required for planting, harvesting, and storage imply at least two organizational features of hunter-gatherer systems electing to incorporate *Zea mays* as a resource. First, localities should be used twice a year when cultivation occurs, to plant in the spring and harvest in the fall. The susceptibility of maize to unplanned germination and the stochastic loss of individual seed vitality over time means that this pattern, once initiated, would have continued without much geographical shifting as groups repeatedly returned to the same location. This repetition is related to the need for storage and the overwhelming likelihood that food would be stored in cultivation areas. The importance of the seed crop, which must exceed the amount needed for consumption and lost to failed germination, places a premium on the preparation of gardens, the anticipation of future needs, and the ability to prevent consumption of entire harvests. Thus the technological capacity to adequately store cultigen seed crops is the second organizational feature that should precede adoption (cf. Flannery 1973, 1986; Binford 1983a).

Cultivation of maize during the growing season—weeding, protection, irrigation, etc.—may not be absolutely necessary to the survival of all of the growing plants. It seems unlikely that the investment of work required to plant domesticates would be made with indifference to crop success, but it is a rather common belief among archaeologists that early agriculturalists in the Southwest simply planted maize in the spring and then returned in the fall to collect whatever plants had managed to survive (e.g., Cordell 1984:178; Ford 1981:13).

However, numerous maize growing experiments in the Southwest indicate that without fairly close attention to the crop, few, if any, plants are likely to complete the growing season (e.g., Mackey 1983; Toll et al. 1986). Besides the more obvious dangers arising from frost, moisture deficiency, heat stress, hail, and floods, there are insects, rodents, large animals, birds, and disease. It is not surprising that New World ethnographic data provide abundant evidence that corn production involves nearly constant monitoring by cultivators (see Forde 1931; Page 1940; Cushing 1974; Ford 1968; Kirkby 1973).

A careful reading of the ethnohistory of certain North American groups does not support the assumption that they practiced untended maize cultivation. When the Pawnees, for example, left their villages after the growing season to hunt bison, older or injured individuals often stayed behind to care for the crops and houses (Weltfish 1965). This case suggests a potentially critical variable in understanding the adoption of domesticates by hunter-gatherers: an age structure permitting otherwise nonproductive group members to assume a role in cultivation. A demographic profile in which the old or young cannot contribute to hunting and gathering because of limited mobility may be ideally suited to the adoption of cultivation with its inherently immobile features. Populations "top heavy" with older individuals are characteristic of homeostatic or "stable" periods of growth (Pianka 1978).

The Apaches are frequently cited as an analog for early southwestern agriculturalists. Seasonally, they moved into the mountains and planted small gardens which they apparently did not tend with much vigor (Fritz 1974; Minnis 1985). The analogy can be misleading, however, because unlike the first southwestern groups to adopt cultigens, the historic Apaches had complex mutualistic and parasitic relations with horticulturalists. The economic objective of these relationships was generally to obtain processed agricultural foodstuffs, thus providing critical access to cultigens without having to depend on their own production strategies. Moreover, the seasonal planting in the mountains probably involved seed crops obtained from horticulturalists, thus relieving the Apaches of reliance on successful crops to ensure the next season's planting. Although this example is not an appropriate basis for arguing that casual maize cultivation was the probable strategy associated with initial adoption, nor that initial agricultural strategies were like Apache strategies, it does point out the significance of the nonconsumptive aspects of successful maize agriculture, such as the production of seed crops.

Another of these less apparent agricultural aspects is the timing of planting. Maize germination is affected by temperature and moisture; warmth and wetness promote germination, cold and dryness suppress or prevent it. In the Southwest, where precipitation is seasonal, successful maturation depends on a precise estimation of soil moisture and climatic conditions at the time of planting. According to Forde (1931) and Page (1940), the Hopis are greatly concerned with the proper timing of planting in relation to a host of environmental factors. Accurately assessing when the danger of frost has largely passed but spring soil moisture has not yet evaporated requires a solid knowledge of environmental conditions throughout the preceding year. This knowledge is obtained through various types of monitoring, but ultimately it requires the ability to assess local conditions near the gardens over extended periods. It is not a requisite, of course, that cultivators monitor the areas in which crops are planted, but doing so will significantly improve the probability of successful planting, and in the uncertain business of maize production, probability is everything.

The potential evolutionary effects of casual or unattended maize cultivation also suggest that it was not a likely strategy in the Southwest. If cultivators harvested only plants that had survived climatic variability, predation by insects, animals, and birds, and competition with wild plants, the result would be plants with a heavy investment in maintenance structures, not in reproductive parts (cf. King 1987). Humans might find themselves cultivating a resource with declining food value and increasingly unpredictable germination patterns. The only apparent way to prevent the loss of some domesticity would be to carefully tend young plants during the germination and sprouting stages to ensure that as much of the seed crop as possible survived.[3] These stages occur over a four-month period. Consequently, it is likely that maize cultivation involved some degree of maintenance during the growing season, especially during the initial growth phases in spring (e.g., Classen and Shaw 1970).

This outline of the basic features of maize cultivation returns us to the question of an appropriate hunter-gatherer economic system into which maize could be introduced without substantial disruption. Repetitive seasonal movement coupled with resource storage and limited geographical movement characterize the hunter-gatherer mobility systems Binford (1980) described as "logistic" or "collecting" adaptations.

---

3. I am grateful to Bruce Smith for suggesting that if casual cultivation generated the physiological changes I have argued, then the appropriate response to maintain domesticity would probably be an investment in protection during the early stages of maturation. I am not sure, however, that Bruce would concur that physiological changes would necessarily result from casual cultivation, and thus he is absolved of any responsibility for that notion.

According to this now familiar and widely used concept, hunter-gatherer systems can be arranged along a continuum of organizational complexity in terms of the degree to which labor is allocated to specialized task groups. "Logistic organization" refers to a settlement system wherein a group moves into a resource area and exploits it through the formation of task groups (Binford 1980:10). Binford also referred to such groups as "collectors" to emphasize the specificity of resource-procurement activities. Logistic systems are a typical response to spatially aggregated resources that are available for short periods of time. Logistically organized groups characteristically send out small parties from a campsite to obtain selected resources some distance away. The settlement patterns exhibited by collectors therefore tend to include a variety of functionally specific sites beyond the residential camp (Binford 1980:12).

In contradistinction to collectors, Binford proposed the term "foragers" for groups that "map onto" resources by moving their residential camps directly to a resource patch. Such strategies appear adaptive to environments with spatially dispersed resources that are available over long periods of time. Foragers move frequently and seldom store food. Resource procurement tends to follow an "encounter strategy" in which there is little predetermined focus on specific food items (Binford 1980:8). Binford summarized this organization as having "high residential mobility, low-bulk inputs and regular daily food-procurement strategies" (1980:9). Foragers generate fewer activity site types than collectors do and rarely use storage caches or stations for special activities such as hunting.

Binford's dichotomy between collecting and foraging represents the idealized extremes of an organizational continuum (Eder 1984) the nature of which is not really in its product—settlement differentiation—but in what Binford described as "labor accommodations to incongruent distribution of critical resources or conditions which otherwise restrict mobility" (1980:15). That is to say, logistic systems employ a complex division of labor to effectively utilize different resources that become available at the same time of year. Logistic settlement organization is an expectable response to what Flannery (1968) has called scheduling conflicts.

Binford's typology for understanding scheduling processes makes a major contribution in its emphasis on anticipation. A logistic system is clearly concerned with adjustment to changes in the location and timing of resources and the location of people vis-à-vis that variability. A critical feature of logistic organization is predictability, both through information gathering and control of resource availability by storage. More succinctly, logistic organization is a means of coping with spatial incongruence and/or temporal conflicts in resource distribution through management of labor and future resource availability.

Binford (1980:15) argued that any change in the environment that increases the spatial incongruence of critical resources favors a logistic settlement strategy. Hunter-gatherers will move to the critical resource with the greatest bulk—that is, the hardest to carry away—and exploit other resources via task groups. Similarly, any condition that increases the number of critical resources will likely require logistic settlement solutions, as would climatic variance leading to increased incongruity among critical resources.

Temporal incongruity is seen as a strong selective pressure for storage (Binford 1980:15). One of the potential results of storage is greater spatial incongruity among resources because of the artifical bulk aggregation in specific localities (Kelly 1983).

Binford's hypotheses for the development of logistic production focus on the environmental changes that produce spatial or temporal incongruity in resource distribution. Since the adoption of domesticates requires relatively complicated storage strategies, the acceptance of agriculture may be especially related to temporal resource incongruity.

This last point is evident in a study by Speth and Spielmann (1982), who note that carbohydrates have important nutritional benefits for human groups subsisting primarily on lean meat diets. In temperate regions, such groups are most likely to rely on lean meat in late spring, before plant resources are available and after stored plant foods have been exhausted. Speth and Spielmann (1982:15) argue that the beneficial effects of carbohydrates are thus greatest in the spring, and stored foods which are high in starch—such as maize—would be a valuable food source at this time. As in any instance of nutritional benefit, it would not be necessary for foragers to recognize that carbohydrates were good for them in the context of a lean meat diet, only that increasing the availability of this resource during certain times had positive effects.

The disappearance of a critical resource, another type of environmental change, also might promote the adoption of agriculture by hunter-gatherers. Rowley-Conwy (1984) saw such a situation in the dispersal of agriculture into Scandinavia. He posited that changing sea levels during the mid-Holocene resulted in the loss of important spring littoral foods and that domesticates were introduced as replacements. An immensely important aspect of this reconstruction is that adoption was predicated on the suitability of domesticates for filling a need and fitting the organization of the recipient groups. Agriculture had been known to coastal Scandinavian hunter-gatherers for some time before they were (or felt) compelled to practice it as the result of losing a major seasonal resource.

There are other archaeological and historic examples of hunter-gatherers who resisted the adoption of known domesticated resources (Akazawa 1982; Zvelebil 1981; B. Smith 1987), adopted available domesticates selectively

(Bogucki 1987), or periodically shifted between foraging and horticultural adaptations (Brooks, Gelburd, and Yellen 1984; Crawford and Yoshizaki 1987). These observations are consistent with Conrad's (1976) position that the degree of investment in behavioral strategies for coping with the environment should generally conform to the degree of environmental uncertainty. If predictability is the basic value in cultigens, their strategic advantage ought to vary with the need to reduce uncertainty (cf. Binford 1983a; Flannery 1986; see also Pryor 1986).

As argued above, a major source of uncertainty for any population is density-dependent competition. In theory, hunter-gatherers had at least four primary responses to competition from increasing density: movement to new areas, intensification of resource procurement, the development of obligatory economic relationships with other groups, and obtaining better environmental information. Movement is probably the easiest and most common response, but we are interested in situations in which movement is geographically restricted by the ecology of the introduced cultigens. Therefore we need consider only the latter three.

Resource intensification means a number of different and not always complementary behaviors to archaeologists (see Bender 1978, 1981). In hunter-gatherer studies, intensification is usually taken as an increase in the range of resource use, particularly resources that may have high procurement costs relative to their economic benefit. In optimal foraging theory, this is equivalent to moving down a rank order of diet items, using those which cost increasingly more in work per unit of return (see Winterhalder and Smith 1982; E. Smith 1983).

With respect to density-dependent competition and restricted mobility, an increase in the use of less desirable or costlier resources is, for the most part, probably the result of loss of access to high-return or highly ranked items which are themselves mobile. Binford (1983a:50) remarked that as hunter-gatherer mobility options are diminished, there is an "inevitable" trend toward "intensification of subsistence strategies within less space. Intensification means using smaller animals, a greater diversity of species, storage of resources with limited access windows but abundant during the period of availability, etc." Similar positions have been taken by Ford (1977) and Bayham (1979).

At a general evolutionary level, increasing population density favors increasing diversity in resource use as a way to enhance both the resistance of a population to environmental stresses and its resilience—the speed at which it is able to return to pre-stress levels (Harrison 1979). In other words, high population density selects for generalist rather than specialist resource-procurement strategies (cf. Pianka 1978). Generalists are less susceptible to minor environmental changes or perturbations because they spread their adaptations among several niches, but they are very susceptible to changes that affect large portions of the environment. Restricted mobility may force hunter-gatherers to become less resource specialized as a result of losing big-return items, but density-dependent selective pressures will increase resource diversity simply as a response to an increasing need for coping with periodic environmental crashes.

The cultivation of domesticates is consistent with shifts toward increasing resource diversity (cf. Christenson 1980). It seems likely, however, that because annual domesticates are usually available for consumption at a time when wild resources are plentiful (early fall), cultivation is a strategy for increasing the range of available resources, through storage, during seasons when wild resource availability is low (Flannery 1986:17).

A third potential response to increasing density—the development of obligatory or formal relationships between groups—is favored by at least two conditions: an increased potential for conflict and/or an increase in social control of access to resource areas. Wobst (1974, 1976) argued that increasing population size among hunter-gatherers will result in denser packing of maximal bands, compressing social boundaries between groups and resulting in less frequent contact.

Wobst (1977) suggested that greater density of maximal bands leads to a corresponding increase in "social distance." Van der Leeuw (1981:268) expanded this theme by arguing that reduced contact can mean irregular or unexpected encounters between groups which do not communicate frequently, a situation which he calls "punctuated interaction."

Punctuated interaction may in turn be linked to Sahlins's distinction between generalized and balanced reciprocity (Wiessner 1982a:69–70). With frequent contact, the exchange relationships underwriting social relations are comprised of relatively informal or generalized sharing, but as social distance increases and contact becomes infrequent or irregular, exchange relationships should become more immediate and thus assume characteristics of balanced reciprocity. Formal exchange relationships are an expectable means of establishing such social bonds.

The need to maintain formalized social interaction in the face of infrequent contact comes in part from the potential for conflict in unpredictable encounters. Intergroup conflict is much more likely when groups do not have an established way of interacting (Yengoyan 1976; Hayden 1982). Likewise, an increase in the number of groups within an area and a decline in the proportion of groups interacting regularly will probably lead to increasingly poor coordination among those groups, so that individual groups will have less knowledge about the activities of some other groups in their region. This in turn means increasing uncertainty about the use of particular resource patches.

Domesticated plants are useful in the context of developing social distance and problems of uncoordinated group activities because they are a source of predictability. The location of the resource is known with absolute certainty, and its temporal availability is known within short time ranges. Stored domesticates, as with any stored resource, are particularly helpful in enhancing predictability because the quantity of available resource is known.

But cultivars may have a more subtle role in the development or functioning of formal relationships or exchange systems. Maintaining alliance bonds between groups is costly in that the activation of a reciprocal obligation incurs a debt. Repayment, which will undoubtedly involve sharing resources or access to resources, may be very unpredictable, making the alliance itself a source of uncertainty (cf. Hayden 1981:523). A logical strategy would be to avoid an imbalance in obligations so that repayments do not become a burden leading to default and severance of the relationship. This is an important internal contradiction in that the system of reciprocity is crucial for providing periodically important assistance, but participation must be regulated to avoid removal from the system by failure to uphold obligations.

As a way of maintaining critical intergroup bonds while minimizing their use, hunter-gatherer groups might begin to focus on locally available but less frequently used resources to avoid procuring resources in areas controlled by other groups, thus activating alliance obligations. Such shifts in resource selection would probably depend on the cost of foregoing preferred resources obtained through alliance relationships.

This proposition may provide some insight into the problem of how hunter-gatherers maintain reciprocal obligations while investing in storage strategies because the principle of generalized sharing appears to be a great impediment to storage among modern hunter-gatherers (Lee 1979:412–14). Surplus production for the purpose of sustaining social relationships could evolve as their contribution to group fitness increased (cf. Bender 1981). Social means for limiting the immediate consumption of harvested resources would probably be predicated on ownership of the resource and the social obligation to share it at some later time. Inappropriate consumption of the resource would then place the consumer at risk of not being allowed to participate in sharing at some critical juncture in the future and perhaps loss of membership in some social networks.

The problems of unpredictable interaction, which may generate conflict among hunter-gatherers and select for ways of diminishing it, are, at least initially, the result of unstructured foraging in the sense of limited coordination between groups. Moore (1981) demonstrated through simulation studies that an area can accommodate higher group densities through coordinated foraging strategies than it can through uncoordinated foraging strategies. In fact, until a population density threshold (determined by carrying capacity) is reached, incremental increases in the number of groups in an area enhance foraging success if groups share information, a result of the synergistic effects of multiple information monitors (see also G. Johnson 1978; Levine 1984; Gatewood 1984; Waltz 1982).

Agricultural strategies are potentially quite advantageous in increasing the quality and quantity of information available to hunter-gatherers because such strategies have well-defined spatial and temporal characteristics and because they can facilitate the collection of other resources. That is, they are both the source of information and the means of acquiring it.

Storage of bulk resources has a tethering effect, tying consumers to storage locations (Binford 1980; Kelly 1983). This effect is not necessarily detrimental and may even allow foragers to search patches more widely and thoroughly than would otherwise be possible because storage extends the accessibility of resources beyond "natural" periods of availability, lengthening the productivity of an area and providing an opportunity to evaluate the activities of other hunter-gatherer groups in the region. In some situations, storage may also permit foragers to assess indicators of future resource distribution, such as local water conditions, animal behavior, or plant maturation, when an area might not otherwise be occupied.

In short, agricultural production is appropriate to all three primary, density-dependent, hunter-gatherer socioeconomic responses, supporting the proposition that a major economic advantage of agriculture is the reduction of environmental uncertainty. Moreover, the economic and social responses to increased density comprise the various organizational requisites for the successful cultivation of the four domesticated plants in the upper Sonoran agricultural complex. If the introduction of domesticates to the prehistoric Southwest were a density-dependent phenomenon among indigenous hunter-gatherers, we can expect density-dependent change and organizational consistency to precede their appearance. On the other hand, if these developments cannot be discerned prior to the arrival of agriculture, we would obviously want to reconsider the proposed construct or the adequacy of the data.

It would be well at this point to bring the discussion back to a more formal evolutionary perspective. Selection operates on variation. If the adoption of maize required a certain range of behavior and organization among recipient foragers, certain kinds of variation ought to have been present. The ecological constraints of fully domesticated maize make this variability a prerequisite for adoption. Logically, however, such variation may have existed long before or after maize was known to Southwest hunter-gatherers; the decision to adopt should have been predicated on organizational consistency but executed as an attempt to reduce economic uncertainty.

3

Archaic Prehistory: Environment, Chronology, and Mobility Organization

In this chapter I want to evaluate the argument that environmental changes increasing the range of critical resources and/or creating temporal and spatial incongruity in resource distribution favor the development of hunter-gatherer subsistence and mobility strategies consistent with the cultivation of annual domesticates. Because temporal incongruity in resource availability is considered a primary selective force for storage strategies, change toward increased temporal complexity should be a key factor in the adoption of domesticated plants.

The goal of this chapter is therefore to assess environmental change during the Archaic period for trends that might have generated conditions suitable for food production. My assumption is not that adoption was the result of environmental change, but rather that such change may have conditioned the acceptance of new resources.

Long-term changes in the southwestern environment have been a traditional research focus in the archaeology of the Archaic period. Most of the early descriptive studies of sites and material culture were collaborative efforts betweeen archaeologists and geologists interested in using the record of environmental change to date archaeological sites, and vice versa (e.g., Sayles and Antevs 1941; Bryan and Toulouse 1943; Antevs 1955). More recently, the collaborative emphasis has shifted to reconstructions of local site ecology as an indicator of possible hunter-gatherer adaptations (Irwin-Williams and Haynes 1970; Simmons 1984).

I offer here a somewhat different approach to the relationship between environmental change and Archaic prehistory, although one that is indebted to these studies: an assessment of temporal patterns in the location and structure of Archaic sites against temporal patterns in the geographical distribution of vegetation zones. If hunter-gatherer organization is responsive to environmental structure, then structural changes—species composition, density, seasonality, and distribution—should covary with changes in the physical indications of settlement systems.

Trends toward logistic production should result in the most obvious indication of hunter-gatherer settlement systems, repetitive site use. Over time the accretion of discarded material from multiple occupations will generally lead to increased site visibility (Binford 1983b:46). At a regional level, the degree of site visibility may correspond to an equivalent emphasis on collecting strategies.

Similarly, logistic systems involving extended use of specific localities are likely to produce a wide range of domestic debris and facilities. Architectural remains may occur if site use involved substantial shelters. Architecture may also serve as a social marker indicating group affiliation with specific areas (McGuire and Schiffer 1983), expectable in systems tied to repeated use of the same locations.

Logistic organization should also involve storage and storage facilities. The extent to which storage facilities appear in the archaeological record depends on the type of resource stored. While skin bags or rock cairns might suffice for some items, they may be inadequate for others, particularly domesticated plants (B. Smith 1985). Archaeologists tend to equate pits with storage, but other, poorly preserved facilities may also have been used, perhaps to a greater extent in highly mobile logistic systems. We should expect the development of storage in association with logistic production and before the adoption of cultigens, but the evidence may not be as obvious as we would wish.

Unfortunately, very little of what is considered Archaic-period archaeology has been chronometrically dated. Most temporal indicators are classes of material culture subjectively assigned to culture-historical periods (Chapman 1980; Cordell 1984; Judge 1981; Simmons 1984). To minimize the inherent ambiguity in site distributions defined by culture-historical markers, I have elected to use only chronometrically dated sites or site occupations. This method requires us to ignore a substantial portion of the published information on sites labelled "Archaic," but it leaves us with a set of sites that can be accurately placed in time. A few years ago this approach, which is clearly tentative, would have been impossible because of the paucity of dated sites. Now, widespread cultural resource management research has provided a corpus of dated sites large enough to begin a statistical consideration of regional Archaic chronologies.

ENVIRONMENTAL CHANGE

Modern patterns of Southwest vegetation are the product of changes which began over ten thousand years ago as the Laurentide and Cordilleran ice masses began to retreat from the northeastern portion of the continent (Bryson, Bareis, and Wendland 1970). With the final dissipation of the Laurentide sheet between 7000 and 6000 B.P., cool, dry summer air masses, which had dominated the western continent, were replaced by warm Pacific air. Atmospheric circulation in the Southwest after 6000 B.P. shifted to a mixed pattern of westerly flow in the winter and strong latitudinal movement of air masses in the summer (Knox 1983; Van Devender 1977).

The current expression of these changes is a pronounced monsoonal pattern in the Southwest, where precipitation occurs primarily in late summer and in winter. A high-pressure system off the Pacific coast generates winter precipitation in the northern Southwest in association with westerly winds, but very little of this moisture reaches the southern areas of the Southwest. In the summer, a high-pressure cell develops over the Gulf of Mexico, cyclonic storms sweep northwestward, and orographically produced rainfall occurs in most montane regions.

The combination of seasonal shifts in precipitation and topographic variation in the Southwest has produced distinct latitudinal differences in plant and animal biogeography. Along the lower Rio Grande Valley, south of thirty-three degrees north latitude, warm temperatures and low winter precipitation created the desert grasslands of the Chihuahuan Desert (fig. 9). In the northern Southwest, cooler temperatures and more winter moisture gave rise to widespread conifer forests and grasslands. In addition, the extensive montane areas of the north increase local topographic relief, resulting in complex zonation of plant communities by elevation and drainage. This ecological contrast reflects a major transformation of regional landscapes over the last ten thousand years, largely the result of a reduction in Late Pleistocene vegetation in the northern Southwest and its replacement by vegetative associations expanding north from the lower Rio Grande Valley.

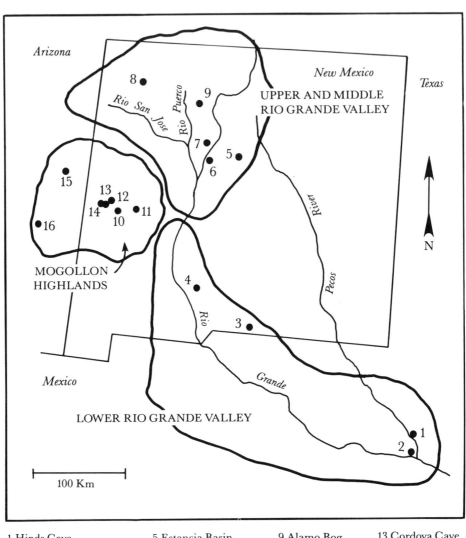

Arizona

New Mexico

Texas

8

9

UPPER AND MIDDLE
RIO GRANDE VALLEY

Rio San Jose

Rio Puerco

7

5

6

River

N

15

13 12

14 11

10

Pecos

16

MOGOLLON
HIGHLANDS

4

Rio

3

Mexico

Grande

LOWER RIO GRANDE VALLEY

1

2

100 Km

1 Hinds Cave	5 Estancia Basin	9 Alamo Bog	13 Cordova Cave
2 Bonfire Shelter	6 Comanche Springs	10 Bat Cave	14 O Block Cave
3 Sacramento Mountains	7 Isleta Cave	11 AKE Site	15 Laguna Salada
4 Gardner Springs	8 Chaco Canyon	12 Tularosa Cave	16 Cienega Creek

Figure 9. Physiographic subareas and localities in the study area.

Pollen evidence from the full-glacial period (24,000 to 14,000 B.P.) indicates that vegetation zones in the Rio Grande Valley and adjacent mountain ranges north of thirty-three degrees latitude may have been 900 to 1400 m lower than they are today (Hall 1985:117). As a result, most of the region was dominated by mesic alpine forests consisting of spruce, Douglas fir, limber pine, and ponderosa pine. Sagebrush communities were more widespread than they are today, and vast areas in enclosed basins such as the Estancia Basin and the San Augustine Plains were covered by lakes (Bachhuber 1982; Harris and Findley 1964; Betancourt and Van Devender 1981; Powers 1939).

In the lower Rio Grande Valley, vegetation during the full-glacial was characterized by xeric woodland savannahs dominated by grasses, pinyon pine, juniper, and oak. Bryant and Shafer (1977) suggested that Douglas fir was present in most parts of southwestern Texas, indicating much cooler and wetter conditions than exist today.

Between 12,000 and 10,000 B.P., postglacial continental increases in temperature and aridity initiated a series of vegetation changes in the Southwest which produced a diminution of alpine zones in the north and subalpine zones in the south. By the Early Holocene (10,000 to 7000 B.P.), the mesic forests in the north were shrinking and being replaced by increasing numbers of pinyon pine (*Pinus edulis*) and juniper, while in the south, the pinyon associations gave way to desert shrub communities (Van Devender and Spaulding 1979; Dering 1979). According to Hall (1985:108), regional pollen spectra from the north include pinyon during the full-glacial, but Van Devender, Betancourt, and Wimberly (1984) argued that pinyon did not appear in the north until about 8000 B.P. as a result of migration from the southern Rio Grande Valley. Macrofossil remains of *Pinus edulis* at Bat Cave occur in layers dated between 12,000 and 8000 B.P. (Wills 1985), indicating that some pinyon was present in northern montane areas by the end of the Pleistocene. It therefore seems likely that pinyon-juniper associations expanded during the Holocene because of indigenous processes and northward migration. The combined effect of these processes would have been a transgression in the range of xeric subalpine vegetation from south to north and from lower to higher elevations (cf. Van Devender, Betancourt, and Wimberly 1984:fig. 3).

Van Devender and Spaulding (1979) argued from the analysis of fossil pack rat middens that pinyon woodlands may have persisted as an extensive zone in the southern Rio Grande until 8000 B.P. Dering (1979), on the other hand, cited pollen and plant macrofossils from Hinds Cave as evidence that during the Early Holocene, pinyon was rapidly confined to relict stands in canyons. Regional vegetation, according to Dering, was typified by increasing grasslands with some xeric species such as cacti, agave, and sotol. Faunal assemblages from the period (Harris 1970) are seen as indicative of sagebrush grasslands, not pinyon woodlands. Generally, the region had a cool climate and heavy winter precipitation (Van Devender and Spaulding 1979:709; Harris 1970:22).

During the Middle Holocene (7000 to 5000–4000 B.P.), generally known as the Altithermal in the West (Antevs 1949, 1955), temperature and aridity reached levels higher than averages for the Holocene or the historic period (Knox 1983; Hall 1985). The environmental effects of these trends are somewhat ambiguous because lowered water tables and consequent erosion from reduced vegetation cover have destroyed much of the regional pollen record in alluvial settings.

However, plant macrofossils from rockshelters in the lower Rio Grande Valley indicate an increase in grasses and shrub vegetation during the Middle Holocene (Dering 1979), a pattern consistent with elevated percentages of cheno-am pollen from preserved alluvial settings (Freeman 1972). Van Devender and Spaulding (1979) suggest that the mid-Holocene saw the development of fully desert grasslands in what is now the Chihuahuan Desert. By 4000 B.P. the desert had essentially attained its modern geographical boundaries.

Mid-Holocene changes in the north seem to have been less dramatic. During this period the last vestiges of Pleistocene lakes (Bachhuber 1982; Weber 1980; Markgraf et al. 1984; Hevly 1964; Powers 1939) were replaced by open grasslands. The reduction of alpine forest zones and the expansion of pinyon-juniper woodlands continued (Van Devender, Betancourt, and Wimberly 1984).

Late Holocene (4000 B.P. to present) paleoenvironmental records from the lower Rio Grande Valley indicate an increase in effective moisture over the Middle Holocene. Pollen from Hinds Cave reflects an increase in grasses (Dering 1979), as does pollen from Gardner Springs (Freeman 1972). The appearance of bison at Bonfire Shelter (2800–2399 B.P.) on the Pecos River confirms an increase in grasslands and probably the incidence of surface water (Dibble 1968; Dillehay 1974; Marmaduke 1978; Schafer 1977).

Evidence for an increase in effective moisture in the lower Rio Grande Valley during the Late Holocene is duplicated in the northern Southwest. Pollen records from the San Juan Basin (Hall 1977; Fredlund 1984), the Jemez Mountains (Stearns 1981), and the San Augustine Plains (Hevly 1980) indicate regional increases in pine forests between 3000 and 2000 B.P. Brief lake resurgences were noted in the Estancia Basin (Bachhuber 1982) and the San Augustine Plains (Weber 1980; Hevly 1980), attesting to greater precipitation and higher water tables (cf. Haynes 1968; Scott 1985). In addition, bison from the Comanche Springs site in the central Rio Grande Valley were dated between 2700 and 2200 B.P. (Fulgam and Hibben 1980), and bison from Bat Cave date to 1800 B.P. It has been suggested that effective moisture increased briefly around 2500 B.P. (Irwin-Williams and Haynes 1970:69), but recent evidence indicates that this phenomenon probably began earlier, implying that the end of the Archaic period (ca. 4000 to 2000 B.P.) was not a period of obvious environmental stress in the Rio Grande area.

These environmental changes undoubtedly influenced indigenous hunter-gatherer economies in many ways, but the most important was the geographical shift in potential resource productivity. Pinyon-juniper woodlands are the most economically productive zones in the Southwest because they represent an abundant critical resource in pinyon nuts (Thomas 1973; Lanner 1981; Ford 1984) and because they support a wide diversity of wildlife (Hevly 1983). Increasing Holocene aridity in the Southwest displaced this major resource zone from the south to the north.

This latitudinal displacement of pinyon-juniper woodlands probably meant a simultaneous increase in their geographical extent—latitudinal and longitudinal expansion on a regional scale and elevational expansion on a local scale. As pinyon and juniper expanded northward (see Van Devender, Betancourt, and Wimberly 1984) over the course of the Holocene, the northern Southwest should have been increasingly productive for hunter-gatherers, and the potential of the southern Southwest should have declined from Early Holocene levels.

Associated with this shift in absolute resource potential was the development of contrasting patterns in the seasonality of resource availability. The southern Rio Grande today is notable for mild winters and hot summers, but seasonality is not pronounced (Marroquin 1977). Vegetation is dominated by xeric species which are highly dispersed in response to moisture scarcity. The reproductive cycles of many of the economically important floral resources found in this environment, such as yucca, agave, and sotol, make them available throughout most of the year (Schafer 1977; Flannery 1968). In the northern Southwest, however, seasonal plant availability is much more restricted, especially in major resources such as pinyon, walnut, and oak, which are gathered in late summer and early fall (Lanner 1981; Hevly 1983).

For hunter-gatherers in the north, these long-term developments would have resulted in greater environmental productivity, but through resources available only at certain times of the year. In the southern Rio Grande region, hunter-gatherers would have experienced long-term declines in the overall productivity of the environment but an increase in floral resources available through large portions of the year.

All else being equal, these environmental changes should have favored an increasing emphasis on foraging strategies by southern hunter-gatherer groups in response to the highly dispersed and relatively unpredictable patterns of maturation in xeric plants. Northern hunter-gatherers, confronted with increasingly predictable and abundant resources, but also with limited periods of access and local patchiness, should have turned to logistic or collecting strategies as effective economic responses.

Another documented long-term change in the southwestern environment was reduced surface water. Lowering water tables and the desiccation of large lakes made surface water increasingly localized. Major drainages such as the Rio Grande, Pecos River, and Rio Puerco probably maintained consistent flow, but the local availability of surface water became increasingly seasonal. Playas and shallow lakes filled from annual surface runoff, and spring flow was controlled by local fluctuations in water table levels (cf. Haynes 1968; Judge 1973).

In the southern desert areas, the extreme scarcity of surface water from high evapotranspiration rates must have been a major year-round constraint on hunter-gatherer mobility, and sources such as the Rio Grande were undoubtedly a primary focus of settlement systems (see Bryant 1974). The problem was far less acute in the northern Southwest, where water deficit became an issue mostly in late spring and early summer. Throughout the Southwest, however, increasing localization of water sources must have affected the mobility of hunter-gatherers.

At lower elevations, a northward expansion of desert flora such as cacti and yucca accompanied the northward expansion of pinyon-juniper over time. This was especially true in the central Rio Grande Valley, where desert-shrub communities extended as far north as thirty-four degrees between the Mogollon and Sacramento ranges. An increase in desert plant species at lower elevations in the north would have provided northern hunter-gatherers with improved access to critical winter and spring plant resources. Where feasible, hunter-gatherers should have been able to move seasonally between areas with winter-spring plant resources and areas with summer-fall resources. As elevational zonation in vegetative communities became more pronounced and water sources more restricted, they probably developed mobility systems that took them from valleys and basins during winter and spring to pinyon-juniper woodlands in upland areas during summer and fall. This pattern was documented historically for the Shoshonis of the Great Basin (Steward 1938; Thomas 1973) and for the Apaches in the southern Southwest (Goodwin 1971; Opler 1941).

The widely held view that the mid-Holocene period of high temperatures and aridity was somehow deleterious to Southwest foragers (Whalen 1973; Nance 1972) raises a possible objection to this hypothesized development. The implicit assumption is that extended drought during the Altithermal reduced vegetation cover and created "dust-bowl" conditions (e.g., Antevs 1955:329, 331; Dick 1965:105), but it was probably the historic dust-bowl years of the 1930s in the West that colored these perceptions. In either case, the Altithermal is commonly seen as a time when hunter-gatherers were under considerable stress from a deteriorating environment, resulting in population decline and shifts to low-return plant foods (Nance 1972).

However, little paleoenvironmental evidence suggests widespread and geographically uniform soil exposure and deflation during the mid-Holocene (see Hall 1985; Gillespie 1985). Although mean annual temperatures and aridity were higher than modern averages, the impact of these factors on the environment must be gauged against the type of vegetative communities and physiographic conditions present in the Southwest during the early Holocene and at the beginning of the Altithermal.

The major effect of increasingly warm and dry climatic regimes during the Altithermal was expansion of pinyon-juniper woodlands and the establishment of open grasslands. Elevated aridity reduced the size of forests and lakes, but the vegetation replacing them—pinyon, grasses, and cheno-ams—was more economically productive. Rather than characterizing the Altithermal as a monolithic period of environmental degradation which had adverse impacts on indigenous hunter-gatherers, it is more consistent with paleoenvironmental evidence to see it as a dynamic period producing a variety of changes with complex but not necessarily negative implications for forager economies.

Perhaps the traditional interpretation of a shift from Paleo-Indian big-game hunting to Archaic small-game procurement should not be seen in negative terms. The continental die-off of large animals at the end of the Pleistocene might have created something of a resource vacuum in the Southwest, which was still heavily forested, cool, and wet. Thus the expanding grasslands and open woodlands of the Holocene may have actually increased the total availability of animal resources, in addition to increasing the availability of plant foods.

Long-term Holocene environmental trends in the Southwest therefore suggest the development of regional differences in hunter-gatherer economic organization corresponding to the establishment of contrasting ecologies. In the northern regions, mobility systems were probably predicated on seasonal movements between lowland and upland zones, involving seasonal emphasis on logistic production. In contrast, southern hunter-gatherers were committed to fewer and less extensive seasonal movements because of the region's greater homogeneity in resource distribution; therefore, logistic strategies were probably less important or pronounced. In the south, riverine areas were critical during dry winter months, and some reduced mobility would be expected, followed by dispersal during summer and fall. With continual increases in resource productivity, the north probably had increasing potential for population growth, while in the south the decline in productivity after the early Holocene likely created conditions favoring relative population stability.

By 4000 B.P. regional environmental boundaries had come to approximate their modern extent, but the period of increased effective moisture between 4000 and 2000 B.P. probably favored increased complexity in plant and animal resource distribution through the continued expansion of pinyon-juniper woodlands and savannahs and the episodic resurgence of basin lakes. Although the appearance of bison in the Rio Grande Valley during this period remains a poorly understood event, the availability of a large game animal in lower elevation areas used primarily in winter and spring undoubtedly had an important effect on hunter-gatherer systems. These late Holocene environmental changes suggest that logistic production by hunter-gatherers may have been strongly favored at this time.

MOBILITY DURING THE PREAGRICULTURAL PERIOD

Documenting hunter-gatherer responses to changes in the environment of the Southwest, if indeed there were any responses, depends on an understanding of temporal and spatial patterning in the organization of economic pursuits. To maximize the reliability of these patterns, I have considered only chronometrically dated site occupations in this discussion, represented by 283 radiocarbon dates obtained from published reports and circulated manuscripts. A growing interest in chronometric dating in the Southwest is responsible for a steady increase in dates from the Archaic, and although this study does not include some recent determinations, it does include dates available through 1984.[1]

To confine the analysis to the Archaic or preceramic period (see Cordell 1984), only dates between 10,000 and 2000 B.P. have been considered. Determinations with standard deviations in excess of seven hundred years were excluded, as were dates obtained from samples of soil humates, bone, shell or other carbonates, and samples processed by solid-carbon techniques, with the exception of several dates from the Mogollon Highlands and the Rio Grande Valley. Contemporaneous dates from the same site were assessed and averaged according to guidelines suggested by Long and Rippeteau (1974).

Each date in the set was corrected for secular variation in carbon-14, as suggested by Klein et al. (1982); the resulting "dates" are the midpoints of the calibrated 95-percent confidence intervals, given according to mean and standard deviation. Where necessary, determinations were also corrected for isotopic fractionation (Stuiver and Polach 1977). Certain time intervals during the Holocene exhibit tremendous variation in the production of atmospheric radiocarbon, especially 6000–5000 B.P. and 3000–2000 B.P. (Suess 1980;

---

1. Details of the selection of radiocarbon determinations can be found in Wills (1985). All the determinations used here were taken from date lists in *Radiocarbon* or other published sources. There are obvious sampling problems in using radiocarbon data in the way I propose, as well as theoretical issues about the actual meaning of a date in terms of human behavior. I am not unaware of these problems, nor do I mean to minimize their significance. In taking this analytic approach, I am not using dates as a test of my model but using that model to look for consistency. This will probably be a thoroughly unhappy exercise for many archaeologists with serious concerns about the Archaic and radiocarbon dating, but I want to consider every possible angle available. If chronology building has any relationship to settlement patterns, then it is worthwhile to at least look at the possible connections. Finally, I have not used the most recent calibration curves (Stuiver and Reimer 1986) because I did not have time to rework the data before publication of this study; however, I do not believe the newly refined calibrations would have significantly altered the shape of the curves given herein.

Ralph, Michael, and Han 1973; Stuiver and Pearson 1986), or about 25 percent of the Archaic period in the Southwest, a problem that dramatically demonstrates the need for calibration (contra Berry 1982:26–27).

These selective criteria increase the reliability of the dates within the sample, but there remains the important question of the reliability of the sample itself in assessing temporal and spatial patterning of Archaic sites. The two issues of paramount importance are site preservation and sampling bias by archaeologists.

Preservation of sites and datable material depends on a host of factors at the time of deposition, including climate, site location, fuel choice, and on-site cultural activities. Postdepositional conditions affecting preservation include erosion and alluviation, soil chemistry, and insect, animal, and human disturbance (Waterbolk 1971; Smiley 1985; Schiffer 1986). It is impossible to adequately address any of these issues, and although I will momentarily reach a conclusion based on archaeological sampling strategies, it is also impossible to determine the extent to which such tactics have biased existing chronologies. As unsatisfying as it may be, for the present time we can only assess chronological patterns for consistency with specified expectations, not the question of how they reflect site preservation and sampling bias.

However, there are persuasive reasons for using radiocarbon dates to assess regional patterns of occupation, as there are for any chronometric method placing sites in temporal order. Rick (1987:55) has presented an eloquent argument for applying radiocarbon assays to occupational patterns in his study of highland and coastal areas of Peru:

> Dates are like self-dated artifacts; because each presumably represents human activity at a point in time, they can be directly compared to each other. Despite intervening biases, I assume that the number of dates is *related* to the magnitude of occupation, or to the total number of person-years of human existence in a given area. Using this premise, it is possible to assess and compare, in a relative fashion, the occupation histories within and between regions.

I take essentially the same position, drawing comparisons between the radiocarbon chronologies of different areas.

The temporal distribution of the entire sample is shown in figure 10. These histograms reflect patterning in radiocarbon determinations that have not been dendrochronologically calibrated to facilitate comparison with results presented by other investigators (e.g., Berry 1982; Berry and Marmaduke 1982). The interval width in figure 10a is 150 years, the mean of standard deviations for the sample, and the 300-year interval in figure 10b is twice that number, or two standard deviations.

```
A  MIDPOINT    COUNT FOR 7.B.P.   (EACH X= 1)

   -10000.0     0  +
    -9850.0     1  +x
    -9700.0     0  +
    -9550.0     2  +xx
    -9400.0     1  +x
    -9250.0     1  +x
    -9100.0     0  +
    -8950.0     0  +
    -8800.0     3  +xxx
    -8650.0     1  +x
    -8500.0     1  +x
    -8350.0     2  +xx
    -8200.0     3  +xxx
    -8050.0     3  +xxx
    -7900.0     3  +xxx
    -7750.0     2  +xx
    -7600.0     5  +xxxxx
    -7450.0     3  +xxx
    -7300.0     4  +xxxx
    -7150.0     4  +xxxx
    -7000.0     2  +xx
    -6850.0     3  +xxx
    -6700.0     7  +xxxxxxx
    -6550.0     2  +xx
    -6400.0     2  +xx
    -6250.0     1  +x
    -6100.0     6  +xxxxxx
    -5950.0     1  +x
    -5800.0     3  +xxx
    -5650.0     3  +xxx
    -5500.0     5  +xxxxx
    -5350.0     1  +x
    -5200.0     3  +xxx
    -5050.0     3  +xxx
    -4900.0     7  +xxxxxxx
    -4750.0     7  +xxxxxxx
    -4600.0     2  +xx
    -4450.0     9  +xxxxxxxxx
    -4300.0     3  +xxx
    -4150.0     6  +xxxxxx
    -4000.0     9  +xxxxxxxxx
    -3850.0     5  +xxxxx
    -3700.0    10  +xxxxxxxxxx
    -3550.0    12  +xxxxxxxxxxxx
    -3400.0     8  +xxxxxxxx
    -3250.0    12  +xxxxxxxxxxxx
    -3100.0     6  +xxxxxx
    -2950.0     8  +xxxxxxxx
    -2800.0    19  +xxxxxxxxxxxxxxxxxxx
    -2650.0    10  +xxxxxxxxxx
    -2500.0    22  +xxxxxxxxxxxxxxxxxxxxxx
    -2350.0    18  +xxxxxxxxxxxxxxxxxx
    -2200.0    27  +xxxxxxxxxxxxxxxxxxxxxxxxxxx
    -2050.0    22  +xxxxxxxxxxxxxxxxxxxxxx


B  MIDPOINT    COUNT FOR 7.B.P.   (EACH X= 1)

   -10000.0     1  +x
    -9700.0     0  +
    -9400.0     4  +xxxx
    -9100.0     0  +
    -8800.0     4  +xxxx
    -8500.0     2  +xx
    -8200.0     6  +xxxxxx
    -7900.0     5  +xxxxx
    -7600.0     8  +xxxxxxxx
    -7300.0     8  +xxxxxxxx
    -7000.0     5  +xxxxx
    -6700.0     8  +xxxxxxxx
    -6400.0     4  +xxxx
    -6100.0     7  +xxxxxxx
    -5800.0     6  +xxxxxx
    -5500.0     7  +xxxxxxx
    -5200.0     4  +xxxx
    -4900.0    14  +xxxxxxxxxxxxxx
    -4600.0     8  +xxxxxxxx
    -4300.0     9  +xxxxxxxxx
    -4000.0    15  +xxxxxxxxxxxxxxx
    -3700.0    20  +xxxxxxxxxxxxxxxxxxxx
    -3400.0    20  +xxxxxxxxxxxxxxxxxxxx
    -3100.0    14  +xxxxxxxxxxxxxx
    -2800.0    29  +xxxxxxxxxxxxxxxxxxxxxxxxxxxxx
    -2500.0    38  +xxxxxxxxxxxxxxxxxxxxxxxxxxxxxxxxxxxxxx
    -2200.0    48  +xxxxxxxxxxxxxxxxxxxxxxxxxxxxxxxxxxxxxxxxxxxxxxxx
    -1900.0     9  +xxxxxxxxx
```

Figure 10. Histograms of uncalibrated radiocarbon dates from preceramic southwestern sites. Left, interval width of 150 years is the average sigma. Right, interval width of 300 years is twice the average sigma.

The histograms indicate the presence of hunter-gatherer groups in the region throughout the Archaic; there are no notable gaps in the distribution. The lower frequency of dates prior to 4000 B.P. is consistent with relatively low population density and/or the effects of time on site preservation. The rapid falloff after 2000 B.P. reflects the tendency of southwestern archaeologists to rely on tree-ring dates to establish time periods after that date, rather than a decline in the number of sites (see Smiley 1985; Schiffer 1986).

There is an apparent decline in the frequency of dates between 6500 and 5000 B.P. compared to the preceding thirty-five hundred years (10,000–6500 B.P.). Berry and Berry (1986:307), who have shown a similar pattern with somewhat different data, argue that it represents a decline in regional occupational intensity, probably related to climatic conditions during the Altithermal. To test the significance of the apparent decrease, we need to determine if the pattern is significantly different from random, given the number of arbitrary time intervals on the graph and the number of dates being plotted. Since the pattern in figure 10a is not significant at a level of .01 ($\chi^2 = 33.75$, DF = 19), there is no compelling reason to view the dip as an indication of prehistoric occupational change or sampling bias. In other words, the "decline" does not represent a significant deviation from general trends.

The pattern described by the histograms is geometric and can be seen clearly in figure 11, a cumulative frequency curve of the same sample. The individual dates in the frequency curve have now been dendrochronologically calibrated, and the lack of distinctive steps or plateaus in the curve again confirms the absence of any periods when hunter-gatherer groups were not present in the region.

However, beyond indicating the presence of Archaic occupations, the only firm conclusion that can be drawn from these aggregate distributions is an increase in the frequency of *dated* sites or dated site components through time. This pattern could logically be attributed to several factors, including better preservation, increased population size, and shifts in settlement mobility.

When the aggregate sample is divided into subregions, several types of variation emerge that may help assess the factors responsible for this pattern. Histograms of calibrated dates from six subregions (fig. 12) suggest significant interregional variation in radiocarbon chronologies. The temporal distribution of dates from the Big Bend area of the lower Rio Grande Valley appears to indicate a relatively consistent frequency of occupations throughout the Archaic, beginning around ten thousand years ago. In the central Rio Grande Valley, from the Trans-Pecos area to the San Juan Basin, patterning in the three subregions (lower Rio Grande, central Rio Grande, San Juan Basin) is very similar, with dated occupations starting at about 8000 B.P. and increasing in frequency thereafter. By contrast, chronologies in the montane areas of the northern Rio Grande Valley and the Mogollon Highlands exhibit distribu-

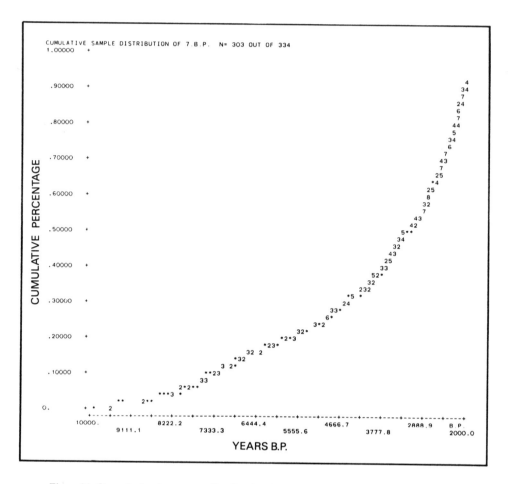

Figure 11. Cumulative frequency distribution for calibrated radiocarbon dates from preceramic southwestern sites.

tions that do not begin until after 5000 B.P., with a few scattered exceptions, and increase rapidly from that point on.

If these regional distributions are transformed to cumulative frequency distributions, an interesting pattern develops. As shown in figure 13, the interregional variation is time-transgressive from south to north and from lower to higher elevations. Dated occupations begin earlier in the southern Rio Grande Valley, but the rate of subsequent increase is much less than in areas to the north. The central Rio Grande Valley and the San Juan Basin have nearly identical patterns of increase, but they increase less than mountain areas. A strong correlative relationship exists between regional patterns and site elevation; 80 percent of the variance in dates is accounted for by the mean elevation of sites within regions (r = .89, r^2 = .80).

SAN JUAN BASIN

Midpoint	Count	
2000.0	13	+xxxxxxxxxxxxx
3000.0	15	+xxxxxxxxxxxxxxx
4000.0	10	+xxxxxxxxxx
5000.0	7	+xxxxxxx
6000.0	7	+xxxxxxx
7000.0	6	+xxxxxx
8000.0	2	+xx
9000.0	0	+
10000.0	0	+
Total	60	

NORTHERN RIO GRANDE

Midpoint	Count	
2000.0	2	+xx
3000.0	3	+xxx
4000.0	2	+xx
5000.0	1	+x
6000.0	0	+
7000.0	0	+
8000.0	0	+
9000.0	0	+
10000.0	0	+
Total	8	

MIDDLE RIO GRANDE

Midpoint	Count	
2000.0	4	+xxxx
3000.0	12	+xxxxxxxxxxxx
4000.0	11	+xxxxxxxxxxx
5000.0	5	+xxxxx
6000.0	4	+xxxx
7000.0	4	+xxxx
8000.0	1	+x
9000.0	0	+
10000.0	0	+
Total	41	

MOGOLLON HIGHLANDS

Midpoint	Count	
2000.0	8	+xxxxxxxx
3000.0	14	+xxxxxxxxxxxxxx
4000.0	2	+xx
5000.0	1	+x
6000.0	1	+x
7000.0	1	+x
8000.0	1	+x
9000.0	0	+
10000.0	0	+
Total	28	

LOWER RIO GRANDE

Midpoint	Count	
2000.0	6	+xxxxxx
3000.0	4	+xxxx
4000.0	8	+xxxxxxxx
5000.0	5	+xxxxx
6000.0	3	+xxx
7000.0	1	+x
8000.0	2	+xx
9000.0	0	+
10000.0	0	+
Total	29	

TRANS-PECOS (BIG BEND)

Midpoint	Count	
2000.0	10	+xxxxxxxxxx
3000.0	11	+xxxxxxxxxxx
4000.0	12	+xxxxxxxxxxxx
5000.0	13	+xxxxxxxxxxxxx
6000.0	12	+xxxxxxxxxxxx
7000.0	16	+xxxxxxxxxxxxxxxx
8000.0	7	+xxxxxxx
9000.0	4	+xxxx
10000.0	3	+xxx
Total	88	

Figure 12. Regional histograms of calibrated radiocarbon dates from preceramic southwestern sites.

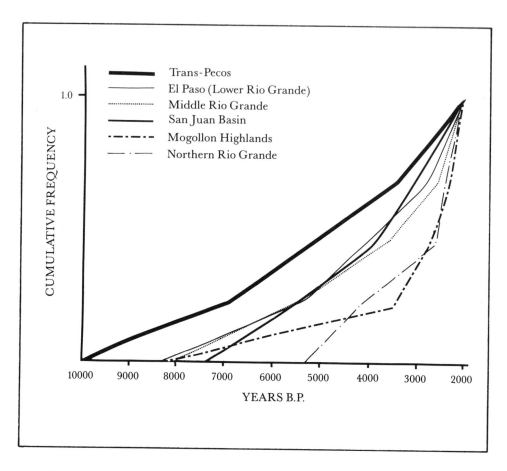

Figure 13. Cumulative frequency distributions of radiocarbon dates from different regions of the study area.

The consistent patterning between radiocarbon chronologies and the latitudinal and elevational differences between regions suggests the effect of some independent variable. An obvious change during the Archaic period exhibiting time-transgressive trends from south to north and lower to higher elevations is the expansion of pinyon-juniper woodlands and open grasslands, or generally, the development of complex vegetation zonation and seasonality in the north and their decline in the south.

This long-term sequence of vegetational change has several logical implications for hunter-gatherer economies that might be partially responsible for the time-transgressive trends in regional chronologies. The probable response to increasing spatial and temporal complexity in economic resources would have been greater reliance on logistically organized modes of production. As a result, mobility systems likely became increasingly based on repetitive use of some key sites or areas, leading to greater archaeological visibility of those locations through accretion of debris and construction.

Southwest prehistorians working in nonceramic archaeology have used the explicit research strategy of investigating sites with the best "research potential" (e.g., Wait 1983; Vogler, Gilpin, and Anderson 1983)—that is, large sites or those with specific kinds of artifacts, such as projectile points, considered diagnostic of particular time periods. This sampling strategy favors the investigation of highly visible sites (Vierra 1980:356). I think it is safe to argue that much of the patterning evident in regional southwestern radiocarbon chronologies reflects the disproportional representation of visible sites over time. In other words, the more visible an Archaic site is to archaeologists, the more likely it is to be sampled for datable material and thus contribute to regional chronology.

The time-transgressive patterns over different regions can therefore be seen as a rough index of changes in site visibility. Because logistic hunter-gatherer organization in the Southwest ought to have become more likely with the increase in resource complexity represented by pinyon-juniper expansion and increased aridity, probably resulting in increased site visibility, interregional variation in radiocarbon chronologies may well be the product of shifts in economic organization and mobility.

The attractiveness of the apparent fit between regional radiocarbon chronologies and expectable shifts in hunter-gatherer organization and mobility should not be taken as a direct indicator of prehistoric demographics. Although radiocarbon chronologies begin at about 8000 B.P. in the central Rio Grande Valley and 5000 B.P. in montane areas, there is evidence in both areas of earlier use by hunter-gatherers. Paleo-Indian sites or artifacts are widespread (but limited in number) in the Rio Grande Valley and in the San Augustine Plains of the Mogollon Highlands, and they occur sporadically in the San Juan Basin (see Judge 1973, 1981; Weber 1980; Broster 1983). On the basis of projectile points, sites dating to the Middle Archaic (7000–4000 B.P.) are also common in the San Augustine Plains, although they are not well represented by chronometrically dated occupations.

In the upland areas, the rapid increase of radiocarbon dates after 4000 B.P. seems associated with an increased use of rockshelters. To some extent, open-air sites have been systematically ignored in favor of rockshelters in upland regions, but there is little evidence for rockshelter occupation until the Late Archaic. The abruptness of this increase thus reflects some bias toward rockshelter excavation, but because those excavations also indicate a change in site-use patterns, the absence or low frequency of chronometric dates cannot necessarily be taken to reflect the absence of hunter-gatherers.

In the Big Bend area, the pattern of site use during the Archaic changed much less than it did in the northern Rio Grande, and the long-term, regular use of rockshelters in the south is evident in the slope of the radiocarbon curve. In contrast, the northern Rio Grande Valley and the San Juan Basin exhibit chronological patterns suggesting increasingly repetitive site use over time, some of which involves rockshelters. Upland areas of the extreme northern Rio Grande and the Mogollon Highlands have extremely sharp curves beginning much later than other areas, partly because of a shift to intensive use of rockshelters. These regional patterns derive directly from the organization of hunter-gatherer mobility, but they may or may not be related to population density.

In addition to radiocarbon chronologies, the distribution of preagricultural sites, features, and some artifact classes supports transgressive regional trends toward apparent logistic strategies in hunter-gatherer economies. For example, projectile point types generally considered diagnostic of temporal periods within the Archaic (see Irwin-Williams 1973, 1979) are not distributed uniformly across the southwestern landscape. Although culture-historical constructs place large-scale limits on the geographical occurrence of point types (e.g., Beckett 1973), associative patterns of smaller scale do become apparent.

During the Early Holocene, point forms corresponding to the Jay-Bajada or Rio Grande series—a large, thick, shouldered type—occur primarily in the northern Rio Grande Valley and adjacent areas. Concentrations have been reported in the San Luis Valley of southern Colorado (Honea 1969; Renaud 1942; Dennis Stanford, personal communication); on terraces above the San Juan River in northwest New Mexico and southeast Utah (Botelio 1955; Chapman 1977; Hadlock 1962; Hunt and Tanner 1960; Mohr and Sample 1959; Vogler, Gilpin, and Anderson 1983); and in the Little Colorado River drainage of east-central Arizona (Longacre 1962; Wendorf and Thomas 1951), the Rio San Jose drainage in west-central New Mexico (Agogino and Hester 1953; Roosa 1967; Honea 1969; Broster 1983), the Rio Puerco drainage in central New Mexico (Irwin-Williams 1973; Hicks 1984), the Estancia Basin of eastern New Mexico (Roosa 1967; Lyons 1969), and the San Augustine Plains of west-central New Mexico (Hurt and McKnight 1949; Wills and Lee 1984). Perennial streams (especially during the Early Holocene) or standing water (lake basins) were common to all these locations.

Middle Archaic point forms, represented by the San Jose, Pinto, and Augustin series, have basically the same distribution as Early Archaic types. During the Late Archaic, a widespread point form appeared, similar to San Pedro (Sayles 1983) and Basketmaker II points (Morris and Burgh 1954). Late Archaic points occur in many localities, but for the first time, a large number occur in rugged upland areas such as the Mogollon Mountains (Martin et al. 1952; Martin, Rinaldo, and Bluhm 1954), the White Mountains in Arizona (Haury 1957), and northeastern Arizona (Parry, Burgett, and Smiley 1985).

The distribution of Archaic points from all periods is generally accompanied by evidence for repeated site use. In the riverine drainages, these sites are usually found in alluvial settings and frequently consist of superimposed hearths (e.g., Agogino and Hibben 1957; Agogino and Hester 1956; Agogino 1960; Dick 1943; Campbell and Ellis 1952) or artifact concentrations in sand dunes (Irwin-Williams 1973; Volger, Gilpin, and Anderson 1983; Moore and Winter 1980; Reher and Witter 1977; Simmons 1984). Late Archaic points also occur in intensively used rockshelters in montane regions.

In sum, the radiocarbon chronologies suggesting intensive use of valley and basin areas during the Early and Middle Archaic, followed by an increase in dated sites in upland areas during the Late Archaic, are confirmed in the temporal frequencies of projectile points associated with those periods.

Another line of evidence, which also seems to correspond to radiocarbon chronologies and projectile point distributions, is the geographical distribution of preceramic structures. Earlier I suggested that house construction might covary with repetitive settlement patterns and surely reflects some degree of logistic foraging. One of the earliest dated houses in the Southwest, if not the earliest, was discovered on the Chama River in the northern Rio Grande Valley. Site OC-8 (Lang 1980) contained a roughly circular struture about 2.1 m in diameter and 15 cm deep. No postholes were discerned, but four burned areas within the structure were interpreted as hearths (Lang 1980:54). A hearth adjacent to the structure produced a radiocarbon date of 5240 ± 130 B.P. (DIC-1783).

Lang (1980:71) suggested that the OC-8 structure was a shallow pithouse associated with at least sixteen extramural pit hearths, a cobble-lined hearth, and a processing or roasting pit. The chipped stone assemblage from these features reflects on-site manufacture of tools, possibly including biface manufacture (Lang 1980:114). Among the lithic materials, however, the most intriguing are over one hundred specimens of ground stone, including eighty-nine manos and ten grinding slabs.

Lang (1980:170) cited the large ground stone assemblage as evidence of plant food processing and suggested that the primary economic activities at the site may have been seed collection and processing. Stratigraphic superimposition of some features and remodelling of others was taken to indicate repeated site use over a period of perhaps three thousand years, during which the basic subsistence tasks at the site did not change.

A site like OC-8 was excavated by Beckett (1973) on a tributary drainage to the Rio San Jose in west-central New Mexico. The Moquino site (D 4013) produced at least two shallow, "pithouse-like" structures defined by dense concentrations of ash, charcoal, ground stone, and hearths. One structure gave a radiocarbon date of 2235 ± 95 B.P. (I-5870), and another dated to 3920 ± 155 B.P. (I-5869; Beckett 1973:130, 135; Berry and Berry 1986:290). Berry and Berry (1986:290) also report dates of 3840 ± 200 B.P. (I-2910) and

4610 ± 350 B.P. (I-2911), although they do not provide any additional information.

The Moquino site is interesting because it indicates repeated and possibly prolonged occupation, food processing by grinding, and lithic manufacture to replace projectile points (cf. Beckett 1973). Located between the pinyon-juniper woodlands surrounding Mt. Taylor and the riverine zone of the Rio San Jose, the site provided relatively easy access to both of these important resource areas.

A series of sites similar to the Moquino site may lie along the Jemez River, about 80 km to the northeast. Agogino and Hibben (1957) reported a number of alluvial and surface "hearths" near Santa Ana Pueblo characterized by large ash concentrations described as "lenses" up to 2 feet thick and 20 feet long (Agogino and Hibben 1957:422; also Agogino and Hester 1956). These features were associated with ground stone and chipped stone debitage dated between 3300 and 2180 B.P. by a series of radiocarbon assays (Crane and Griffin 1958, 1960). The setting of the Santa Ana sites is similar to that of the Moquino site, with the Jemez Mountains to the north and the valleys of the Jemez River and Rio Grande to the north and east.

Other Late Archaic pithouses have been documented in the El Paso area, where O'Laughlin (1980) reported twelve house structures dating between 4500 and 2160 B.P. on the western slopes of the Franklin Mountains, about 3 km from the Rio Grande. These houses were small, shallow, and round, averaging about 3 m in diameter and 10 cm in depth. They appeared to occur in clusters of two to five structures, some burned, and some with evidence of multiple, superimposed floors. Trash and storage pits were associated with these structures, and the artifact inventory listed ground stone and chipped stone tools. Burned floral remains included species available in spring and fall, and Fields and Girard (1983:207) reported evidence for the procurement and processing of succulents (cacti, agave), which may have been collected during winter months.

Late Archaic pithouses are also found in southeastern Arizona, where they may be more numerous than in other areas occupied during this time period. Several sites have been excavated in the San Pedro River and Matty Canyon areas, apparently dating between 3000 and 2000 B.P. (Sayles 1983; Huckell and Huckell 1985). Some of these structures had deep, bell-shaped pits and burials.

Documented pithouses dating to the Late Archaic seem to occur in a geographic belt extending from southeastern Arizona through eastern Arizona and into the Black Mesa region of northeastern Arizona (Gumerman 1966; Wendorf 1953). Aggregations of pithouses are known from Hay Hollow Valley (Fritz 1974) and on Black Mesa (Nichols and Smiley 1984; Smiley 1985). The

Cienega Creek site, a nonarchitectural, open-air Archaic site in eastern Arizona, exhibits intensive and repeated occupations (Haury 1957). Many of these pithouses produced evidence of maize cultivation, although this evidence is not directly related to the adoption of maize in the Southwest, which occurred earlier.

To summarize these settlement data, we see the first evidence of some degree of extended site occupation in the northern and central Rio Grande Valley about 5000 B.P. By 4000 B.P., site occupation in the El Paso area, where winter-spring encampments would be expected, seems to reflect repetitive and perhaps annual occupation. The El Paso sites may also provide the first evidence of extended group aggregation. Pithouse sites with deep pits and burials date between 3000 and 2000 B.P. in eastern Arizona, and Late Archaic occupation of the Cienega Creek site reflects repeated site use. In general, these Archaic house sites occur at intermediate or low elevations (below 1800 m) in areas posited as the winter-spring component of logistical foraging systems.

CONCLUSION

At the beginning of this chapter I argued that environmental shifts toward increased temporal and spatial complexity in resource availability would favor logistic economic organization. An overview of documented paleoenvironmental trends suggests that increases in temporal complexity *and* an increase in productivity took place, conditions that would encourage logistic mobility and possibly population growth. Trends in radiocarbon chronologies, while difficult to separate from collection biases, are at least consistent with temporal and geographical patterns of vegetative change. Likewise, the spatial and chronological distribution of Archaic projectile points, sites, pithouses, and ground stone occur in patterns mimicking these long-term environmental changes and radiocarbon chronologies. The rather abrupt appearance of intensive Late Archaic occupation in upland regions occurs during a period of overall resource increase. Consequently, it is apparently unrelated to any discernable environmentally induced stress. Indeed, the possibility of a shift toward the use of upland areas during a period of increased carrying capacity suggests that we look to social and demographic factors rather than just environmental conditions to explain the presence of agriculture in montane regions.

4

Archaic Prehistory: Projectile Points

and Population Interaction

I suggested in the preceding chapter that temporal and geographical patterning in the distribution of chronometrically dated preceramic sites in the
Southwest might reflect patterns of increasingly restricted residential group
mobility. This interpretation does not directly address the question of why an
organizational change in mobility occurred, although environmental change
and/or increasing population density seem likely explanations. The conservative view would favor environmental change, given the apparent correlation
between long-term shifts in regional vegetation and patterning in regional
radiocarbon chronologies.

It is difficult, however, to use site distribution to address alternative or complementary causality in the form of density change. Although site distribution
is directly related to organizational variance, distributions can also change
irrespective of density, and increasing density need not result in organizational
modifications. Consequently, to determine whether density-dependent factors
influenced Archaic economies, we need a measure of density independent of
site distribution.

Boundary maintenance, an important density-dependent behavior, meets this criterion. Increasing density leads to higher levels of competition and resultant selective pressures for controlling information about resource availability and access to resource patches (Dyson-Hudson and Smith 1978; Cashdan 1983; cf. Pianka 1978). The specific means whereby these general objectives are accomplished by hunter-gatherers can be viewed in terms of establishing and maintaining social distinctiveness. This may take place at a number of levels, but for analytic purposes there are primarily two, the individual and the group. Density-dependent increases in competition should favor the increasing clarity of social categories at both levels.

In competitive situations, social affiliation must be communicated between potentially competitive or cooperative social units or categories. Messages about the identity of individuals and groups are the means of this recognition and thus the dynamic feature of social boundaries. Transmitting, receiving, and decoding social messages are therefore interrelated behaviors which should covary positively in intensity and significance with density.

A tremendous amount of social information about affiliation beyond the nuclear family is found in "stylistic" behaviors or markers. We intuitively recognize "style" as certain forms of variation within behavioral or material classes having a function (intentional or not) in communicating information about the self-perception of the people exhibiting the pattern. Wiessner (1984:192) says that we generally view style as an expression or display of social personae.

In principle, archaeologists have had little difficulty transferring this intuitive understanding of style to prehistory, assuming almost universally, for example, that it serves as a marker of group membership. They are less of one mind, however, in deciding if style plays an active role in social interaction or if it is merely a passive byproduct of social distinctions (see Plog 1983; Hodder 1982; Sackett 1986).

In this study I follow the position outlined by Wobst (1977) and others (Binford 1962; Wilmsen 1973; Plog 1980; Wiessner 1982b, 1984; Conkey 1978; Hodder 1979, 1982; Braun and Plog 1982; Sinopoli 1985) that style can be an active cultural phenomenon and that it can be defined as the formal variability in behavior or material culture that participates in the exchange of social information. I am especially interested in the communication of information between the kinds of mobile hunter-gatherer groups that might establish social boundaries: minimal bands, maximal bands, and language groups (see Wobst 1974, 1976, 1977; Lee 1979; Wiessner 1982a).

Wobst (1974) suggests that strong boundary maintenance between minimal bands is unlikely because at this level groups are usually too fluid in membership to permit long-term group cohesion; individuals come and go in a constant demographic shifting and adjustment (Lee 1979). Maximal bands and language groups, however, may be stable enough over time to develop a sense of group distinctiveness. Wobst (1974, 1976) has shown that the maximal band is probably equivalent to a social network within which any adult member can be assured access to a mate. These "mating networks" are fairly constant in size (or at least in their minimum size) regardless of overall population size or density, so that increasing density should result in a closer packing of networks (see also Braun and Plog 1982:511).

An increase in the number of networks or maximal bands within a fixed geographic area should cause contact between distant bands to decline and contact between proximate groups to increase. According to Wobst (1977:323), the emergence of different patterns of group interaction within a region means that information about group affiliation will be transmitted in different ways; some groups become more likely targets for receiving information than others. In general, groups close enough to know something about another group, but still distant enough for irregular or unpredictable contact, are most likely to receive social information.

The ethnographic record of hunter-gatherers plainly documents the importance of style in mediating social interaction. Unfortunately for archaeologists, the limited material needs of mobile hunter-gatherers (Sahlins 1972) manifests in largely nonmaterial stylistic behaviors, falling mainly within the realms of language (Hill 1978) and ritual (Yengoyan 1972, 1976). Nevertheless, hunter-gatherers are known to invest social information in stylistic variations of material culture, particularly items likely to be exchanged between individuals (Wiessner 1982a, 1982b).

Hodder (1979) argued that economic stress among tribal pastoralists in the Beringo district of western Kenya generates conditions favoring group corporateness or cohesion in reference to outsiders. Where groups have identical economies and compete for the same resources, social boundaries between them are clearly distinguished, frequently by way of variation in material culture. The style of various items and their frequency often show distinct breaks at the boundaries between groups (1979:447). Hodder suggested that items of material culture can be a medium of communication between individuals and groups and may be especially important in symbolizing and supporting social relations during times of stress. Tension arising from intergroup friction is likely, in his view, to select for increasing expression of group identity or affiliation through style, and he finds high population density a major factor in promoting tension, presumably through competition (1979:447).

Hodder (1982:187) also suggested that in the ethnographic record of "traditional" or nonindustrial societies, "Groups may support and justify competitive interaction in areas of stress by emphasizing overt material culture differences." In general, he noted the importance of interaction between competitive groups; boundaries are not barriers, but lines of distinction helping to define the relationships between groups. Boundaries are thus flexible, depending on social context. Although material culture may be discontinuous in relation to group boundaries, it is more common for behavior to covary with them. Among mobile hunter-gatherers, we are likely to find boundary maintenance expressed in material items that move through exchange or population mobility, and distributions of those items will probably not be localized (cf. Wobst 1974, 1981).

Among the limited array of material culture characteristic of modern, mobile hunter-gatherers, weapons often seem to convey social information, probably because they are fundamental to hunter-gatherer adaptations and because they are likely to be displayed or exchanged in intergroup interaction. Wiessner (1982a), Larick (1985), and Sinopoli (1985) examined stylistic variation of spears and arrows in ethnographic and ethnohistoric settings. Collectively, they found that attributes of projectile points and shafts are frequently used to express social identity, ranging from differences between linguistic groups to differences between age cohorts within a group. A fascinating insight emerging from these studies is that stylistic investment is enormously flexible, so that nearly any feature or characteristic of an object may have social significance, but features with significance in one social context may have little or no meaning in another. Despite the potential difficulties posed by this observation, for the moment I only wish to justify the assumption that hunter-gatherers do use weapons to communicate aspects of social identity.

Stone projectile points (i.e., hafted bifacially retouched blades) are present throughout the Archaic record in the Southwest. Projectile points are, in fact, one of the few artifacts diagnostic of this period, although more often than not, they are temporally ambiguous. Nevertheless, because they are visible during group interaction and have the potential for stylistic variation, they are appropriate for considering density-dependent patterns of hunter-gatherer interaction.

From this position it is a simple matter to return to Hodder's argument that increasing competition and associated stress select for symbolic behavior that helps delimit the social status and roles of interacting groups and individuals (see also Conkey 1978:67; Hayden 1981; G. Johnson 1983). If density-dependent change in hunter-gatherer competition and interaction did take place during the Archaic period in the Southwest, symbolic investment in material culture—including weapons—may have covaried positively.

In general, we should not expect to discern maximal bands or their spatial boundaries in the material archaeological record. Such social manifestations were undoubtedly too short lived to be evident in the precise distribution patterns of material culture (Wobst 1981). Likewise, social boundaries may or may not have been geographical, and if so they are not necessarily represented by physical markers. We can, however, reasonably expect to find evidence of boundary maintenance or behavior in style.

Although this seems like a reasonable expectation, it belies the difficulty of identifying style in the lithic material culture of prehistoric cultural systems. Stylistic features of lithic artifacts often have distinct utilitarian value, and the encoding of social meaning may be arbitrary and coterminous with task-related functions, thus masking any social significance (Binford 1986; Sackett 1986; Lechtman 1976).

I propose that style in projectile points can be inferred first from attributes or features not obviously dictated by function or inconsistent with task performance (i.e., representing an impediment to apparent function, such as knife blades too thin to be used in cutting without breaking). This is a fairly common approach to delineating style in archaeological contexts (e.g., Dunnell 1978). Second, we might expect style to be represented by changes in the overall amount of morphological variation within a geographical area over time. The problem with this second criterion is that morphological variation may reflect shifts in task specific functions; for example, variability in overall blade length may indicate the use of several types of knives for a equal range of cutting tasks or the effects of blade reduction through use and resharpening. The possibility also exists that morphological variation will reflect cultural "drift," or isochrestic style, as defined by Sackett (1982). I have tried to minimize these difficulties by comparing assemblages from sites in similar environmental settings, thus controlling in some limited way for the probable range of on-site activities and tool function, and by focusing on hafting elements, thereby basing comparisons on the portion of the point least likely to be modified by repair. By definition, variation by drift reflects social boundaries; therefore, for this analysis it seems a moot point whether social meaning is imparted to objects deliberately by their makers.

DATA COLLECTION

The southwestern Archaic is nearly synonymous with variation in projectile point forms. This is especially true in the Rio Grande Valley and its tributaries, where there are no exclusive diagnostic markers for the preceramic period other than projectile points. Moreover, the recognition of cultural phases within the Archaic period depends completely on different kinds of projectile points (e.g., Irwin-Williams 1973, 1979). The perception that projectile point types coincide with culture-historical periods is so pervasive that when chronometric dates from sites are inconsistent with the presumed ages of associated projectile points, there is a tendency to see multiple periods of occupation. The result is that no independent confirmation of points as temporal markers is possible.

To minimize some of these inherent classificatory problems, I have selected a series of bifacial blades from west-central New Mexico archaeological sites which I believe can be assigned to three sequent blocks of time. These periods, defined by the three major climatic divisions of the Holocene, are the Early Archaic (ca. 10,000 to 7000 B.P.), the Middle Archaic (ca. 7000 to 4000 B.P.), and the Late Archaic (ca. 4000 to 2000 B.P.).

The projectile points assigned to the Early Archaic were selected because they had been previously classified by other researchers as diagnostic of this time period and/or because there was a demonstrable basis for their age. Specimens from the Lucy site (Roosa 1956, 1967), the Quemado site (Honea 1969), and the Atarque site (Museum of New Mexico site files) are dated by local geologic relationships, and specimens from the Arroyo Cuervo area (Hicks 1984; Irwin-Williams 1973) are presumably associated with radiocarbon determinations.

Middle Archaic projectile points used in this analysis include the original San Jose type specimens from the Grants, New Mexico, area (Bryan and Toulouse 1943); specimens from the Ojo los Huertos site (Comanche Springs) near Belen, New Mexico (Dick 1943; Hibben 1951); specimens from the Rio Rancho sites west of Albuquerque (Reinhart 1968); and specimens recorded by the University of Michigan in the San Augustine Plains from 1981 to 1983.

Chronometrically dated Middle Archaic points are not common. Indirect dates suggest a range of 7000–3000 B.P. (Ferguson and Libby 1963; Lang 1980; Lister 1953), although a date of 7630 $\pm$ 140 B.P. (A-809) was reported from a "San Jose level" at Armijo Shelter in central New Mexico (Haynes, Grey, and Long 1971:14). The specimens from Ojo los Huertos are presumably older than 2700 B.P. (Fulgam and Hibben 1980), and the Rio Rancho artifacts probably predate 2100 B.P. (Reinhart 1968). The San Augustine series is dated between 6000 and 3000 B.P. on the basis of the location of sites relative to fossil shorelines and the location of similar specimens in Bat Cave.

Throughout the Southwest, the typical Late Archaic projectile point has an expanding stem and a convex base with broad side notches or deep corner notches (fig. 14). The specimens considered here were found at radiocarbon-dated sites in the Mogollon Highlands; all date between 3000 and 2000 B.P.

Dimensional attributes used in this study are shown in figure 15, and the site locations are given in figure 16. The geographical extent of the analysis decreases through time, so that the Early Archaic area is over twice as large as that encompassed by the Late Archaic points.

I would like to emphasize at this stage that this sample is designed to assess collections from sites that can be reasonably dated or which have served as the typological basis for culture histories. It is not a random sample, and the results cannot be considered statistically valid for all of the time spans or periods represented. Although I will generalize from these data, the results ultimately apply only to the sites being studied.

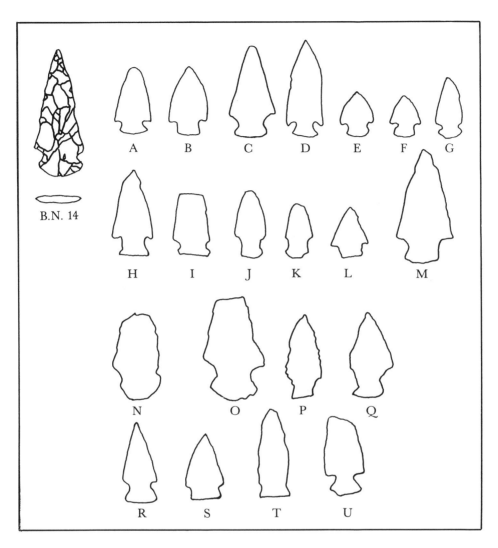

Figure 14. Late Archaic projectile points. BN14, San Pedro point from Bat
Cave. *a–g*, Basketmaker points from Durango, Colorado (Morris and Burgh
1954). *h–k*, San Pedro points from southeastern Arizona (Windmiller 1973).
l–m, San Pedro points from northern Mexico (Fay 1956, 1968). *n–q*, Unnamed
points from El Paso, Texas (O'Laughlin 1980; Fields and Girard 1983). *r–u*,
San Pedro points from Bat Cave (Dick 1965).

PROJECTILE POINT VARIATION

Irwin-Williams (1973, 1979) argued that there are two temporally distinct
projectile point types from the Early Archaic in the northern Southwest. The
Jay point, a heavy, shouldered form with a straight or convex base (fig. 17),
was used between 7900 and 6700 B.P. The Jay was replaced by the Bajada

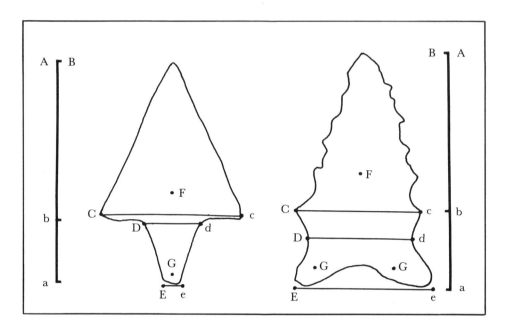

Figure 15. Projectile point measurements used in the analysis. *A–a*, Total length. *B–b*, Blade length. *a–b*, Stem length. *C–c*, Shoulder width. *D–d*, Neck width. *E–e*, Base width. *F*, Blade thickness. *G*, Base thickness.

point, which differs primarily in having an indented base (fig. 17). Bajada points were said to date between 6800 and 5200 B.P.

The temporal distinctions between the Jay and Bajada types—and hence evidence for a derivative relationship—have not yet been demonstrated chronometrically. A comparison of the size of Jay and Bajada specimens in the collections examined for this study failed to reveal any statistically significant differences (p = .05) between the two in any attribute except neck width (table 6). The difference in neck width reflects a tendency for indented base specimens to covary slightly with constricted necks. Consequently, for the purposes of this study, straight-convex and indented base specimens have been combined in one group.

A size comparison of collections from different Early Archaic sites also failed to discern any significant differences, despite considerable distances between sites (table 7). The intersite consistency in this analysis is strikingly repeated when the combined specimens from the twelve sites used in this study are compared to a large sample of Early Archaic projectile points from the Arroyo Cuervo region of west-central New Mexico (Hicks 1984). The two samples, which cover an area of 20,000 km², are so consistent in average values and variance that they appear to reflect manufacture by strictly standardized criteria.

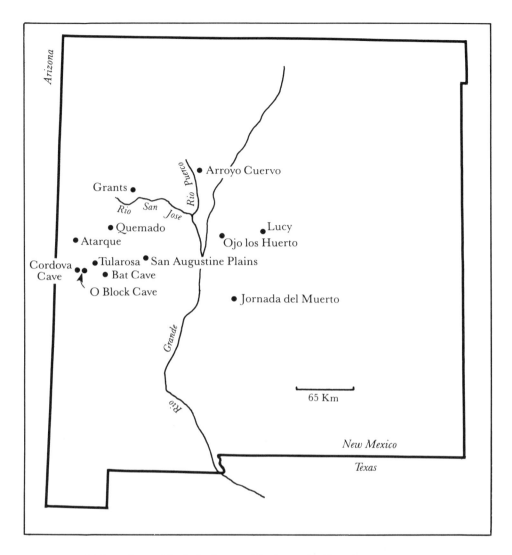

Figure 16. Locations of Archaic sites used in the projectile point analysis.

The great consistency in point-form dimensions from Early Archaic sites corresponds to limited variation in qualitative aspects of morphology. Early Archaic specimens appear to represent a single type, almost always made of basalt (83.0 percent) and with no edge modification (tables 8 and 9). The heavy stem, thick blade, and frequent reworking of broken tips probably indicates that task function and durability were primary manufacturing concerns.

Middle Archaic projectile points, in contrast, exhibit a much higher degree of morphological and raw material variation than Early Archaic points. As seen in table 10, at least two different stem configurations indicate correspondingly different hafting techniques. One stem configuration—indented

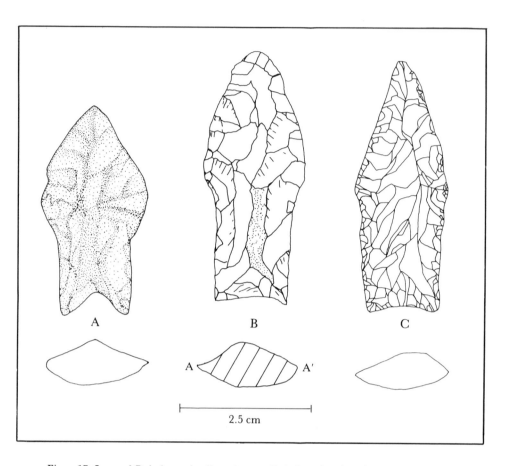

Figure 17. Jay and Bajada projectile points. *a,* Bajada point, basalt, Museum of
New Mexico 7009/11. *b,* Jay point, basalt, Museum of New Mexico 6150/11C.
c, Jay point, chert, Museum of New Mexico 6150/11B.

*TABLE 6. Mann-Whitney U Statistic for Differences between Jay and Bajada
Projectile Points*

	N	U	Significance
Length	30	79.50	0.5000
Blade length	29	58.00	0.1771
Stem length	29	64.50	0.2499
Shoulder width	26	55.50	0.5957
Neck width	29	53.50	0.0430
Base width	30	81.50	0.2312
Blade thickness	28	60.50	0.4725
Base thickness	30	52.50	0.2136

TABLE 7. Mann Whitney U Statistic for Differences between Early Archaic Sites

	U	Significance
Atarque (N = 10) and Lucy site (N = 7): distance = 250 km		
Length	30.00	0.4194
Blade length	30.00	0.4194
Stem length	30.00	0.4194
Blade width	14.00	0.2178
Stem width	20.00	0.2178
Blade thickness	26.00	0.0818
Base width	23.00	0.1448
Base thickness	18.00	0.2178
Quemado (N = 7) and Jornada del Muerto (N = 4): distance = 200 km		
Length	10.00	0.2788
Blade length	9.50	0.4697
Stem length	10.00	0.6515
Blade width	11.50	0.6515
Stem width	2.50	0.0879
Blade thickness	7.00	0.0879
Base width	0.00	1.0000
Base thickness	8.00	0.5718

base with an expanding stem—is similar to that of the traditional San Jose and Pinto types. The second stem form, a combination of convex base and contracting stem, corresponds to traditional Augustin and Gypsum Cave classifications (see chapter 1). In addition, the Middle Archaic collection exhibits a large proportion of specimens with edge modification (28.7 percent) and a wide diversity of material types (tables 8 and 9).

A comparison of indented base-expanding stem projectile points from different Middle Archaic sites indicates significant differences in basal attributes but little variation in blade dimensions (table 11). There are also some differences in overall length and blade length, but these are interdependent measurements, and the differences are probably the result of different resharpening and breakage patterns. Therefore, they are probably not important to this analysis (cf. Thomas 1981)

These dimensional patterns in Middle Archaic indented base-expanding stem specimens suggest that the form of the haft varied significantly between sites, despite gross morphological similarity. A consideration of proportional

TABLE 8. *Percentage of Lithic Material by Period for Archaic Sites*

Early Archaic (N = 30)		Middle Archaic (N = 128)		Late Archaic (N = 93)	
Basalt	83.0	Basalt	35.9	Basalt	35.5
Quartzite	6.3	Obsidian	30.5	Chert	25.8
Obsidian	5.4	Rhyolite	16.4	Chalcedony	15.1
Chert	4.4	Chert	11.7	Obsidian	14.0
Chalcedony	0.9	Petrified wood	3.1	Rhyolite	8.7
		Chalcedony	1.6		
		Jasper	0.8		

TABLE 9. *Blade Edge Modification by Period for Archaic Sites*

	Early Archaic N	%	Middle Archaic N	%	Late Archaic N	%
Unmodified	27	90.0	86	66.7	88	94.6
Serrated	—	—	32	24.8	3	3.2
Scalloped	—	—	5	3.9	1	1.1
Unknown	3	10.0	6	4.7	1	1.1

differences between hafting elements, represented by ratios between measurements, seems to confirm this suggestion. Major differences between sample areas seem to be in the width of the base relative to neck and shoulder width (table 12). When hafted, wide bases would protrude more and be more visible than would narrower bases.

The large number of edge-modified points and the wide range of raw material in the Middle Archaic can also be interpreted as an emphasis by the makers on visible features, but this emphasis varied between sites. For example, while point assemblages from the Grants area and the San Augustine Plains had several serrated specimens, the Ojo los Huertos collection from the Rio Grande Valley had none.

Of special interest in the Middle Archaic point assemblages is choice of raw material. Chemical analysis of obsidian points from the San Augustine Plains and Ojo los Huertos (Nelson 1984) indicates that Gwynn Canyon obsidian

TABLE 10. *Haft Form by Period for Archaic Sites*

Early Archaic			Middle Archaic			Late Archaic		
Haft Form	N	%	Haft Form	N	%	Haft Form	N	%
St-Cn	10	33.3	Ex-Cn	32	31.4	Ex-Cv	30	42.3
Ct-Cn	9	30.0	Ct-Cv	30	29.4	Cr-Cv	11	15.5
St-St	5	16.7	Ex-Cv	13	12.7	Ex-Cn	7	9.9
Ex-Cn	2	6.7	Ex-St	7	6.9	Sd-Cv	7	9.9
Ct-St	2	6.7	No-Cv	6	5.9	Ex-St	6	8.5
Ct-Cv	1	3.3	Ct-Cn	4	3.9	No-Cv	3	4.2
St-Cv	1	3.3	No-St	2	2.0	Cr-St	3	4.2
			Ct-St	2	2.0	No-St	1	1.4
			St-Cv	2	2.0	Ct-Cv	1	1.4
			St-St	1	1.0	St-St	1	1.4
			Cr-Cv	1	1.0	Cr-Cn	1	1.4
			Cr-Cn	1	1.0			
			St-Cn	1	1.0			

Stem Form: St = straight   Cr = corner notched   Base Form: Cn = concave
Ex = expanding   Sd = side notched   Cv = convex
Ct = contracting   No = none   St = straight

TABLE 11. *Kruskall-Wallis Tests for Differences between Expanding Stem and Concave Base Projectile Points from Middle Archaic Sites*

Dimension (cm)	N	Kruskall-Wallis Statistic	Significance
Length	44	5.8749	0.05
Blade length	43	6.7482	0.03
Stem length	43	0.2215	0.90
Shoulder width	37	0.6043	0.74
Neck width	44	1.6201	0.45
Base width	44	7.4349	0.02
Blade thickness	39	3.4709	0.18
Base thickness	44	14.1190	0.00

NOTE: DF = 2, N = 44

*TABLE 12. Mean Values for Projectile Point Stem Proportions in Middle
Archaic Sites*

	Base to Neck Width	Shoulder to Base Width
Grants	1.12	2.18
San Augustine Plains	1.34	1.12
Ojo los Huertos	0.95	1.29

(found 30 km southwest of Bat Cave) dominates in the plains, while the Ojo los Huertos points are made of Obsidian Ridge obsidian from the Rio Grande gravels. The obsidian points from the Grants sites have not been analyzed, but presumably the obsidian came from the local Grants Ridge source (see Findlow and Bolognese 1982). Interestingly, differences in the proportion of obsidian points in each assemblage reflect differences in the use of local cherts.

Contracting stem points with convex bases from Middle Archaic sites exhibit less variation between sites than expanding stem-concave base points. Specimens from LA 50827 and BR-39 (Reinhart 1968) are very similar in form (table 13). LA 50827 is an open-air campsite in the San Augustine Plains, and BR-39 is a possible habitation site on the western terraces of the Rio Grande, nearly 160 km to the northeast. Some variation in length attributes is evident between the two samples, but there are no other significant proportional differences, indicating that the shape of the projectile points does not vary.

In the San Augustine Plains, the expanding stem-concave base points and contracting stem-convex base points are apparently at least partially contemporaneous. Limited stratigraphic evidence from Bat Cave suggests some chronological overlap. However, the two forms are usually not found in equal numbers on individual sites; one or the other commonly dominates. Contracting stem forms may be younger on the whole than expanding stem forms, based on radiocarbon dates for the latter in northern New Mexico (Lang 1980) and the former in the southern Rio Grande Valley (Marmaduke 1978). This is, nonetheless, a tenuous chronological distinction. It may be more significant that expanding stems are found far more frequently north and west of the San Augustine Plains, and contracting stems to the south and east.

Data from Late Archaic sites reveal an intriguing trend toward widespread similarity in projectile point form, especially in hafting technique, but a corresponding shift toward tremendous heterogeneity in point size. These patterns can be seen through two analyses: first, a qualitative consideration of

TABLE 13. *Mann-Whitney U Test for Differences between Contracting Stem Points from Sites LA 50827 and BR-39*

	U	Significance
Length	10.00	0.0058
Blade length	10.00	0.0052
Stem length	33.50	0.0052
Shoulder width	100.00	0.5000
Neck width	59.00	0.0802
Base width	112.00	0.5000
Blade thickness	42.00	0.0706
Base thickness	93.50	0.0810
Shoulder-base width ratio	86.50	0.5000
Neck-base width ratio	77.00	0.5344

morphological differences between widely separated site areas, and second, an assessment of size variation between sites in a small local region.

I will consider morphological differences in projectile point samples from the Cienega Creek site (Haury 1957); Tularosa, Cordova, and O Block Caves in the Mogollon Highlands (Martin et al. 1952; Martin, Rinaldo, and Bluhm 1954); and BR-16, the type site for the Rio Rancho phase in the central Rio Grande Valley (Reinhart 1967, 1968). The approximate time spans for each data set, based on radiocarbon dates, are given in table 14.

Projectile points from these 116 Late Archaic samples are almost entirely expanding stem or notched forms (96.6 percent)—again, I consider notching to be a special type of expanding stem. The Rio Rancho phase points are notched from the corner at an angle of about 40–45 degrees to the long axis of the point. The Cienega Creek and Mogollon points, in contrast, have lateral indentations, which are closer to perpendicular.

The Late Archaic samples also vary in the proportion of different material types and in blade edge modification (table 15). Many of the obsidian projectile points from the Mogollon rockshelters are made of Gwynn Canyon obsidian, the closest source, but from visual identification and chemical analysis of Late Archaic specimens from Bat Cave, it is apparent that Red Hill and Mule Creek sources are also represented. The obsidian at Cienega Creek may have been obtained from eastern Arizona, but it was imported to the site. The evidence, albeit limited, of nonlocal obsidian use in the Late Archaic projectile point samples deviates from the apparent Middle Archaic focus on local

TABLE 14.   *Radiocarbon Time Range for Selected Late Archaic Sites*

Mogollon rockshelters	2800–1800 B.P.
BR-16 (Rio Rancho phase)	2900–2100 B.P.
Cienega Creek	3200–1900 B.P.

TABLE 15.   *Percentages of Qualitative Projectile Point Attributes for Late Archaic Sites*

	Mogollon Sites (N = 93)	Cienega Creek (N = 40)	BR-16 (N = 9)
Haft form			
Expanding stem-convex base	67.7	90.0	56.0
Expanding stem-concave base	11.3	10.0	44.0
Edge Modification			
None	95.7	63.0	100.0
Serrated	4.3	37.0	—
Material type			
Obsidian	14.0	67.0	—
Other	86.0	23.0	100.0

sources. This change may reflect the development of exchange relationships between different areas, rather than the direct procurement of raw material, especially because the overall proportion of obsidian in the Late Archaic samples declines in the Middle Archaic samples, even though the Late Archaic sites are closer to the same sources.

Having noted these gross qualitative differences between geographically widespread Late Archaic sites, it is instructive to look at dimensional variation between the contemporaneous and nearby Mogollon rockshelters. The results of a comparison of basic measurements are summarized in table 16. It is clear that despite their proximity in time and space, the samples vary significantly in every measurement except shoulder width and blade thickness.

Several factors may account for the lack of consistency. An obvious one would be an increase in the range of projectile point functions, for example, their use as knives, gravers, and other nonprojectile tools. Another might be

TABLE 16. *Kruskall-Wallis Tests for Differences between Projectile Points from Tularosa, Cordova, and O-Block Caves*

	N	Kruskall-Wallis Statistic	Significance
Length	109	11.59	0.0030
Blade length	84	7.62	0.0222
Stem length	84	12.58	0.0019
Shoulder width	80	4.38	0.1120
Neck width	80	20.81	0.0000
Base width	72	3.69	0.0033
Blade thickness	91	4.17	0.1241
Base thickness	81	7.08	0.0289

sloppy workmanship. Late Archaic points are often less precisely made than earlier points, sometimes exhibiting thick cross-sections from overlapping step fractures. Then again, if notching is a more efficient method of replacing broken points, it may imply high fracture rates, which in turn might correspond to less overall investment in point manufacture. Given the uniformity in morphology between the three Late Archaic samples, variation in size probably represents a combination of functional and technological factors.

The overall increase in blade length evident in Late Archaic projectile points may provide some insight into these different possible constraints. If a projectile point is considered analogous to a rod—a cylinder whose length exceeds its diameter—certain ballistic principles may be applied in assessing the significance of increased length. Increasing the length of a rod relative to its diameter decreases the velocity required for it to penetrate a target (Zukas et al. 1982:209). Hafting contributes more to the effective diameter of a projectile point than other aspects do. In Middle Archaic points, the base is frequently wider than the blade, placing the effective diameter at the base and possibly inhibiting effective penetration. In Late Archaic points, however, the blade is always wider than the base, so that the base presents little or no impediment to penetration. Together with elongation of the blade, this modification suggests that Late Archaic points may have evolved toward greater efficiency.

Evans (1957) conducted a series of experiments on the accuracy of arrows with projectile points of different sizes. He found that increasing the size or weight of the point increased the accuracy of arrows at long distances. The distal (nock) end of an arrow acts as the stabilizer or steering mechanism in flight. A heavy projectile moves the center of gravity in the arrow forward to the proximal end, thus decreasing air friction along the distal end. The result is greater accuracy.

Evans (1957:83) also discovered that increasing the velocity of an arrow increases accuracy because the degree to which the distal end acts as a stabilizer increases with the square of velocity. Following Zukas et al. (1982), it might be possible to achieve the effect of increasing velocity by decreasing resistance to penetration. Hence the shift in Late Archaic projectile points to large, elongated forms may reflect an attempt to increase accuracy.

An emphasis on functional efficiency indicates a need for better weapons and tools. Such an enhancement of subsistence technology is expectable with a decline in mobility and a need for better extractive capabilities.

POINT STYLE AND SOCIAL BOUNDARIES

The trends in morphological and dimensional variation evident in the projectile point samples examined in this study seem consistent with expectations for density-dependent changes in style. During the Early Archaic, when population was apparently rather low, projectile points exhibit an astonishing similarity over wide areas and an emphasis on task function and durability. These Early Archaic patterns are a reasonable correlate of a demographic situation featuring small, highly mobile groups with little or no investment in boundary maintenance, or at least not enough to be encoded in lithic technology.

In the Middle Archaic sample, the increase in variation over the Early Archaic specimens represented by different hafting techniques, diversity in material selection, nonfunctional modification of the blade, and differences in size and proportional relationships within the two morphological types corresponds to an increase in the number of known and dated sites. The environmental settings of Middle Archaic sites parallel those of the Early Archaic, and the period probably saw some degree of population increase. The dramatic shift in projectile point variation suggests that during the Middle Archaic, distinctiveness became more important than in the Early Archaic.

Projectile point variation within the Late Archaic sample appears to indicate a decline in the widespread morphological heterogeneity seen in the Middle Archaic, although coupled with increased changes in size. In other words, the Late Archaic projectile points were widely similar in shape but could be vastly different in size, even within a single site. These two trends suggest that points played less of a role in boundary maintenance and more of a utilitarian role. This Late Archaic pattern probably means that the social boundaries between groups had become well established and easily recognized, so that the history of relations between groups became the basis for mediating social interaction. If so, mobility patterns may have become regular, that is, seasonally or annually predictable for given groups. Regular mobility might in turn imply less flexiblity in resource procurement, which—if it resulted in more intensive use of local resources—might select for more efficient extractive technology.

Bleed (1986) provides a means for addressing this apparent technological development in the Late Archaic point sample by distinguishing between "maintainability" and "reliability" in hunter-gatherer weapons. He offers these terms to characterize the optimal design of weapons, which varies according to different procurement systems. Reliable weapons are made to work in any possible situation, whereas maintainable weapons can be quickly modified for different tasks. Bleed (1986:739) argues that a key to reliability is overdesign, as in an exceptionally sturdy and precisely constructed weapon. Redundancy is a hallmark of overdesign. Maintainable weapons, which tend to be simpler, "have modular design so that failed components can be removed and replaced with a spare part that makes the entire system functional" (1986:740).

According to Bleed, reliability is characteristic of procurement systems based on encounter tactics (foragers) and maintainable weapons are found with more highly organized procurement (collectors or logistic organization). In other words, extended procurement forays favor weapons that can be quickly adapted or repaired in a wide range of hunting and processing contexts.

The pattern I have delineated for the Late Archaic points in this study seems consistent with an emphasis on maintainability, at least compared to Early and Middle Archaic points, because of an apparent concern with expedient manufacture and replacement. Bleed's apparent view of such a pattern as a response to logistic foraging strategies lends additional support to the position that the Late Archaic shows an increasing trend toward logistical procurement organization.

If relatively predictable patterns of group positioning as implied from changes in projectile point form and a focus on the extractive value of efficient and flexible weapon systems appear during the Late Archaic, then it is the time when we would expect the adoption of cultigens to be possible. This is not to say that such a change in mobility would in any way require the adoption of domesticates, but that conditions which would permit adoption appear to be in place by the Late Archaic.

5

The Transition to Food Production

in the Mogollon Highlands

This chapter is designed as a prelude to the presentation of current evidence related to the beginning of agriculture in the Mogollon Highlands. Several critical expectations for the development of preagricultural hunter-gatherer systems in the Southwest have been presented and evaluated in the preceding chapters, but here I attempt to focus at a much more local level, and specifically on subsistence activity. Because there is still very little empirical evidence of the preagricultural period in the Mogollon Highlands, much of what I present is hypothetical. Nevertheless, a consideration of probable preagricultural patterns allows us to evaluate the limited archaeological record available from that period and the nature of changes that may have occurred with the introduction of domesticates.

Throughout the Holocene period, the San Augustine Plains were surrounded by coniferous forests, with spruce-fir-ponderosa pine associations giving way to ponderosa pine-Colorado pinyon-juniper woodlands as modern semiarid conditions prevailed. The lake occupying the basin of the plains was shallow and alkaline during the early part of the Holocene, but during the mid-Holocene it dried completely, and the resulting flats were colonized by a wide range of grasses and shrubs. Relatively high water tables characterized the basin even after the lake was gone, producing permanent springs along the northern margin. Seasonally inundated playas became prominent features after lake desiccation, and palynological evidence suggests that elevated precipitation between 3500 and 2000 B.P. generated small, permanent bodies of water and permitted pinyon woodlands to extend onto the basin floor (Hevly 1980).

The ecological conditions of the montane region around the San Augustine Plains that emerged during the mid-Holocene were significantly different from those of the Late Pleistocene-Early Holocene. Spruce-fir forests do not produce especially abundant food resources because most of the plant biomass is invested in trees; the density of game and potential economic plants is consequently low. In contrast, the expansion of pinyon-juniper woodlands and the development of extensive grasslands for grazing herbivores represented a tremendous increase in the availability of food resources for hunter-gatherers.

A roster of major food items that increased in the Mogollon Highlands during the mid-Holocene includes pinyon nuts, walnuts, acorns, various fruits and berries, grasses, chenopods, and amaranths. In addition, the density of deer, antelope, elk, mountain sheep, rabbit, and small game undoubtedly increased as favorable habitats developed, particularly the extensive ecotone around the plains basin.

Pinyon nuts and walnuts have extremely high nutritive value. The seed of a Colorado pinyon (*Pinus edulis*), for example, is 14 percent protein, 62–71 percent fat, and 18 percent carbohydrates; walnuts have respective values of 15 percent, 68 percent, and 12 percent (Lanner 1981:101). A pound of shelled *Pinus edulis* nuts contains 2,880 calories. Estimating roughly, a good collector can gather thirty or more pounds of shelled nuts per day (Lanner 1981:102–103). Both pinyons and walnuts occur in masts or "crops," where numerous trees produce an extremely concentrated food source.

Despite the mid-Holocene increase in the abundance of these important resources in the Mogollon Highlands, most of them were available only from late summer to early fall. The seasonal cornucopia that occurs in early autumn in the southwestern mountains was tempered for hunter-gatherers by what Binford (1983b:50) called a "limited access window": the environment becomes bountiful, but only for a relatively brief time.

Moreover, the simultaneous maturation or aggregation of so many different resources placed generalized foragers in a quandary. Given the variety and abundance of resources, how did they allocate labor and time in their procurement? Flannery (1968) described the decisions made by hunter-gatherers in resource procurement as "scheduling," wherein labor is distributed among different kinds of resource collecting in a manner that presumably brings the best return.

Some of the critical food resources in the uplands are precisely the ones which can present the most difficult scheduling decisions. Pinyon is notorious for annual variation in the quantity of nut masts. The Colorado pinyon appears to average about one good mast every four years, somewhat better than the singleleaf pinyon's (*Pinus monophylla*) average of seven years in the Great Basin (see Thomas 1973). Grasses mature in response to local weather conditions, and the time when seeds are ripe but have not yet fallen from the plant may last only a few days or weeks. Predicting these patterns is clearly difficult.

Animal concentrations vary from year to year by locality, and the abundance and quality of game can decline dramatically following severe winters or outbreaks of disease. Indeed, the harsh and frequently prolonged winters at higher elevations in the Southwest may deplete resource availability the following autumn. Exceptionally cold, snowy, or long winters can decimate game populations and suppress or delay plant maturation. In other words, although montane areas are highly predictable sources of autumnal wild food resources, any given resource may or may not be available in any given place, time, and quantity.

For prehistoric hunter-gatherers in the Southwest, upland areas would have been extremely attractive collecting areas during late summer and early fall, as they were for the Great Basin Shoshonis (Steward 1938; Thomas 1973) or the southwestern Apaches (Opler 1941; Castetter and Opler 1936). However, to effectively exploit the benefits of montane autumnal resources, hunter-gatherers would have had to accommodate unpredictability and the simultaneous occurrence of different key resources at the local level. It seems likely that group mobility, flexibility in group membership, and a wide-ranging knowledge of resource areas were the basis for successful use of upland regions. Therefore, hunter-gatherer bands were probably able to adjust demographically and spatially to resource patterns as they encountered them each year.

Although montane areas far exceed the productivity of other zones in the Southwest in early autumn, they are not attractive during other seasons. The severe winters and low edible biomass make survival precarious during winter and spring. In contrast, areas of lower elevation such as the Rio Grande Valley are warmer and exhibit a wide range of important winter-spring plant foods.

Agave, sotol, and mesquite, critical lowland resources, do not occur at higher elevations. In addition, the density of cacti is much higher in the hotter, more arid low-lying regions. These xerophytic, heliophyte plant species have long periods of maturation and prolonged fruiting as adaptations to low precipitation, characteristics that make them available to hunter-gatherers over an extended period of time, particularly during winter months (see Bryant 1977).

Agave (*Agave* sp.), for example, is found in the hot Sonoran Desert and can be collected at any time of year. Flannery (1968) has described agave procurement in Mexico, noting that the leaves are collected after the plant has flowered, a development that softens plant tissues and begins a natural fermentation. Cactus fruits tend to appear in late spring, but their leaves can be eaten at any time. Mesquite, a woody legume found in alluvial soils that was of great importance to historic Apache groups, produces pods during late summer and early fall.

Spring occurs earlier at lower elevations than it does in upland areas, resulting in an earlier availability of many plant species, the roots and shoots of which are used as greens. Large montane stream systems fed by runoff from melting snow support dense concentrations of wildlife and plants in gallery zones, or bosques. Throughout the arid Southwest, regardless of season, perennial or nearly perennial streams represent a relatively reliable source of game, fish, birds, plants, and fuel.

Given the distinct seasonal differences in resource availability between upland and lowland areas in the central Southwest, it seems likely that regional hunter-gatherer populations adopted systems of seasonal movement that took them from lowland winter-spring camps to upland summer-fall camps. Groups may have left valleys and basins from early summer to midsummer, following the time-transgressive maturation of plant resources upslope (fig. 18) and eventually arriving in forested areas in early fall to hunt and to collect pinyon nuts, walnuts, berries, and grass seed. By late fall these groups would have moved back down to lower elevations, possibly encountering a second pinyon harvest on the pediment slopes and foothills above the Rio Grande and other streams—a result of the longer growing season in warmer areas. Some winter camps were probably located on the foothills or stream terraces, where pinyon could be cached and fuel was obtainable, and many hunter-gatherer bands likely dispersed into warmer desert regions to take advantage of winter succulents. Winter demographic patterns in most parts of the central Southwest were probably characterized by widespread population dispersal. The leaves and fruits of desert succulents and legumes will not store for more than a few days or weeks, making it impossible to sustain a prolonged occupation with these resources alone. In contrast, spring resource concentrations in riverine areas may have permitted periodic aggregation.

Although this is a completely hypothetical reconstruction of preagricultural hunter-gatherer systems based on logically expected relationships between foragers and their environment, there is some empirical evidence to support it. Paleo-Indian artifacts (ca. 11,500 to 9500 B.P.) have been found in numerous locations in the San Augustine Plains. Folsom, Hell Gap, and Cody complex projectile points have been documented at several sites (Hurt and McKnight

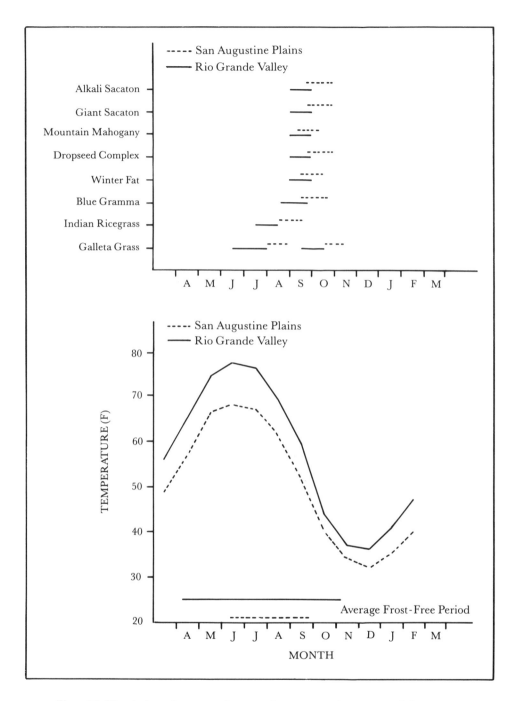

Figure 18. The timing of grass-seed maturation compared to average daily temperatures in the Rio Grande Valley near Socorro, New Mexico, and in the San Augustine Plains. *Top*, Seed maturation by month for selected grasses. Data from Bureau of Land Management (1981, 1983). *Bottom*, average daily temperatures and frost-free periods. Data from Eisenhood (1979).

1949; Wills and Lee 1984; Robert Weber, personal communication; Dennis Stanford, personal communication), and one Folsom site has been partially excavated (Beckett 1980).

In the western portion of the San Augustine Plains, near Bat Cave, both Paleo-Indian and Archaic sites seem to occur near water sources, including still-active springs along the northern edge of the basin and playas on the floor and along the southern border. Judge (1973) hypothesized that Paleo-Indian sites in the Rio Grande Valley were situated near water as a strategy for hunting game that congregated there.

During the Paleo-Indian period, it is likely that much of the central San Augustine Plains was inundated, or at least very swampy, and thus not suitable for campsites. Predictably, Paleo-Indian projectile points occur primarily on beach terraces and in areas around the margins of the Early Holocene lakes.

The location of Archaic-period (ca. 9500 to 2000 B.P.) sites in the San Augustine Plains shows a marked change from Paleo-Indian distributions. Archaic sites are found in a diversity of local settings, including hillslopes, beaches, the basin floor, and river valleys and canyons in the surrounding Mogollon Mountains. The sites are frequently quite large (greater than 1,000 m²) and exhibit surface scatters of debitage, projectile points, unifacial tools, ground stone, and fire-cracked rock. In the case of basin floor sites, all these lithic materials had to have been transported some distance, often as much as 2 km.

A good example of a large open-air Archaic site on the basin floor, LA 50827, is located 1.7 km northwest of Bat Cave and dates somewhere between 4500 and 3500 B.P. on the basis of associated projectile points. The site consists of debitage, unifacial and bifacial chipped stone tools, ground stone, and fire-cracked rock distributed in a large oval (fig. 19). Cores, projectile points, and retouch fragments are numerous (table 17), suggesting that primary core reduction and biface manufacture occurred at the site. The nearest source of the rhyolite used for many implements is 3 km southeast, and all the obsidian comes from Gwynn Canyon, 33 km southeast.

The mean weight of chipped stone artifacts from LA 50827 was 5.70 g, with a range of 0.04–75.53 g; cores accounted for most of the specimens weighing over 17.0 g. Of the 281 specimens, 39 percent exhibited at least one utilized edge, and 16 percent had two utilized edges. The edge-angle mode for both primary and secondary edges was 72 degrees. Ethnographic studies in Australia suggest that tools with edge angles of 60 degrees or more are used for woodworking or scraping (Gould, Koster, and Sontz 1971; Gould 1980). Parry (1980) found that utilized stone tools at Garnsey Bison Kill in southeastern New Mexico with edge angles between 70 and 90 degrees were consistently associated with secondary processing areas.

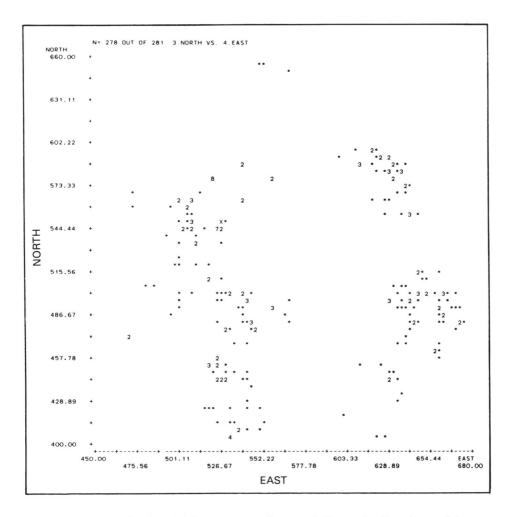

Figure 19. Distribution of chipped stone artifacts, excluding projectile points, at LA 50827. The grid system is in meters.

In addition to chipped stone, fifty-two pieces of ground stone were recorded at LA 50827, all grinding slabs. The average utilized surface area composed 70 percent of the working side but varied between 0 and 100 percent. Grinding slabs were made of volcanic tuff, basalt, and rhyolite, all available within 1 to 3 km of the site.

These data give us some idea of how the site may have been used. Apparently, a good deal of tool manufacture took place, and raw material was brought in from local sources. The pattern of edge modification in unifacial tools suggests that secondary butchering and/or woodworking also occurred at

TABLE 17. *Lithic Artifacts from Bat Cave (1981–83) and LA 50827*

	Bat Cave Preceramic Occupation Surfaces		Bat Cave Preceramic Pit		North Shelter Preceramic Pit		LA 50827 Surface	
	N	%	N	%	N	%	N	%
Biface	2	2.4	0	—	1	0.4	2	0.6
Core	4	4.8	0	—	0	—	25	7.7
Blade	1	1.2	0	—	1	0.4	1	0.3
Flake	69	83.3	81	86.2	120	47.4	136	42.0
Angular fragment	5	6.0	9	9.5	83	32.8	34	10.5
Biface fragment	1	1.2	0	—	3	1.2	1	0.3
Retouch fragment	1	1.2	3	3.2	45	17.8	76	23.5
Hammerstone	0	—	0	—	0	—	2	0.6
Projectile point	0	—	1	1.1	0	—	47	14.5
Weight (g)								
Range	0.01–31.43		0.02–1.98		0.01–7.84		0.04–75.53	
Mean	2.58		0.39		0.38		5.70	
S.D.	5.22		0.44		0.85		11.15	

the site—that is, game and/or wood were carried to the camp from procurement areas. The large number of projectile points indicates that broken points were rehafted at the site and new points manufactured to replace them.

On the basin floor, LA 50827 was probably in an advantageous place for grass seed (primarily *Sporobolus*) collection on the treeless playas, and it is likely that the grinding slabs were transported to the site for seed grinding. The lack of use-wear on many of the rock slabs found at the site suggests they were left there in anticipation of return visits. Abundant fire-cracked rock, evidence of boiling or roasting, had to have been carried in from at least 1.5 km. All of these relationships seem to indicate that the location of the site was so important that its inhabitants brought raw material to it rather than establishing the campsite near the raw material sources.

The large size of LA 50827 and the large oval distribution of artifacts may indicate repetitive site use and/or use by a relatively large group. The emphasis on grass seed procurement, suggested by the location of the site and the production of ground stone, reflects a late summer or early fall occupation.

An Archaic-period component at the Ake site (Beckett 1980) in the eastern San Augustine Plains has produced radiocarbon dates of 3360 ± 160 B.P. (UCR-982A) and 3440 ± 150 B.P. (UCR-982B) from a buried hearth. The projectile point assemblage includes forms similar to those at LA 50827, but stratigraphic mixing with Folsom material in the sandy sediments apparently made it impossible to discern distinct occupations. The hearth was constructed in a time of standing water and extensive pinyon-juniper savannah in the area (Hevly 1980), at least indirectly indicating that the site was positioned to take advantage of these two important resources.

A possible nonceramic lithic scatter is located on a ridge top near the SU ceramic site in the San Francisco River Valley. Dense chipping debris, much of it obsidian, is associated with scattered oval manos. Although there has been no investigation of this site, it is located in a pinyon-juniper stand and may have been used for collecting pinyon nuts. It is clear from the presence of Gwynn Canyon obsidian in San Augustine Plains sites that foraging parties made extended trips into the mountain forests, but as yet there are no conclusive Archaic sites in these areas predating the appearance of agriculture. The Wet Legget site (see chapter 1) is aceramic, but recovered materials were not chronometrically dated.

Despite the lack of research, it is obvious that the San Augustine Plains contains a remarkably high density of Archaic-period projectile points (Hurt and McKnight 1949; Dick 1965; Beckett 1980; Wills 1985; Fromby 1986). By and large, however, the proveniences of these specimens do not extend outside the plains until the Late Archaic.

In sum, the spatial pattern of Archaic-period sites in the Mogollon Highlands is what we would expect if late summer and fall resources conditioned site location. There is currently no evidence that would imply spring or winter occuption in sites without any evidence of agriculture. Consequently, it seems reasonable to accept that this hypothetical preagricultural settlement system was seasonal, while acknowledging that there is as yet no direct evidence of any specifically seasonal occupation in any clearly nonagricultural Archaic sites.

6

The Mogollon Highlands

as a Case Study

As noted in chapter 1, many of the earliest agricultural sites in the Southwest are found in the Mogollon Highlands, including Bat Cave, Tularosa Cave, Cordova Cave, and Cienega Creek. Prehistorians have argued that mesic conditions in this mountainous area made it the most favorable location for the first southwestern agriculture (e.g., Woodbury and Zubrow 1979; Ford 1981; Minnis 1985). Recent archaeological research (Wills 1985) in the Mogollon Highlands conducted by the University of Michigan Museum of Anthropology has provided a wide variety of new cultural and paleoenvironmental information about the period in which cultigens were introduced into the region. My interpretation of these data differs from previous constructs in viewing environmental conditions as a necessary but independent variable in the process of introduction and considering a change in the regional character of the human population to be its most significant motivation.

SITE USE AND SETTLEMENT CHANGE

The stratigraphic sequence of a single prehistoric site represents the history of deposition and modification in the accumulation of sediments and material in that particular location (Binford 1980; Gifford 1981). The "archaeology" of a site is the archaeologist's interpretation of the processes responsible for the stratigraphy, a perspective usually derived from only a portion of the site's content and often seen from the vantage of postexcavation cross-sections of deposits. Combinations of artifacts—usually termed assemblages—are defined on the basis of coassociation in excavation contexts; material found close together is assumed to have been affiliated before deposition (Speth and Johnson 1977). The archaeological understanding of a site depends on the assumptions made in linking the depositional structure to the artifactual content.

To assess information from a single prehistoric site or a series of sites, the investigator has to be aware that the history of accumulation of material may not trace very closely the overall pattern of cultural change within the social system using the site, or as Binford (1982:16) argued, "there is no necessary relationship between depositional episodes and occupational episodes." The factors initially conditioning the pattern of discarded cultural material relate to the position of the site within the regional settlement system. As many archaeologists have demonstrated, the types of artifacts and the spatial utilization of a site depend upon how many people were at a particular site, why they were there, and how long they stayed (e.g., Gould 1980; Yellen 1977; Binford 1978, 1980). Ultimately, understanding the structure of a site depends on understanding the role that site played in the socioeconomic system.

No archaeological site will exhibit patterns that exactly reflect *all* the disparate cultural and environmental factors that conditioned architecture or the discard of material. Although researchers have spent considerable effort on the practical and theoretical issues surrounding site formation and interpretation (Binford 1972, 1980; Schiffer 1976, 1983; Gifford 1981), they are generally agreed that the ability to understand the processes responsible for site structure varies by the level of explanation sought. It may be extremely difficult, for example, to "explain" the exact events surrounding site use at any precise instant in time.

At the level Binford (1978:486) called "general system change," there may be no direct connection between the role of a site in the settlement system and changes within that system. Binford (1978:486) cited Vierra's work in highland Peru as an example of site stability in the context of economic transition. Vierra excavated a rockshelter which gave evidence of the shift to agriculture in the region, but which demonstrated no significant changes in the lithic assemblage before or after this development. Binford suggested that the site was an important hunting stand and remained so even after the hunter-gatherers using it began to produce food. He concluded that hunting may have become less important thereafter, but the use of the site did not vary despite major changes in the overall economy.

Binford's theoretical point is that sites utilized only at particular times in conjunction with focused procurement strategies may be less sensitive to major changes in the economy than sites used for a range of activities. Similarly, sites occupied in conjunction with specific social activities, such as ceremonial locales, might not reflect economic change in any discernable manner. When considering the extent to which a site represents change within an entire social system, these factors have to be acknowledged.

The development of explanatory models for early agriculture in the Southwest has been predicated on straightforward evolutionary interpretations of individual site sequences. In the half dozen or so sites considered to show sequential changes in socioeconomic adaptation associated with early cultivation, every sequence is based on arbitrary excavation units, not on the definition of individual episodes of site use or occupation. Differences between assemblages are defined by arbitrary levels, or between cultural phases, by diagnostic artifacts. There has been little, if any, effort to relate site stratigraphy to the overall social system responsible for that stratification, and only very recently has there been a concern with occupational episodes (e.g., Waber, Hubbell, and Wood 1982; Human Systems Research 1972; Simmons 1984).

This chapter will attempt to bring individual early sites in the Mogollon Highlands into a regional context. I will consider three issues of paramount importance in assessing early food production: changes in patterns of hunter-gatherer movement, evidence of resource storage, and indicators of systemic shifts in site function.

BAT CAVE

Geomorphology

Bat Cave, a complex of adjacent rockshelters eroded from a massive volcanic conglomerate by waves from Pleistocene Lake San Augustine, is located in the southwestern part of the San Augustine Plains (fig. 3). The shelters occur at an average elevation of 2,093 m, about 39 m above the present surface of the plains. Between 12,000 and 10,000 years ago, the cliff face above the Bat Cave complex collapsed, creating a large barrier of jumbled boulders in front of the shelters and forming a catchment responsible for subsequent deposition of sediments in the shelters. Before and after the rockfall, packrat and mouse fecal material covered lag deposits of beach gravels in the shelters. At the time of collapse, a layer of yellow sediment was generated from the rapid weathering of exposed and crushed rock surfaces. Over the yellow layer, a complex mixture of colluvium and organic sediments was deposited, and cultural features such as hearths, most of which appear to postdate 6000 B.P., were superimposed throughout.

Originally, the geologic sequence in the shelters was described in three parts: the basal beach gravel, the yellow sediment ("buff sand"), and a "midden" deposit. The description gave the impression of three extensive layers occurring in every part of the shelter complex and grading distinctly from one to the next (Dick 1965:11). The depositional history of the shelters is actually considerably more complex. Sediments were characterized primarily by cultural content rather than geologic structure, and the interpretation of site chronology was based on artifacts recovered from arbitrary excavation levels without regard for depositional processes. Thus the nature and origin of the sediments seemed unimportant.

Antevs (1955:329) felt that the yellow sediment in Bat Cave was an aeolian deposit produced during the Altithermal, when denudation exposed large areas of soil, creating windborne dust and eventually the yellow layer. He estimated that the Altithermal lasted from 7500 to 4000 B.P. (1955:329), and the yellow sand became an important chronological marker for archaeological material at the site. Radiocarbon dates eventually dated the top of the yellow layer at about 6000 B.P., confirming his estimate.

Several factors confound the original interpretation, however. First, the sediments in the San Augustine Plains are overwhelmingly comprised of silts and clays from weathered volcanic rock; there is no nearby source of sand. Second, there is no evidence of aeolian transport in the grains composing the sediment. And third, an identical sediment can be observed today weathering from behind bedrock spalls. It therefore appears that the yellow sediment was produced at the site. This does not mean that it does not date to the Altithermal, nor that Altithermal climate had no effect on its creation. It does mean that the situation is complicated, and the sediment has probably been continuously produced since the caves were formed. As we will see later, attention to this sort of detail is vastly relevant in understanding the cultural remains.

History of Excavation

Bat Cave was excavated in 1948 as part of Harvard University's Upper Gila expedition (Dick 1965; Brew and Danson 1948) and again in 1950 by the University of Colorado. The 1950 project was designed to secure radiocarbon samples for dating the stratigraphic distribution of material recovered in 1948. The first field season opened a large area in the talus slope below four small shelters (1A, 1B, 1C, and 1D) and excavated most of them (fig. 20). The second field season removed deposits only from shelters 1B and 1C.

The University of Michigan Museum of Anthropology initiated limited testing at Bat Cave in 1981, followed by more extensive test excavations in 1983 as a joint project of the University of Michigan and the National Geographic Society. The new investigations were intended to obtain information on the nature of early cultigens at the site, taking advantage of technological and theoretical developments in archaeology after 1950. In the following section, the results of the original project and the new research are briefly described to outline changes in site use apparently associated with the shift from hunting and gathering to hunting and gathering with the addition of food production.

Main Shelter Stratigraphy and Chronology

Excavations by the University of Michigan in the main shelter (fig. 20) exposed two well-defined periods of prehistoric occupation represented by compact, superimposed surfaces associated with cultural features, artifacts, and subsistence remains. The older surface is preceramic, the younger apparently spans the preceramic and ceramic time periods. A series of geologic layers containing occupational rubbish separates the two cultural strata.

The lower surface was composed of numerous thin layers of mixed ash, charcoal, and unburned organic debris such as twigs and rodent feces. Five hearths were associated with the surface, four of which overlapped (fig. 21). A large, conical pit with a flat bottom was the earliest feature affiliated with the surface; it had been filled in and covered by later activities. The excavated portions of the surface covered 2.25 m², and the continuation of the surface into unexcavated grid squares indicated a minimum extent of 5 m².

Two radiocarbon dates from a single hearth indicate a Late Archaic age of between 2840 and 2570 B.P. (table 18). The later date probably represents the actual firing of the hearth more accurately because it was taken from saltbush (*Atriplex*), a species less likely to be as old at death as oak (*Quercus*), the material composing the other sample. Apparently the surface was built up over an extended time, probably as a result of broadcasting ash from the hearths and subsequently trampling it into a dense, hard feature. The direct imposition of ash layers indicates fairly regular reuse; the area seems to have been deliberately cleaned, or little time was allowed for the accumulation of debris between occupations. The stratigraphy of the pit also suggests that some intentional "housekeeping" occured.

The pit contained grass stems and inflorescences, knotted yucca, fragments of cordage, pieces of twisted rabbitskin blankets, articulated limb segments of rabbits (especially legs), some lithic debitage, a broken projectile point, and several maize cobs and squash seeds. Cobs from the bottom of the pit dated to

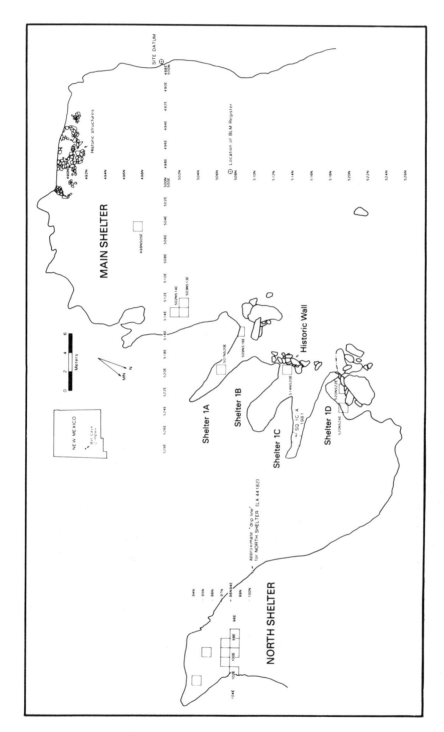

Figure 20. Plan view of Bat Cave (LA 4935) and the north shelter (LA 44182).

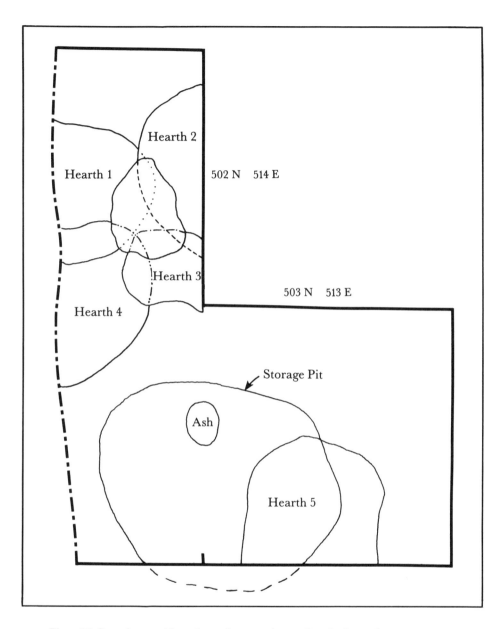

502 N   514 E

503 N   513 E

Figure 21. Superimposed hearths and occupation surface in the main shelter, Bat Cave. Hearth 1 dates to 2840 ± 130 B.P. (A-3662). The storage pit is sealed by a later surface dated at 1980 ± 120 B.P. (A-3661).

TABLE 18. *Radiocarbon Dates from Bat Cave and Tularosa Cave*

Site	Date (B.P.)	Lab No.	Year	Material	Location
Bat Cave	1752 ± 250	C-165	1948	uncarbonized plants	stratum I, shelter ?
Bat Cave	1907 ± 250	C-173	1948	uncarbonized plants	stratum II, shelter ?
Bat Cave	2239 ± 250	C-172	1948	uncarbonized plants	stratum III, shelter ?
Bat Cave	2249 ± 250	C-164	1948	uncarbonized plants	stratum IV, shelter ?
Bat Cave	2862 ± 250	C-170	1948	uncarbonized plants	stratum V, shelter ?
Bat Cave	1610 ± 200	C-567	1950	charcoal	stratum I, shelter C
Bat Cave	2816 ± 200	C-569	1950	charcoal	stratum III, shelter C
Bat Cave	2048 ± 170	C-570	1950	charcoal	stratum IV, shelter C
Bat Cave	5605 ± 290	C-571	1950	charcoal	stratum V, shelter C
Bat Cave	5931 ± 310	C-573	1950	charcoal	stratum VI, shelter C
Bat Cave	840 ± 80	A-2799	1982	charcoal	hearth, shelter A
Bat Cave	1470 ± 40	A-2789	1982	charcoal	503N 513E, main shelter
Bat Cave	1670 ± 100	A-3657	1984	charcoal	occupation floor, north shelter
Bat Cave	1710 ± 100	A-3660	1984	charcoal	occupation floor, north shelter
Bat Cave	1980 ± 120	A-3661	1984	charcoal	occupation floor #2, main shelter
Bat Cave	1990 ± 100	A-3663	1984	charcoal	hearth, shelter B
Bat Cave	2260 ± 135	A-3659 ·	1984	charcoal	99N 98E, unit 40, north shelter
Bat Cave	2510 ± 120	A-3658	1984	charcoal	hearth, north shelter
Bat Cave	2570 ± 80	A-3789	1984	charcoal	hearth, main shelter
Bat Cave	2840 ± 130	A-3662	1984	charcoal	hearth, main shelter
Bat Cave	2340 ± 420	A-2791	1982	maize cupule	main shelter
Bat Cave	2460 ± 220	A-4183	1984	maize cupule	north shelter
Bat Cave	2690 ± 90	A-4185	1984	maize cupule	stratum V, shelter C
Bat Cave	2780 ± 90	A-4166	1984	maize cupule	north shelter
Bat Cave	3010 ± 150	A-4167	1984	maize cupule	main shelter
Bat Cave	3060 ± 110	A-4189	1986	maize cupule	stratum VI, shelter C

TABLE 18. *(continued)*

Site	Date (B.P.)	Lab No.	Year	Material	Location
Bat Cave	3120 ± 70	A-4188	1984	maize cupule	stratum IV, shelter B
Bat Cave[a]	3740 ± 70	A-4187	1984	maize rachis	stratum VI, shelter C
Bat Cave	2630 ± 90	A-4182	1984	squash seed	north shelter
Bat Cave	2980 ± 120	A-4186	1984	squash seed	stratum IV, shelter B
Bat Cave	2140 ± 110	A-4184	1984	bean	stratum IV, shelter C
Tularosa Cave	1930 ± 140	A-4180	1984	maize cupule	square 2R1, level 13
Tularosa Cave	1940 ± 90	A-4181	1984	maize cupule	square 2R2, level 14
Tularosa Cave	1900 ± 70	A-4178	1986	squash seed	square 2R2, level 14
Tularosa Cave	2470 ± 250	A-4179	1984	bean	square 3R2, level 11

SOURCES: Libby (1955); Dick (1965); Long et al. (1986); Richard I. Ford, personal communication; Austin Long, personal communication. Some additional radiocarbon dates from Bat Cave and Tularosa Cave are not reported herein but will be available in a forth coming Bat Cave site report.
[a]Sample A-4187 is considered unreliable due to possible contamination during curation. See discussion in text.

2340 ± 420 B.P. (A-2791) and 3010 ± 150 B.P. (A-4167), consistent with the radiocarbon dates from the hearth. The clear definition of layering in the pit fill (fig. 22) points to successive dumping episodes, although it is also possible that the pit was lined with grass and that the collapse of the lining produced some layering. Because the pit was closed by a layer of ash associated with the top of the occupation surface, the contents date to midway in the accretion of the surface, after the construction of the pit and before its closure.

It seems that the lower occupation surface was produced by at least four periods of use, each associated with the construction of at least one hearth. The compactness of the constituent surface features and the lack of intervening sediment indicates that relatively short intervals passed between occupations, although there is no reliable way to estimate their duration.

The few plant remains associated with the hearths included walnut shell fragments, pinyon shells, juniper seeds, and *Opuntia*. Charcoal from the hearths consisted of oak and saltbush (*Atriplex*). This ensemble of species is typical of pinyon-juniper woodland, and oak would have been likely on the rocky slopes around Bat Cave. There is no similar association within 10 km of the site today, and then only in sheltered, well-watered canyons, indicating that conditions during the late Archaic occupation of the lower surface were wetter.

This conclusion is confirmed by the plant remains recovered from the pit. In addition to the species associated with the occupation-surface hearths, the

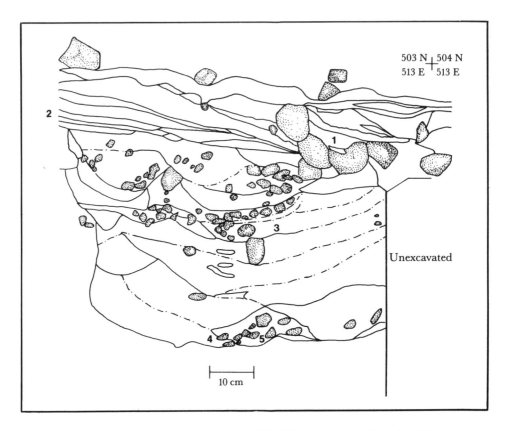

Figure 22. Profile of filled pit in square 503N 513E, Bat Cave. *1*, Hearth, 1470 ± 40 B.P. *2*, Dung, 1980 ± 120 B.P. *3*, Rabbit fur, 2680 ± 110 B.P. *4*, Maize cob, 2340 ± 420 B.P. *5*, Maize cob, 2930 ± 150 B.P.

pit contained sunflower seeds and flowers, yucca seeds, chenopod seeds, *Suaeda* (seepweed) seeds, cattails (*Typha latifolia*), and at least four grass species. The aquatic species indicate the presence of local standing water, probably in the playas along the fringe of the basin, where water from rainfall, runoff, and springs collected.

After the final period of use, a series of loosely consolidated sediment layers accumulated on the occupation surface. They contained a range of cultural material, including maize cobs, but the volume of noncultural organic material and the lack of features signify that the material was probably deposited by animals.

The upper occupation surface was built on this debris. Radiocarbon dates of 1980 ± 120 B.P. (A-3661) and 1470 ± 40 B.P. (A-2789) bracket the beginning and end of use. This surface was equal in area to that of the earlier surface, but not as thick, and it appears to represent several events widely spaced in time rather than numerous short-term occupations. There are three epi-sodes indicated in this surface, the first separated from the last by perhaps four hundred years.

The earliest use on the upper surface was contemporaneous with hearth 1 (fig. 21), and the second occupation is evident in hearth 2, a large, rock-lined feature. Two subsequent hearths (3 and 4), built over hearth 2, are associated with ceramics. This occupation surface was therefore established about 2000 B.P., possibly as the result of a single occupation, and then reused several cen-turies later. Although each hearth contains lithic debitage, the associated artifacts are few, further suggesting that these later periods of use were not as intensive as the earlier period. Historic deposits rest almost immediately on the prehistoric layers, indicating that little or no prehistoric use of this part of the site took place after about 1600 B.P.

Plant remains from the upper surface, which are even fewer than those from the lower surface, are dominated by juniper. Squawbush (*Rhus trilobata*) char-coal from a hearth in front of shelter 1B produced a date of 1990 ± 100 B.P. (A-3663). This species, typical of rocky slopes, must therefore have been pre-sent when the upper preceramic surface was occupied. Squawbush still grows at the site today.

North Shelter Stratigraphy and Chronology

Although the geomorphology of the north shelter (fig. 20) is very different from that of the main shelter, their archaeological sequences are quite similar. A preceramic component in the north shelter dates between 2500 and 2200 B.P., separated from an early ceramic occupation (ca. 1700 B.P.) by nearly a meter of culturally sterile colluvium. Like the main shelter, the north shelter preceramic component is characterized by hearths and a pit associated with maize and squash.

An active talus cone is building up in the north shelter—its salient geologic feature. Deposition has been rapid at times, although apparently not during the last one thousand years. The cone has nearly blocked the entrance to the shelter, providing excellent protection from the outside and making the site difficult to see from the basin below.

Only 1 m² (a single grid square) of the north shelter preceramic component was excavated (fig. 20). Within that area, two small hearths were found, one in the fill of a large, circular pit (fig. 23). The pit was excavated into cultural layers predating 2510 ± 120 B.P. (A-3658). Several radiocarbon assays (sam-ples A-3659, 4183, 4166, and 4182 in table 18) indicate that the pit filled fairly soon after its construction.

Only part of the pit fill was excavated in 1983 because of the unconsolidated nature of overlying sediments. However, it appears that the pit filled in much

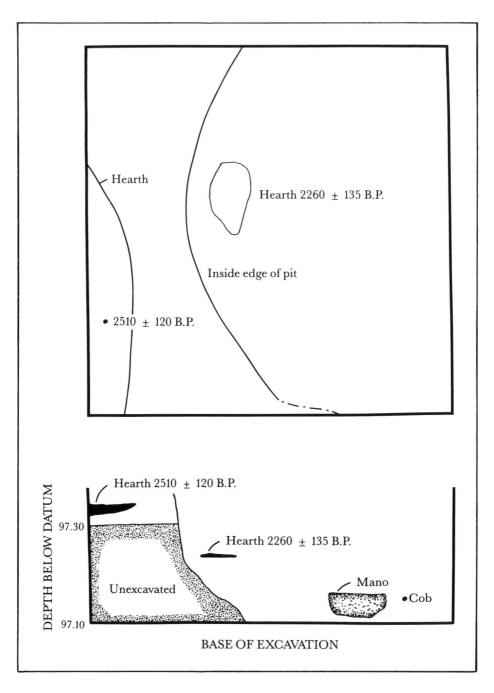

Figure 23. Plan view and cross-section of partially excavated preceramic pit in square 99N 98E, north shelter, Bat Cave.

the same manner as the preceramic pit in the main shelter did, in a series of dumping episodes. Pieces of ground stone, lithic debitage, maize cobs, squash seeds, squash rind and stem fragments, and charcoal were mixed with small rocks and fine, unconsolidated sediment, which together suggest the sort of casual camp cleaning and discard typical of modern hunter-gatherers (Yellen 1977; Binford 1978; Gould 1980).

Charcoal from the preceramic units included juniper, pinyon, oak, *Atriplex*, *Fallugia*, and *Abies*. By weight, the *Atriplex* charcoal predominated. These species, like the plant remains from the main shelter, indicate the former presence of pinyon-juniper woodland and the typical rocky substrate species characteristic of the site area today.

The preceramic use of the north shelter apparently ended about 2200 B.P., followed by rapid sedimentation in the shelter (approximately 7 cm every one hundred years) from colluvium spilling into the cave from the cliff above. The ceramic occupation began approximately 1700 B.P. (samples A-3657 and 3660 in table 18). These dates all apply to a shallow structure discovered near the eastern wall of the shelter, apparently built about 1700 B.P. and abandoned within the next decade or so. There is no convincing evidence that the shelter was occupied thereafter in prehistoric time.

The presence of ponderosa pine (*Pinus ponderosa*) is an interesting aspect of the early ceramic occupation. Ponderosa dated at about 1700 B.P. occurred as a layer of needles directly under the surface of the structure and as large fragments of charcoal in the structure fill, but nowhere else in the Bat Cave complex. Ponderosas currently grow no closer to the site than about 8 km to the south in sheltered canyons. The occurrence of the species at 1700 B.P. may therefore represent a mesic episode in local climatic history, an implication supported by the appearance of large numbers of bison bone in the Bat Cave complex during the ceramic period.

Small Shelter Stratigraphy and Chronology

Most of the Harvard excavations took place in the area of the small shelters, and all of their cultigens and radiocarbon samples were recovered from these shelters. The University of Michigan excavated test squares in shelter 1A and in front of shelters 1B and 1D, but nearly all the preceramic deposits in these areas had been previously excavated or removed by vandals. Consequently, we must rely almost exclusively on the original field records in reconstructing the preceramic stratigraphy of the small shelters. There is a pressing need for such a reconstruction because the original description of the shelters presented only summary data, most of it distinguishing between ceramic and nonceramic excavation strata (Dick 1965). Although it was standard practice to concentrate on comparisons between arbitrary excavation units rather than discrete geologic or cultural features when Bat Cave was first studied (e.g., Haury 1950; Martin et al. 1952), it will not serve the present discussion because we need to assess contextual associations between artifacts and subsistence remains. Fortunately, much of the primary data upon which the Bat Cave summary was based are still available, permitting a refinement of the previous description.

The cultigens and radiocarbon samples came almost entirely from shelters 1B and 1C. Some botanical material came from shelter 1A, but only a small area was excavated, and all the deposits appear to have been ceramic in age: a radiocarbon sample collected in 1981 from a hearth resting on bedrock in shelter 1A assayed at 840 ± 80 B.P. (A-2799). No perishable material was recovered from shelter 1D or the talus slope (Dick 1965:13). For these reasons, most of the remaining discussion will concern shelters 1B and 1C.

Shelters 1B and 1C were originally excavated in 12-inch arbitrary levels, sometimes divided into 3-inch levels to facilitate defining a ceramic chronology (Dick 1965:10). The excavation followed no grid provenience system because of the small and awkward configuration of the shelters, but it was conducted in squares of approximately 6 feet on a side. Depth measurements were taken from a red line painted on the cave walls at the surface level.

Although shelters 1B and 1C appeared to be separate before excavation, the removal of sediment revealed the top of a single shelter. According to the elevation of the red line in the two shelters, the original surface of the sediments in front of 1B was higher than the surface in front of 1C, producing a down-slope from 1B to 1C running parallel to the front of both shelters (fig. 24). Yet the elevation of the red line also indicates that the surface level of sediments *inside* 1B and 1C was lower than in front.

This difference in elevation is critical in interpreting the archaeology of the small shelters because the original cultural stratigraphy was defined by excavation units numbered sequentially from the original ground surface. Thus, excavation level I in the site report (Dick 1965) is actually an aggregate level composed of the first 12 inches of excavated sediments in every part of the site, that is, all the material from level I in shelters 1A, 1B, 1C, 1D, and the talus slope. The same procedure applied to each numbered level. In adjacent excavation areas such as shelters 1B and 1C, the same numbered levels are not necessarily contiguous with each other because of the difference in the initial surface elevation. Mangelsdorf, Dick, and Camara-Hernandez (1967:3) aptly point out the artificial character of the resulting units, which form the back-bone of the site interpretation:

> Because there was no obvious stratigraphy in the cave corresponding to cultural phases, the material was removed in arbitrary strata of 12 inches each: 0-12 ", 12-24 ", etc. Since three different sections of the cave were excavated and since the sterile sand representing Antevs'

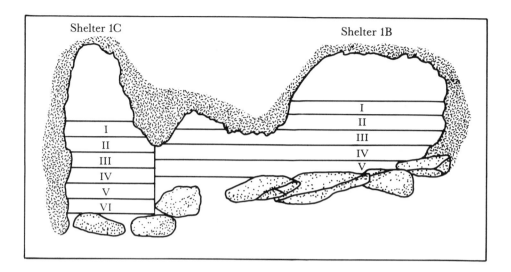

Figure 24. Reconstruction of excavation levels in Bat Cave shelters 1B and 1C, at the deepest point in the sediments. Each excavated level is 12 inches. This profile face represents the termination of excavation in 1948.

dry level on which the cave deposits rest, occurs at different levels in different parts of the cave, it might be supposed arbitrary levels in one section would not correspond to those in another. In Section 1B [shelter 1B] for example, the sterile sand occurs at 36" while in 1C it is found at 60". However, the cobs in the 24-36" level of 1B are similar to those in the 24-36" level of other sections. Consequently we have averaged the data on cobs and kernels according to the arbitrary level in which the specimens were found.

Note that the sterile sand (yellow sand) was found at the base of level III in shelter 1B and at the base of level V in shelter 1C. While these comments refer specifically to the maize, they can be applied to all the excavated cultural remains from Bat Cave. When the red line is mapped by its absolute elevation, the sediments in shelter 1B are 45 cm higher than those in shelter 1C. Given the configuration of the shelters and the fact that the original project did not use a transit during the excavation, it is understandable that such an error was made.

In figure 24 the shelters have been redrawn from a 1981 transit map of the red line at the original surface. Depths were taken from the original field notes, and the boulders were plotted from the Harvard project photographs. The map demonstrates the lack of correspondence between excavation levels in the two shelters. It also shows that perishable material should not have been found below level IV in shelter 1B proper or below level V in the area between

1B and 1C which was treated as 1B during excavation. Therefore, shelter 1C was the only part of Bat Cave where any perishable remains, including maize, could have been found in level VI. Also, it is important to note that material from the lowest levels in shelter 1B would correspond in depth to material from the first three levels in shelter 1C—that is, primarily to the ceramic levels in 1C.

In terms of the cultural stratigraphy in the shelters, this reconstruction of the excavation levels has profound implications. A significant aspect of the new profile can be seen in the lower levels of shelter 1C, where a large pit originates at the base of level III and cuts down into the rockfall and beach gravel layers at the base of the profile (fig. 25). No apparent cultural features exist below this point; the geological context of excavation level VI is clearly Pleistocene or early Holocene, except for the portion of the pit that intrudes to this point. Consequently, it is unlikely that archaeological materials such as maize would be found in situ at level VI, and it is very *likely* that portions of

Figure 25. Previously unpublished photograph of the large pit in the rear portion of Bat Cave shelter 1C. The top of the pit originated in excavation level III and extended into level VI. The bottom of the pit cuts into a layer of Pleistocene beach gravels on the bedrock floor of the shelter. (Courtesy National Anthropological Archives, Smithsonian Institution.)

the archaeological collections from levels V and VI in shelter 1C came from the intrusive pit.

A sample of uncarbonized wood recovered from level V in 1948 produced a date of 2862 ± 250 B.P. (C-170). Given the geology of the shelters, it almost certainly came from shelter 1C, meaning that it also came from a level into which the pit extended. In 1950 a charcoal sample collected from level III, immediately above the pit (figs. 24 and 25), gave a date of 2816 ± 200 B.P. (C-569). Dick (1965:18–19) attempted to explain this discrepancy in terms of different rates of deposition between the front and the rear of the shelter. However, it is clear that the 1948 sample could only have come from the area of shelter 1C below the 1950 sample because the 1948 excavation went below level IV only in that section of the shelter (original project field notes). Despite the possibility that the samples were mixed, the dates represent a minimum age, given that radiocarbon determinations are statistical averages, and thus the discrepancy cannot be explained by different depositional rates. The difference would make sense, however, if the charcoal sample above the pit came from a hearth constructed shortly after the pit was filled. In other words, because the two dates are not statistically different, the two sample proveniences are probably about the same age. Given their stratigraphic separation, for this to be possible the two samples would have had to originate in about the same place.

This introduces the second fundamental issue in reconstructing the stratigraphy of the small shelter—dating. Two sets of radiocarbon dates were produced from the original project, one submitted in 1948, the other in 1950. The first set consisted of five samples of uncarbonized plant material (table 18): one with only maize cobs, three with only wood, and one with mixed cobs and wood. These samples were selected by the project botanists in the laboratory without consulting the project archaeologist (Dick 1965:18). Plant material was taken from excavation levels in different parts of the site and combined; no record was kept of the plants used or the site areas they came from. Only the sample from level V can be reasonably located in the site; the other four samples, in which material of different ages may have been mixed together, must be disregarded.

The quality of the original samples concerned the director of the radiocarbon laboratory that processed them, Willard Libby, and in 1949 he suggested that more samples be obtained to establish the validity of the original set (Peabody Museum archives). The 1950 excavations at Bat Cave were designed specifically to retrieve confirmatory dates (Dick 1965:viii).

Five of the six new samples consisted of charcoal pooled from arbitrary excavation levels in a 5-foot-square block of deposits in front of shelter 1C, at the dripline of the cliff (fig. 20). The other sample came from the rear of shelter 1C, above the deep pit. There is a critical argument, however, against correlating material from levels inside and outside shelter 1C simply on the basis of equivalent depth below surface. Geologic deposition in the small shelters was affected by the pile of boulders that had spilled into the site during cliff collapse and subsequently kept colluvium from entering the shelters. Sediment backed up against this barrier, but sedimentation behind the rocks, at the rear of the shelter, was largely biologic in origin—mainly rodent feces. Colluvium began to accumulate in the rear of the shelters when the barrier was breached. However, the deposition of sediments in the shelters was always a simultaneous mixture of geologic and biologic processes. A hearth discovered at the bottom of the sediment block, apparently at the level where colluvial sediment (particularly the yellow sediment) began to extend around and over the boulders, produced a date of 5931 ± 310 B.P. (C-573)—perhaps the most reliable assay from the original excavations. Another sample, obtained one level higher, dated to 5605 ± 290 B.P. (C-571). Consequently, it seems reasonable to place the deposition of the yellow sediment layer in the small shelters before 6000 B.P., based on the dates above it.

This layer would correspond to excavation levels IV or V in shelter 1C, in which artifactual material can be assigned a date of 6000 B.P. only if it occurs in situ within the same geologic unit. Because the project field notes record only a few stone tools in the "upper few inches" of the yellow layer, and because the hearth dated 5931 B.P. rested on top of the yellow sand, it seems safe to assume that cultural deposition took place later. Thus there is good reason to question correlating the 6000 to 5600 B.P. range with all of the archaeological material from levels V and VI in shelter 1C.

Stratigraphic Summary

The earliest evidence of human occupation at the site seems to occur at about 10,000 to 9000 B.P. in the main shelter but postdates 6000 B.P. in the small shelters. Between 10,000 and 2800 B.P., the site complex may have been used sporadically by small bands of hunters. Broken projectile points and flake tools were almost the only artifacts recovered from deposits falling in this time frame. Unfortunately, there is some ambiguity about the age of these specimens, most of which were found in shelter 1C where the large pit cuts deeply into older sediments. For the moment, we can only argue that before around 2800 B.P., direct evidence of site use is extremely limited.

Between 2800 and 2200 B.P., however, we find large pits associated with hearths in three different parts of the rockshelter complex. We also find that each pit was apparently abandoned and allowed to fill with discarded material, seemingly in part through active site cleaning. The pits in the main shelter, the north shelter, and probably shelter 1C contained cultigens. Site use continued after the pits were filled, and there is evidence of a hiatus of several hundred years in the north shelter. The guano deposit that covered the pit and hearth complex in shelter 1C is tantalizingly suggestive of the separation between ceramic and preceramic deposits in the other parts of the site, but their congruence cannot be demonstrated. In the main shelter, the rhythm of preceramic occupation appears episodic, with periods of repeated and perhaps regular use. But again, this pattern cannot be extended to the entire site.

The final, ceramic phase of occupation is estimated from several radiocarbon dates to have lasted a thousand years, from 1800 to 800 B.P. The ceramic deposits are dense with hearths, but the density of artifacts is not great. The ceramic occupation began at a time of locally mesic climatic conditions, as ponderosa pine apparently advanced into the pinyon-juniper woodlands surrounding the site during the Late Archaic.

The first well-documented evidence of agriculture is associated with the features marking the preceramic shift from occasional to intensive, repetitive site use at 3000 to 2800 B.P. Because of the depositional complexity of the small shelters, none of the cultigens collected in 1948–50 can be reliably dated to before 3000 B.P. on the basis of the arbitrary excavation levels in which they were recovered. And as we will see later in this chapter, new dates on a set of original maize specimens also fail to support the dates derived from charcoal in the same levels.

Lithic Technology

Unless cultivation requires some new type of tool, the adoption of cultigens and the lithic technology of the adopting population do not necessarily covary. Southwest Archaic peoples had grinding tools, and it is improbable that maize cultivation directly required any other stone tools. Therefore, in examining the lithic assemblage from Bat Cave, a significant change between the precultigen Archaic component and the initial period of cultivation should be the result of a change in the role of the site, not a need for new technology. A major premise of this study is that no real investment in time or energy would have been necessary to accommodate domesticates, and this includes tool manufacture and use. The pattern that should be evident, if this assumption is correct, is a continuation of existing technology. If the role of the site changed in response to cultivation, the lithic assemblage from the incipient period of food production should not be especially different from that of the preceding period, except as a reflection of a different set of on-site activities.

Because of the problems posed by the intrusive pit in shelter 1C, the hearth and associated ground stone fragment in the main shelter are the only unambiguously precultigen cultural materials at Bat Cave. The early radiocarbon dates and the early biface types undoubtedly reflect use of the site complex prior to the introduction of cultigens, but the excavation procedures prevent a clear distinction between precultigen and cultigen artifacts. Nevertheless, it is possible to extract some relevant information about the precultigen lithic technology.

For example, according to the field notes, no ground stone was recovered below level III in shelter 1C, and only two specimens were recovered in preceramic contexts in shelter 1B, one a complete, oval mano, the other a fragment of a similar mano. These pieces were recovered on top of the beach gravels, suggesting an age between 6000 and 3000 B.P.

Of the total lithic assemblage recovered from the Bat Cave complex in 1948–50, only fifty-one pieces of chipped stone (exclusive of projectile points) were recorded from levels V and VI for the entire site (i.e., shelters 1B, 1C, 1D, and the talus area). This means that at most, only 9 percent of the total lithic assemblage (N = 1079) could have come from precultigen levels. If the site's precultigen cultural period lasted about 7000 years, the fifty-one chipped stone tools would represent an average discard rate of 7.3 tools per 1000 years. Consequently, the evidence of lithic technology during this period is slight. All of the possible precultigen specimens were scrapers or bifacial knives, suggesting cutting and/or woodworking. It is impossible to ascertain whether manufacture or maintenance of tools also took place because no debitage was saved.

In contrast to the sparse distribution of ground stone and unifacially flaked tools in the probable precultigen deposits located in 1948–50, there were numerous projectile points and bifaces. Of 193 projectile points recovered from shelter 1C, 110 (57 percent) were found in levels IV through VI.

In sum, the available data on stone tools from the early occupation of Bat Cave indicate by their very limitations that on-site tool production was not extensive and that the primary activity seems to have been the replacement or rehafting of broken projectile points. The significance of this lack of lithic material can be seen by comparing Bat Cave and LA 50827, a nearby precultigen site described in the previous chapter.

The contrast between the two sites is striking (see table 17). Both give indications of projectile point repair and probably cutting and/or woodworking, but at LA 50827 there is evidence of primary core reduction, biface manufacture and retouching, grinding, and, as inferred from large amounts of fire-cracked rock, boiling. Several families probably camped at LA 50827, sending out collecting and hunting parties during the day that returned to the basecamp at night. Other sites like LA 50827 are scattered around the margins of the San Augustine Plains. Bat Cave, on the other hand, seems to have been a temporary hunting camp, or perhaps simply a resting spot, considering the slight evidence of activities other than projectile point replacement.

The earliest dated association between lithic material and cultigens at Bat Cave occurs between ninety-three specimens of debitage and the hearths making up the lower occupation surface in the main shelter (table 17). Ninety pieces (97 percent) were unmodified flakes or angular fragments; the other three pieces were biface thinning flakes. Nearly all the debitage was a local gray chalcedonic rhyolite (66 percent) or local chert (14 percent). The average weight of pieces in the assemblage was 0.39 g, ranging between 0.02 and 1.98 g, although approximately 90 percent of the pieces weighed less than 1.0 g. The size distribution, coupled with the absence of cores or bifaces, suggests that the assemblage was the product of the secondary stages of biface manufacture or resharpening and maintenance of tools.

The only biface from this occupation surface, a large expanding stem point typed as a San Pedro, was found in the fill of the pit. Also found in the pit were thirty pieces of debitage with an average weight of 0.20 g and a range between 0.01 and 0.57 g. Like debitage from the hearths, most of the pit specimens were local rhyolite or chert (90 percent). Ten flakes were biface reduction flakes, and eight were resharpening flakes, suggesting some tool manufacture.

Early cultigens are also associated with lithic material in the north shelter. Of 253 chipped stone specimens recovered from the preceramic pit in square 99N 98E, 80 percent were flakes or angular fragments. The presence of forty-five retouch fragments is the major difference between this debitage and that of the main shelter.

The weight of lithic materials from the north shelter has a mean of 0.38 g and a range of 0.01 to 7.84 g—comparable to figures from the main shelter. The range is exaggerated by the three bifaces; 90 percent of the pieces in the assemblage weigh less than 1.0 g, as in the main shelter. The debitage is dominated by local chaledonic rhyolite and chert (71 percent), although more chalcedony (16 percent) was recovered here. Since there were no cores in the north shelter preceramic deposits, it would appear that bifaces were manufactured from partially prepared blanks or preforms.

The pattern of lithic technology from the dated early cultigen deposits in the Bat Cave complex differs significantly from the pattern preceding the appearance of cultigens. The material associated with cultigens indicates biface manufacture and maintenance, with some utilization of waste flakes, but little evidence of scraping or cutting—perhaps reflecting the failure of the original project to save debitage and thus distorting the overall picture. However, the unifacial tools found in the lower levels are not present in the preceramic deposits containing domesticates, although they are common in the late ceramic levels in association with bison remains.

Because cores and projectile points are common at LA 50827 and thus a component of the local Middle Archaic technology, but not common in the Late Archaic agricultural deposits at Bat Cave, it seems likely that the shift to cultivation seen at Bat Cave produced a change in site use. Maintenance such as repair of bifaces took place around the shelter camp, and butchering probably occurred near the kill sites, whereas before, the site had only been used to replace broken points. Because the data from LA 50827 indicate a greater range of lithic reduction and tasks than data from the period of cultigen introduction at Bat Cave, it is probably reasonable to assume that the use of Bat Cave at this time represented only a partial transferal of basecamp activities. Bat Cave probably had a somewhat more specialized role than LA 50827; rather than being abandoned, other activities probably took place at other, specialized localities. Consequently, based on the lithic data, it would appear that the shift to food production in the region meant that large, multipurpose campsites were broken up into smaller, specialized campsites.

Bat Cave and other rockshelters on the edges of the San Augustine Plains probably became important to cultivators because they provided protected places where seed crops could be stored. Moreover, they were close to arroyos and drainages, where runoff and soil conditions were most advantageous to cultivation. Rockshelters were probably occupied during the fall harvest, when it would have been necessary to spend several days drying the maize. But much of what took place in camps on the basin floor, such as grass processing and animal butchering, may not have happened as frequently in the rockshelters. In fact, there is little evidence of grinding or butchering in the Bat Cave lithic material.

Perishable Remains

In the absence of unambiguous perishable remains from precultigen contexts, it is a moot question whether perishable remains at Bat Cave reflect changes associated with agricultural adaptations. Field notes from the 1948 excavation mention only sandal fragments in the lowest excavation levels, but it is possible that perishables from the early agricultural occupation can help elucidate site use patterns.

The only reliable context for perishables with preceramic cultigens is the large pit in the main shelter. Within the pit, fragmentary rabbit fur blankets or robes represented the most common class of artifact. These fragments, found throughout the feature, consisted mostly of single strips of twisted fur or sometimes two strips twisted around each other. Often, knots of yucca or leather were attached to the ends of individual strips, probably as binding elements. Only a few strips exceeded 30 cm in length, and most were shorter than 20 cm. The various fragments had a combined length of approximately 12 m and weighed 3.25 kg.

The fur seems to represent the by-products of blanket or robe repair. Many strips were crumpled into balls, as if thrown away. Numerous rabbit bones, often in the form of articulated limbs, were scattered throughout the pit, but vertebrae and crania were rare, perhaps because the rabbits were killed away from the site and the pelts brought back. It appears that old portions of robes in need of repair were removed and discarded, new sections were inserted, and excess fur was thrown away.

In addition to the rabbit fur and bones, the pit fill contained fragments of leather, some of it sewn with yucca cordage, dozens of fragments of yucca cordage, small pieces of porcupine skin, leather sandal fragments, numerous feathers, and strands of shredded yucca leaves. At the base of the pit, a large rock was tied with yucca strips—possibly a deadfall trap. Clearly, yucca was collected and shredded for making cordage. One would expect such items at a basecamp, where raw material is returned to the camp for preparation and use. There was no such evidence in the excavation levels that may have been precultigen in age.

Faunal Remains

According to Dick (1965:91), very little bone was found below the ceramic levels at Bat Cave. A cursory examination of the original bone (Peabody Museum and Colorado University collections) from the lower levels shows that it consisted mostly of rabbit and prairie dog.

Rabbit and prairie dog bones were also found in the main shelter, along with porcupine quills. Bison remains are numerous in the ceramic levels, but none were found in preceramic levels. Likewise, large game such as elk, mountain sheep, mule deer, and pronghorn were found in ceramic levels, and there is no definite association of these species with preceramic deposits.

In short, little can be determined about the change to agricultural use of the site from the faunal remains except in a negative sense. Despite the abundance of projectile points, few large mammals were represented. If large game was hunted, it seems to have been butchered away from the site.

Faunal remains recovered from the 1981–83 excavations have not yet been completely analyzed, but the sample associated with the initial agricultural occupation seems to be dominated by rabbits.

Wild Plant Remains

Wild plant remains collected during the 1948 season were reported by C. Earle Smith (1950), who identified thirty-nine genera or species (table 19). Each genus can be found in the region today, though several are no longer growing near Bat Cave. Smith listed cattail, walnut, and aspen, indicating more water than is present around Bat Cave today. Walnut shell fragments were among the most common plant remains recovered. Pinyon is mentioned, but Smith did not provide provenience or numerical data. Amaranth, goosefoot, sunflower, and yucca were abundant, in addition to thirteen grass species.

Smith (1950:175) assumed that humans introduced all the plant remains to the site, a conclusion we now have to reject in light of the evidence of packrat

TABLE 19.   *Non-cultivated Plant Remains by Excavation Level from the 1948 Investigations at Bat Cave*

Plant	Stratum					
	I	II	III	IV	V	VI
Amaranthus hybridus						x
Ribes sp.			x		x	x
Suaeda suffrutescens		x				x
Juglans major[a]	x	x	x	x	x	x
Yucca sp.[a]	x	x	x	x	x	x
Atriplex canescens	x	x	x	x		x
Populus tremuloides					x	
Yucca baccata				x	x	
Bouteloua gracilis				x	x	
Sporobolus airoides	x	x	x	x	x	
Bouteloua hirsuta	x	x	x	x	x	
Quercus grisea	x	x	x	x	x	
Amaranthus powelli	x	x		x	x	
Opuntia sp.	x	x	x	x		
Poa secunda			x	x		
Typha latifolia			x			
Festuca kingii			x			
Chenopodium sp.			x			
Poa fendleriana	x	x	x			
Trisetum wolfii	x	x	x			
Lycium sp.	x	x	x			
Artemisia spp.	x	x	x			
Cucurbita foetidissima	x		x			
Eupatorium sp.	x		x			
Muhlenbergia rigens	x		x			
Scirpus olneyi		x				
Scirpus validus		x				
Oxytropis sp.		x				
Ptelea sp.		x				
Rhamnus sp.		x				
Pericome caudata		x				
Calamagrostis inexpansa	x	x				
Asclepias sp.	x	x				
Quercus gambelii	x	x				
Elymus salina	x					
Sitanion hystrix	x					
Sporobolus wrightii	x					
Monarda sp.	x					
Verbesina sp.	x					
TOTAL	23	22	19	11	10	6

NOTE: Species were listed as present or absent in the original report (Smith 1950) rather than as counts per level. The species are presented in this table as a frequency seriation to show overall plant diversity by level.

[a]This species is described by Smith (1950) as occurring "throughout the deposits," but it is not clear whether he actually meant every excavation level.

and other rodent activity. As Smith noted, however, the assemblage does indicate that modern vegetation encompasses the range of species found in the site deposits. Notably, he did not find ponderosa pine.

It is difficult to use the 1948 botanical data in determining human plant procurement strategies, in part because material from different shelters was combined by excavation level. Also, the provenience system given in Smith's report was changed after publication. The first botanical report on Bat Cave maize (Mangelsdorf and Smith 1949) designates the arbitrary excavation levels as strata I through VI. Stratum I was the lowest excavation level, 60 to 72 inches below the surface. Smith used this system in 1950. After the 1950 excavation, however, the numbering system was reversed, as in table 19, and stratum I became the highest level, 0 to 12 inches below the surface (Dick 1965).

This recording change must be kept in mind when interpreting Smith's 1948 data (there was no botanical report for 1950). Very few of the species were actually recovered from the lower levels of the site, a pattern that can easily be misconstrued if the number change is not taken into account.

Floral remains collected in 1981–83 have not yet been completely analyzed.

Cultigens

It is certainly fair to say that the archaeological study of agricultural origins in the New World began with the surprising discovery of ancient corn at Bat Cave in 1948 and 1950. In a long and distinguished series of studies, Mangelsdorf (1950, 1958, 1974) argued not only that the Bat Cave maize was ancient, but also that it provided the physiologic evidence of the evolution of maize from its wild ancestor.

The two fundamental interpretations of the maize revolve around the age of the plants and the evidence of change under cultivation. Age is obviously critical to understanding the adoption process because it permits us to relate the maize to archaeological changes. The role of humans in the breeding of maize is equally significant as a means of interpreting the social and economic constraints on cultivation strategies.

During the course of analysis, the age of the first set of maize from Bat Cave has been estimated several times, most recently at 2300–2000 B.C. (4300 B.P.) (Mangelsdorf 1974:149; Mangelsdorf, Dick, and Camara-Hernandez 1967:2–3). Dick (1965:95) previously raised the possibility of an earlier date, noting that the excavation level producing the "the most primitive maize recorded from Bat Cave" was associated with radiocarbon dates ranging "from not later than 3049 B.C. or 3655 ± 290 years and not earlier than 3981 ± 310 B.C." These dates are based on the unreliable correlation between level VI in front of shelter 1C and level VI in the rear. Consequently, I favor a date of between 2500 and 2300 B.P.

A sample of four cobs recovered during the 1948–50 excavations was recently examined at Harvard University by Richard I. Ford, and cupules were submitted to the University of Arizona Radiocarbon Laboratory for nuclear accelerator assay. The resulting dates range from 3740 to 2690 B.P. (samples A-4187, 4188, 4189, and 4185 in table 18). Unfortunately, the cobs had been treated with some unidentified lacquer in the field and were simply soaked in warm water before the assays were conducted. Although the new dates fail to support Dick's age estimates (at least for the lowest level in shelter 1C), they cannot be considered reliable because of the possibility of contamination.

Now let us examine the evolutionary sequence. Mangelsdorf considered cob length and diameter the best indications of evolutionary changes in the Bat Cave maize (Mangelsdorf and Smith 1949; Mangelsdorf 1950, 1974; Mangelsdorf, Dick, and Camara-Hernandez 1967). A progressive increase in size from the oldest levels in the site to the youngest was taken as the result of casual field cultivation. Decreased competition from wild plants provided an insulated environment in which gradual evolution was facilitated without any deliberate intervention by humans other than the removal of competing weeds. The recovery of the most "primitive" appearing cobs in the lowest levels was cited as evidence of this process.

However, the mixing of cultigens and artifacts from Bat Cave—first in the field, through the use of arbitrary excavation levels, and second in the laboratory, where excavation levels were combined without regard for what part of the site they represented—gives us good reason to question this evolutionary outline. Despite the protest that no serious distortion was created (Mangelsdorf, Dick, and Camara-Hernandez 1967:3), the nature of the site stratigraphy makes this conclusion untenable.

Beyond the methodological question, however, there are more direct means of assessing and rejecting this sequence. For example, Mangelsdorf (1974:151) himself suggested that a misidentified immature specimen or the tip of an undeveloped cob may have led to the definition of "primitive" maize. In fact, only 8.6 percent of the 766 cobs recovered from Bat Cave in 1948 were whole. Ford (1981) considers the "primitiveness" of the Bat Cave maize to have been exaggerated.

Perhaps most interesting, however, are patterns in the size of the maize. Figure 26 shows the vertical distribution by level of the variable Mangelsdorf considered most sensitive to maize evolution. Note that the figure shows increase in *variation* (cf. Mangelsdorf and Smith 1949:246), with the smallest and the largest specimens occurring in the youngest deposits. The mean for the lowest levels is the smallest in the sample, but it seems clear that the difference between means is not very great, and that it is probably the product of a greater size range, not of evolutionary development (cf. Minnis 1985:332).

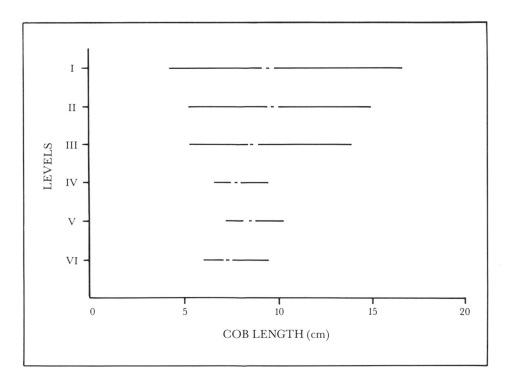

Figure 26. Cob length measurements by excavation level, Bat Cave, 1948. The dot represents the mean; the bar represents the range.

We are left then with very different conclusions about the original maize than first proposed. The cobs are probably no older than 2800 B.P., and the evidence of evolutionary change is by no means clear.

The most reliable information about the early maize at Bat Cave comes from the 1981–83 excavations. This maize is still being studied and will be reported in detail in a forthcoming site report. Ford (Wills, Ford, and Speth 1984) reported that all the Bat Cave maize belongs to the chapalote series and has primitive characteristics, but nevertheless is similar to maize found in later Pueblo contexts. Most of the cobs appear to be tillers or unfertilized, as Mangelsdorf's data suggest. In a sample of forty-two cobs recovered in 1983 from prehistoric contexts, the average length was approximately 4.2 cm, and the average maximum diameter was about 0.97 cm.

The four dated 1981–83 cobs range in age from 3010 to 2340 B.P. (samples A-4167, 4166, 4183, and 2791 in table 18). Unlike the 1948–50 cobs, those collected by the University of Michigan were not treated with any preservative, and the resulting assays can be considered reliable. Moreover, these accelerator dates are consistent with conventional radiocarbon dates on charcoal from the same features and stratigraphic sections (table 18).

The original project also recovered squash (*Curcubita pepo*) and beans (*Phaseolus vulgaris*). A squash seed and bean from the 1950 excavations were recently assayed and produced dates of 2980 and 2140 B.P., respectively (table 18). These specimens had apparently not been treated with preservative and can be considered reliable. Accelerator assays for squash seeds found in 1983 are consistent with the 1950 sample (table 18).

Possibly the most interesting feature of the Bat Cave cultigens is that maize and squash occur together in the deposits and features. No beans were recovered in 1981–83, and it is difficult to determine the exact provenience of beans found in 1948–50. Thus it seems clear that at Bat Cave, maize and squash were cultivated together from the time they first appear in the site stratigraphy, but beans are not evident until sometime later.

TULAROSA CAVE

Tularosa Cave is located 38.7 km northwest of Bat Cave but only 16 km west of the San Augustine Plains (fig. 16). The site is situated at an elevation of 2049 m on a steep, south-facing hillside overlooking Tularosa Creek. The relatively narrow valley expands somewhat just below the cave, forming a small floodplain where farmers grow maize today. Local vegetation consists mainly of ponderosa pine and pinyon forest, although cottonwoods and a variety of riparian species such as cattail and reed grass grow along the creek.

Tularosa Cave is a fairly small rockshelter consisting of a single chamber eroded from volcanic tuff. An enormous pile of boulders in front of the shelter indicates an overhang collapse sometime in the past. The bedrock floor of the site slopes from the back to the front, and as at Bat Cave, colluvial and biologic agents were simultaneously responsible for the accumulation of shelter sediments.

Tularosa Cave was first described by Hough (1907), who excavated to bedrock in parts of the site and removed five burials. According to him, the site had been vandalized before he arrived. In 1950 Martin and his associates (Martin et al. 1952) excavated much of the remaining deposits and established the chronological basis for the northern Mogollon ceramic period. In addition, they recovered over thirty thousand maize cobs, many from preceramic levels—the greatest number of specimens yet recovered from an early agricultural site in the Southwest.

Stratigraphy and Chronology

As at Bat Cave, the deposits from Tularosa Cave were described according to their cultural content rather than geologic sediments or cultural features. Each excavation level (20 cm thick; 2 by 2 m square) was assigned to a chronological phase based on the type of pottery recovered from it. Although Hough (1907:75) noted two "beaten" floor surfaces in the cave fill, which Martin also reported, all cultural material was collected by arbitrary levels except when a number of pits were discovered in the bedrock floor of the shelter. Objects from these pits were recorded as such. The lack of precultigen deposits at Tularosa Cave is critical. Because the lowest excavation level and the deepest bedrock pit contained abundant maize, it appears that the first use of the site was associated with agriculture.

Hough's excavations surely disturbed a considerable portion of the site, introducing a certain amount of ambiguity about the reliability of context (see Bullard 1962). Nevertheless, Hough implied that most of his excavations took place in the ceramic component of the site, so the preceramic levels probably remained relatively intact.

In figure 27, the distribution of "prepottery" excavation units is plotted over the pits in the cave floor. The gap between the two clusters of preceramic levels corresponds to a steep slope in the bedrock, which apparently prevented sediment accumulation (Martin et al. 1952:75). The pits along the west wall of the shelter in squares 4L1 and 5L1 were assigned to the Georgetown phase (A.D. 500–700) and the Pinelawn phase (ca. 300 B.C.–A.D. 500), respectively, as determined by pottery recovered from the excavation levels. Because the floor pits clearly belong to the concentration of pits occurring in adjacent preceramic levels, we can conclude that Hough or vandals had previously exposed the pits dated with pottery, given that the depth of deposits in this part of the shelter was about 50 cm.

The Tularosa Cave preceramic levels do cover the eleven floor pits, which range in diameter from 25 to 125 cm and in depth from 17 to 60 cm. Two and possibly three postholes were associated with the pits. A sample of maize cobs from the pits in square 2R1 produced a date of 2223 ± 200 B.P. (Martin et al. 1952:74, 468). Berry (1982:28) wanted to change this date to 2473 ± 200 B.P. to correct for the C-4 photosynthetic pathway in maize, and his date will be used here. Other radiocarbon dates, including several recently obtained accelerator assays on cultigens, bracket the deposits above the pits between 2400 and 2000 B.P. (table 18). Therefore, the preceramic component at Tularosa Cave appears relatively well confined between 2500 and 2000 B.P., contemporaneous with the agricultural occupation at Bat Cave.

The preceramic excavation levels at Tularosa Cave contained a wider range of material culture than they did at Bat Cave. Ground stone, especially manos, was common at Tularosa Cave, and unifacial flake tools were more abundant (tables 17 and 20). The variety of perishable artifacts, such as basketry, cordage, sandals, and wooden tools, was also greater, and these items were frequently found intact, which was not the case at Bat Cave. These quantitative differences cannot be attributed to the volume of excavated sediment because more was excavated at Bat Cave.

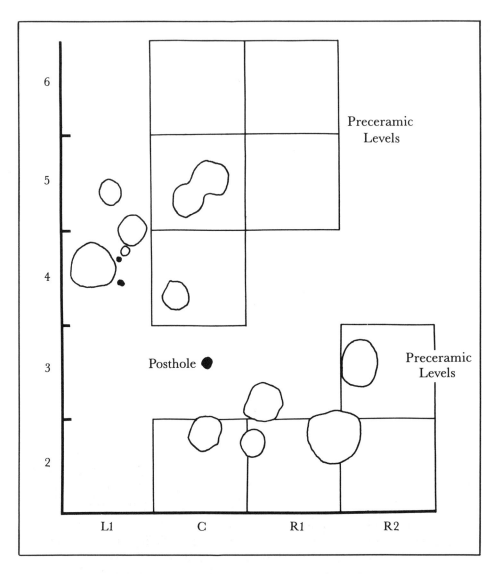

Figure 27. Distribution of preceramic excavation levels and floor pits at Tularosa Cave.

Fifteen snares—an important artifact class absent from Bat Cave—were recovered from the preceramic levels at Tularosa Cave (part of what may have been a deadfall trap was found at Bat Cave in 1981). Snares are a passive technology, set and left by the trapper. Successful trapping, which depends on relatively long-term or stable use of a particular area (Rowley-Conwy 1984:301), is often associated with family or group ownership of a trapping territory. Trapped animals are usually small, and in temperate regions, trapping takes place mainly in fall and winter.

TABLE 20.   *Lithic Artifacts from Tularosa, Cordova, and O Block Caves*

Lithic Type	Tularosa Cave			Cordova Cave			O Block Cave		
	N	%	D[a]	N	%	D	N	%	D
Scraper	76	65.5	4.30	167	73.6	2.94	56	71.8	2.69
Drill	6	5.1	0.34	18	7.9	0.32	5	6.4	0.24
Graver	0	—	—	3	1.3	0.05	1	1.3	0.05
Biface	19	16.4	1.08	20	8.8	0.35	5	6.4	0.24
Mano	9	7.8	0.51	9	4.0	0.16	3	3.8	0.14
Rubbing stone	3	2.6	0.17	3	1.3	0.05	0	—	—
Slab metate	0	—	—	2	0.0	0.04	1	1.3	0.05
Basin metate	3	2.6	0.17	3	1.3	0.05	6	7.7	0.28
Metate fragment	0	—	—	2	0.9	0.04	0	—	—
Grinding slab	0	—	—	0	—	—	1	1.3	0.05
TOTAL	116			227			78		

SOURCES: Martin et al. (1952); Martin, Rinaldo, and Bluhm (1954). These counts do not include small debitage, apparently not collected.
[a]D = density per m³.

Faunal remains from the preceramic levels at Tularosa Cave may reflect trapping, as rabbits are the most common species (Heller 1976:26). Artiodactyls, however, are the most important dietary animal resource in the assemblage, contributing perhaps 84 percent of the animal protein represented (table 21). According to Heller (1976:70), the presence of high proportions of immature artiodactyls indicates a late summer or early fall occupation. The total minimum number of individuals (MNI) is not great, however, averaging about one deer and three rabbits per hundred years. Nonetheless, evidence of hunting is far more extensive at Tularosa Cave than at Bat Cave.

A major difference between Tularosa Cave and Bat Cave can also be seen in the collections of maize. A total of about twelve hundred cobs was found at Bat Cave, including perhaps six hundred from preceramic levels; at Tularosa Cave, the preceramic sample alone exceeds fifteen hundred for just two excavation squares (2R2 and 3R2).

Harvesting and storage were clearly important activities at Tularosa Cave during the preceramic, as evident from husks, stalks, and unshelled cobs; 409 cobs were recovered from one pit in square 3R2 (Cutler 1952:407; Field Museum of Natural History records). Cultivation undoubtedly took place on the floodplain immediately below the shelter. The large cobs at Tularosa Cave indicate that harvesting occurred after full maturation of the plants.

TABLE 21. *Faunal MNI from Preceramic Levels at Tularosa Cave*

Species	MNI[a]	Edible Meat Weight (kg)[b]
Sylvilagus sp.	13	10.20
Lepus californicus	3	4.10
Spermophilus variegatus	2	0.95
Cynomys sp.	7	4.45
Neotoma sp.	3	0.95
Ondatra zibethicus	1	0.95
Thomomys sp.	1	0.32
Erethizon dorsatum	2	9.53
Canis sp.	1	5.67
Urocyon cinereoargenteus	2	4.08
Felis sp.	1	27.22
Lynx rufus	1	5.67
Odocoileus sp.	5	226.80
Antilocapra americana	2	74.84
Ovis canadensis	1	—
Antilocapra-Ovis	2	90.72
Meleagris gallopavo	1	3.81

SOURCE: Heller (1976).
[a]Based on White (1953): most common element present.
[b]Based on the MNI.

The emphasis on cultivation at Tularosa Cave and the evident range of domestic activities and maintenance tasks point to its use as a late summer and/or early fall basecamp. Shelled cobs—and thus, unparched seeds—may have been stored as seed for spring planting. The presence of a possible structure within the cave suggests that it may also have been occupied during the winter. Salwen (1960:215) argued that the padded leather sandals found at Tularosa Cave by Hough and Martin indicate winter hunting.

Tularosa Cave is close to a number of important natural resources. The perennial stream below the site is the locus of several major economic items, including muskrat, beaver, waterfowl, cattails, reedgrass, and fish; it would have been a focal point for wildlife in the surrounding pine forests. Walnut and pinyon were prominent in the Tularosa Cave deposits, as were various berries. The vast grasslands of the San Augustine Plains, with their grazing herbivores, could have been reached in a walk of a few hours. In contrast to the frigid winters on the San Augustine Plains, the climate of the sheltered Tularosa River Valley would have been somewhat more moderate, and Tularosa Cave has a southern exposure.

In short, it appears that Tularosa Cave was occupied during fall, winter, and spring, possibly for the express purpose of cultivation. Hunting parties operated at some distance from the shelter, at least to hunt pronghorn on the San Augustine Plains. As at Bat Cave, the small size of the shelter suggests that it was used by a relatively small group, but it also may have been used more intensively.

CORDOVA CAVE

Cordova Cave is located 72.5 km southwest of Bat Cave on the western slope of the San Francisco River Valley (fig. 16). The shelter, formed by runoff erosion of the soft volcanic tuff, is situated at an elevation of 2376 m, approximately 303 m above the valley floor. The local vegetation is identical to that of the ponderosa-pinyon forest surrounding Tularosa Cave except for the lack of a nearby riparian community and a greater proportion of species adapted to rocky substrate, such as *Opuntia* and oak.

The cave consists of a single, relatively narrow chamber. The basal sediments in the shelter were a thick layer of tan sand—a unit that produced very few artifacts, almost none of them perishable. Ashy layers containing charcoal occurred directly on top of the tan sand, and a distinct layer of white ash emanated from a large hearth near the top of the deposits. The upper 20 cm of fill contained mostly recent rockfall and vegetation debris.

Over half the excavated levels in Cordova Cave were considered preceramic. Pottery was so sparse in the ceramic levels that the excavators abandoned their standard practice of assigning phases based on ceramic types, simply dividing the levels into plain ware and late pottery units.

When the site report (Martin et al. 1952) was published, no dates were available for the site. Martin and his colleagues estimated that "Cordova Cave was occupied before the beginning of the Christian Era," or about 500 B.C. to A.D. 1. Fortunately, the excavators collected radiocarbon samples whenever possible, even though they were not processed. One of these samples, from the deepest excavation level (square 3R1, level 11), recently produced a date of 2810 ± 60 B.P. (Beta-9761). This time span may be a bit too long, however. The charcoal submitted for the date was ponderosa pine, and the specimen may well have been considerably older than the date it was burned. There is no way to correct for such a problem. For the sake of caution, the sample might be estimated to date between 2600 and 2500 B.P., and the preceramic component between about 2800 and 2000 B.P., assuming that the shelter was utilized throughout the Late Archaic.

The stone tools recovered from the preceramic levels at Cordova Cave parallel those at Tularosa Cave in the range of types and the proportions of each tool class to the whole assemblage. Both sites produced large numbers of bifacially retouched blades, including projectile points (Martin et al. 1952:200–282).

The paucity of perishable artifacts from the preceramic levels makes any interpretation based on their attributes a dubious endeavor. Two fragments of basketry and one piece of cloth constitute the entire assemblage. On the other hand, the absence of such material may itself be significant. The excavators attributed the lack of perishable artifacts to two factors: dampness in the basal tan sand layer and a large fire between A.D. 1 and 500, which "may have smouldered for some time like a fire in a peat bog, slowly working downward" (Martin et al. 1952:79).

There are problems with these two explanations. No evidence verifies the presence of dampness in the tan sand layer. The interpretation was made despite the presence of large quantities of bone and plant material, and not on the basis of independent geologic or biological data. The slow fire undoubtedly destroyed some artifacts, but its total extent was rather limited. Also, plant remains were recovered from the levels in question, and it is unlikely that the fire would have burned cultural items only.

A more interesting explanation might look to the density of all classes of artifacts from the site, which is fairly low. The excavators even suggested that the site was not occupied very much after A.D. 1. It appears that the cultural inventory reflects a low intensity of site use and probably a very specialized function, which could account for the narrow range of artifacts. It would be useful to examine the faunal data in this regard, but the bones were not analyzed.

Plant remains from Cordova Cave were studied and reported subsequent to the site report (Kaplan 1963). Wild plant species present in preceramic levels were listed in Kaplan's report (table 22), but the cultigens have not been studied. Kaplan did note that *Zea mays* was present in all levels of the site, and cobs, kernels, husks, and stalks were found in every level (1963:352). If the cultigens were distributed throughout the excavation levels, then they might date as early as 2800 B.P. It is unclear, however, if Kaplan's levels refer to the cultural distinctions of "Pre-pottery," "Plain Ware," and "Late," or to individual excavation units. In the former case, cultigens might not have occurred through the entire preceramic sequence. It seems that maize was found in at least some preceramic levels, but how much is unknown.

In sum, Cordova Cave seems to have been primarily a hunting station during the preceramic period (cf. Linskey 1975; Hunter-Anderson 1986). As for

TABLE 22.   *Percentages of Plant Remains from Cordova Cave*

Species	Prepottery	2000–1250 B.P.	1250–850 B.P.
Zea mays (cobs)	30	27	53
Lagenaria siceraria	6	41	53
Cucurbita foetidissima	14	60	26
Juglans major (nuts)	16	24	60
Yucca "compactions"	15	42	43
Agave "compactions"	5	42	53

NOTE: For an explanation of the formula by which these percentages were obtained, please see Kaplan (1963).

the presence of cultigens, hunters may have simply brought corn into the site during periods of temporary use. Or, like so many rockshelters in the Southwest with ceramic-period deposits, macrofossils from the younger layers may have moved downward in the deposits into older layers. Without directly dating the specimens, it is almost impossible to resolve these matters with confidence.

O BLOCK CAVE

O Block Cave is one of a series of rockshelters located on the eastern slopes of the San Francisco River Valley, approximately 71 km west of Bat Cave and only 5 km south of Cordova Cave. At an elevation of 1900 m, the site is only 60 m above the valley floor. Local vegetation consists of ponderosa pine and pinyon with a thick understory of oak.

O Block Cave is eroded from a volcanic conglomerate cliff. The shelter apparently formed as the bedrock matrix weathered and the large constituent clasts, especially large boulders, fell out. A fault running through the cave probably contributed to the exposure and weathering of the bedrock. As a result, the cave has a rather high ceiling, but it is not very deep.

O Block Cave was excavated in 1952 by the Field Museum. Nearly all the sediments in the site were removed during that research, which was reported in a brief summary of the fieldwork (Martin, Rinaldo, and Bluhm 1954). The University of Texas conducted new excavations at the site in 1986. O Block Cave is seldom included in the inventory of early Southwestern agricultural sites, doubtless because the cultigens recovered were never analyzed, and the site was not dated at the time the site report appeared. However, maize was recovered at the site in a preceramic context, and in 1960 two early radiocarbon dates were published. While the data as they now exist are relatively scant, O Block Cave should be considered along with Bat Cave, Tularosa Cave, and Cordova Cave as an example of agricultural beginnings in the Mogollon Highlands.

Excavation at O Block Cave followed the method used at Tularosa and Cordova caves, proceeding in 20 cm arbitrary levels and 2 by 2 m squares. Of the sixty-nine excavation units at the site, twenty-seven were preceramic, for a total sediment volume of 5.4 m³. Some geologic stratification was observed; at the base of the deposits, a layer of buff-colored sediment was presumed to have weathered from the bedrock (Martin, Rinaldo, and Bluhm 1954:26). Above this, a thick series of ashy layers contained discrete hearths, much like the ones at Bat Cave. Modern plant detritus and bedrock breakdown overlay this ashy sediment. Unfortunately, no profile drawings were kept (Martin, Rinaldo, and Bluhm 1954:29). Although it seems likely that the basal buff sediment was associated with preceramic material, the contact between it and the ashy layers cannot be correlated with the excavation levels.

However, the preceramic levels can be dated. A charcoal sample from square C2, level 7, the deepest excavation level, produced a date of 2780 ± 100 B.P. (M-717), and a sample from level 4 dated to 2600 ± 100 B.P. (M-718). The level 4 sample came from a level defined as Pinelawn phase, a ceramic occupation, suggesting some mixture. Together, these two dates give at least a good estimate of the earliest perceramic occupation, even though a clear continuity between 2600 B.P. and the first ceramic-period use of the site cannot be established.

The chipped stone from the preceramic levels at O Block Cave, like that of Cordova Cave, is dominated by scrapers (table 20). Most of these tools are unifacially retouched flakes with little formal modification other than the working edge. There were several manos present, as well as six basin metates, one slab metate, and a grinding slab. The density of these classes of artifacts did not vary much between O Block, Cordova, and Tularosa caves.

A large number of animal species was found at O Block Cave, and a list of species by number of bones is shown in table 23. The diversity is high, but clearly, deer and antelope were the major food source. These figures should be taken as a relative indicator of the species present because material from only three squares was analyzed.

In the absence of any botanical analysis, it is rather difficult to assess the significance of the O Block Cave cultigens. The Field Museum collections include specimens of maize cobs and husks from square C-2, level 4, and all the levels above, so maize might have occurred at the level dated to 2600 B.P. As noted above, however, this level was assigned to a ceramic phase, indicating

TABLE 23. *Faunal Inventory by Preceramic Level at O Block Cave*

	Square A2	Square B1	Square C2	Total[a]
Sylvilagus sp.	8	5	26	39
Lepus californicus	4	1	7	12
Spermophilus sp.	2	0	0	2
Neotoma sp.	0	0	10	10
Ondatra zibethicus	0	1	1	2
Thomomys sp.	0	0	8	8
Odocoileus hemionus	3	3	13	19
Antilocapra americana or				
Odocoileus hemionus	40	47	67	157
Unidentified mammal	24	11	50	85

SOURCE: Martin, Rinaldo, and Bluhm (1954).
[a]Counts are number of elements; MNI was not calculated.

disturbance. Consequently, it is not clear if any preceramic cultigens were present. Based on the data from nearby Cordova Cave, it would be safe to assume there were, but because the material was not given much consideration, probably not very many specimens.

Like Cordova Cave, it appears that O Block Cave was primarily a hunting station during the Late Archaic. Consequently, it seems that Cordova Cave and O Block Cave had different structural roles in the regional subsistence-settlement system from those of Bat Cave or Tularosa Cave. Cordova and O Block were probably utilized when such use did not conflict with cultivation at major agricultural stations.

CIENEGA CREEK

The Cienega Creek site, 180 km west of Bat Cave, is located at an elevation of 1,878 m in a small valley in the White Mountains of eastern Arizona (fig. 16). Although situated within the Mogollon Highlands, it is probably too far west to have been directly connected to social networks encompassing the region around Bat Cave and Tularosa Cave. Nevertheless, the archaeology at Cienega Creek has important implications for understanding regional hunter-gatherer agricultural adaptation during the Late Archaic.

The site, excavated by Haury (1957), produced perhaps the most stunning alluvial Archaic site sequence in the Southwest, with clear superimposition of features separated by distinct episodes of sediment deposition. *Zea mays* pollen reported from preceramic portions of the site has commonly been cited as one of the earliest occurrences of maize in the Southwest (Martin and Schoenwetter 1960). Unfortunately, the first set of radiocarbon dates from the site exhibited internal discrepancies which have caused many investigators, including Haury (1957:23), to urge caution in accepting the reported dates. It is equally unfortunate that the discussion about the reliability of the dating has overshadowed the remarkable archaeological record at the site.

Haury (1957) defined four geomorphologic surfaces at Cienega Creek, two of which were associated with preceramic material. During the Archaic, Cienega Creek was clearly a campsite occupied repeatedly over time, as evident from the large number of features. The most intriguing was a large pit containing the remains of at least thirty-six cremations interred individually.

Twelve radiocarbon samples were submitted for assay, eight to the University of Arizona and four to the University of Michigan. The two laboratory results were extremely inconsistent. The Arizona samples were older than the Michigan samples from the same layers by as much as one to two thousand years. A reanalysis of the Arizona samples gave results that agreed more closely with the Michigan dates (Damon and Long 1962).

However, samples from bed C-3 gave earlier dates than D-1, directly beneath it (fig. 28). Damon and Long (1962:243) suggested that the D-1 material may have been contaminated, but did not consider it likely. They assumed that the assays from bed C-3 were reliable. Berry (1982), on the other hand, questions the dates from bed C-3, arguing that the anomalous dates may have been derived from charred wood washed into the site from an older, eroded geologic context.

In any case, it is unnecessary to invoke geologic processes to account for the anomalies. In figure 28, a schematic profile of the Cienega Creek site is shown with a plot of the relevant radiocarbon dates. Haury (1957:24) suggested that the wood in pit 8 was probably older than the feature in which it was found, which was probably also true of the 3190 ± 160 B.P. sample in bed C-3. A third anamolous date, 2900 ± 150 B.P. (A-26B), was obtained from the third laboratory analysis of the original sample, which had been contaminated (Damon and Long 1962:242). If A-26B is rejected as unreliable and the other two samples are old wood (see Schiffer 1986; Smiley 1985), the remainder of the stratigraphy is chronologically consistent.

The basal occupation at Cienega Creek apparently dates to about 3000 B.P. (Berry estimates 2500 B.P.), and the preceramic occupation spans 3000 to 2000 B.P. It appears that the cremations occurred primarily in the latter part of the preceramic sequence, probably between 2100 and 1900 B.P.

The evidence of maize at Cienega Creek, limited to pollen, was reported by Martin and Schoenwetter (1960). *Zea mays* pollen was found as deep as 280 cm

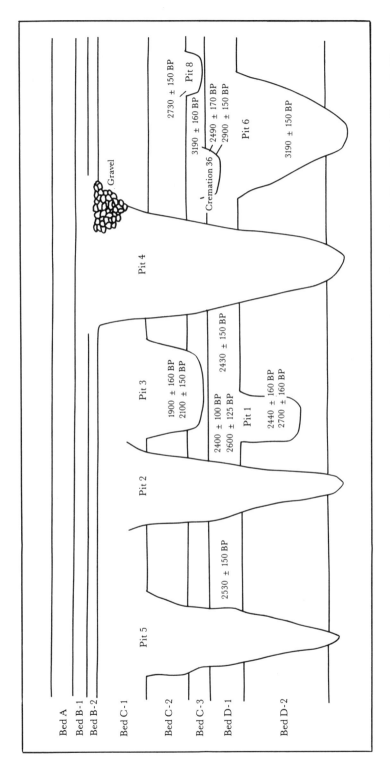

Figure 28. Schematic profile of geologic beds, cultural features, and radiocarbon dates at Cienega Creek. Compiled from figures 5, 23, and 24 in Haury (1957).

in bed C-3. Martin and Schoenwetter cited the extant dates for the D-1 bed as the basal dates for the site, following Haury's preference for the original Arizona dates over the Michigan dates (1960:33). Martin and Schoenwetter did not attribute maize pollen to bed D-1; instead, they assigned it to the Chiricahua stage, including D-1 only by implication. If the deepest sample was taken at a depth of 280 cm, then D-1 may not have been represented in the pollen sampling (see Haury 1957:figs. 5, 23, 24). Berry's (1982) criticism of the Cienega Creek pollen analysis fails to acknowledge that the reanalysis of the radiocarbon data took place after the publication of the pollen results. The dates reported in 1962 would now assign the early pollen to 3000–2000 B.P.

However, Berry makes a far more fundamental attack on the Cienega Creek maize pollen study, charging that preceramic pollen at the site was "likely" the result of contamination from overlying ceramic levels. Several large pits (presumably wells) were excavated into the preceramic deposits from ceramic layers, and maize pollen may have entered the lower levels (Berry 1982:22). But Berry also acknowledges that the pollen samples came from a single column. For his contamination proposition to be correct, he must assume that the pollen column was taken in a pit, which he does not demonstrate, and which seems highly improbable.

Schoenwetter (cited in Berry 1982:22) thinks that because *Zea mays* was present in all levels, but in greatest numbers in the lowest levels, contamination may not have been the source of pollen in the preceramic beds. Berry counters by arguing that the amount of pollen was too small to allow a statistical evaluation of significant differences between beds, which he takes to indicate a poor association between maize and the preceramic deposits (1982:22). His rejoinder suffers the glaring problem of not explaining what kinds of statistically verifiable differences would indicate contamination; significant or not, the preceramic levels will continue to have more pollen than the ceramic levels.

Berry's consideration of potential problems with the Cienega Creek preceramic pollen is useful, but his conclusion (1982:23)—that contamination explains the presence of preceramic pollen better than the original interpretation, maize cultivation during the Archaic—seems unwarranted by his own discussion. A conservative interpretation should regard early agriculture at the Cienega Creek Site with skepticism, but currently there is no compelling reason to dismiss a preceramic date. A rough date of 2500 B.P. appears entirely reasonable, especially given earlier dates in the Tucson Basin (Huckell and Huckell 1985; Long et al. 1986) and at Bat Cave.

Agriculture is not the only significant aspect of the Cienega Creek site. At least forty-seven cremations were present in the excavated portion of the site, thirty-six of which occurred in pit 3. Cremations were placed in the pit individually, and the pit was left open between interments (Haury 1957:11).

Some cremations were placed in shallow pits near pit 3, and all the cremations were in baskets (1957:14). Cremation 36, the earliest, was found in bed C-3, probably dating to about 2400 B.P., and pit 3 was used between 2100 and 1900 B.P.

The use of the site as a crematorium and especially the prolonged use of the single pit indicate a close association between the social group using the site and the site itself. That association may have lasted a thousand years during the Archaic, and when cremations began, the relationship took on a highly symbolic aspect. Pit 3 undoubtedly was used by a single group, the symbolic correlate of which is ownership or hereditary affiliation with the site area (cf. Saxe 1970).

In terms of agriculture, the site seems to have been occupied before evidence of cultivation appears in the stratigraphy. Cremations may have started even before the inhabitants adopted cultigens, but the intense social ties to the site evident in the cremations of pit 3 surely occurred in the context of cultivation. The sequence at the site therefore appears to reflect a localized social group with an increasing investment in land tenure or territorial affiliation toward the end of the Archaic.

No Archaic sites near Bat Cave have been found comparable to Cienega Creek, perhaps because excavation in the eastern Mogollon Highlands has focused on rockshelters. Nonetheless, the evidence from the Cienega Creek site may increase our knowledge of Late Archaic settlement systems throughout the uplands of the central Southwest. Apparently, montane forests were the scene of developing regional associations between social groups and specific areas. The patterning at Cienega Creek is a good example of social localization, which would be expected with mobility restriction and which should have preceded or accompanied the appearance of cultigens. The occurrence of maize after the Cienega Creek site had become a repeatedly occupied campsite with buried cremations may be one of the best indicators of the relationship between mobility and the acquisition of food production in the Southwest now available.

7

Early Agriculture

in Regional Perspective

At the beginning of this book I argued that the critical value in the early domesticated plants introduced into the Southwest was a matter of predictability, not productivity. Although the yield of these plants was not especially high, the ability of cultivators to control their location and temporal availability—including delayed or prolonged use through storage—was a major change in the relationship between foragers and their food resources. Given this assumption, I inferred that the conditions favoring the adoption of cultigens by hunter-gatherers would be generated by increasing levels of uncertainty in environmental productivity and that a primary source of uncertainty would be variation in population density.

General trends or temporal patterns in several aspects of the Archaic archaeological record in the central and northern Southwest support these propositions to the extent that they are consistent with expectations for some density-dependent socioeconomic transformations. Starting with an overview of long-term environmental changes, I suggested that throughout the Archaic period there was an increase in the overall productivity of the Southwest's environment and the complexity of spatial and temporal patterns of resource availability in the central and northern portions. These changes represented an increase in the potential productivity of the northern and central Southwest over time. For logical and empirical reasons I have eschewed the commonly held view that mid-Holocene peaks in temperature and perhaps aridity were necessarily deleterious to hunter-gatherer populations. In fact, I propose that the population began to grow rapidly during that period as critical complementary seasonal resources such as pinyon and desert succulents expanded numerically and geographically.

An examination of the geographic distribution of radiocarbon-dated Archaic sites reveals chronological trends that apparently parallel postulated shifts in regional vegetative zones. I argued that the hunter-gatherer response to increasing temporal and spatial complexity in resource availability would be greater emphasis on logistic foraging strategies, which would, in turn, result in repetitive use of particular localities. Radiocarbon chronologies seem to reflect such developments, as increasing frequencies of dated sites show a south to north transgressive pattern consistent with a similar trend in the expansion of pinyon-juniper woodlands and savannahs.

In addition, the geographic evidence of dwellings (pithouses) and concentrations of projectile points and ground stone indicate a general system of group mobility throughout the Archaic in which stream drainages were key areas. Upland or montane regions have revealed less evidence of dense site and artifact concentrations until the Late Archaic. These data fit well with hypothetical mobility between upland and lowland areas as vegetative contrasts became pronounced during the Holocene. Seasonality in the Southwest would evoke a "typical" hunter-gatherer system, in which lower-lying areas provided key resources from winter through midsummer and upland areas were resource rich in late summer and autumn.

To establish whether these probable changes in Archaic societies took place as adjustments to the environment or whether they might also have been the result of demographic structure, I considered stylistic variation in projectile points as markers of density-dependent boundary behavior. My assumption was that projectile point style might reasonably reflect efforts to maintain social boundaries. I expected that increasing density would reduce foraging success and increase the need for clearly defined social or group markers. In other words, population density varies positively with resource competition, and hunter-gatherers are likely to react to competition by enhancing information about competitors.

A variety of ethnographic studies confirm that projectile points are deliberately used to convey social information by way of style and are therefore potential markers of boundary maintenance (although not necessarily physical boundaries). Collections of projectile points from the central Southwest grouped by Early, Middle, and Late periods of the Archaic suggest a high degree of stylistic investment toward the latter part of the Middle Archaic. Specimens from the Late Archaic, which is defined by most authorities on the basis of projectile point variation, suggest very little emphasis on style and perhaps a shift toward increasing technological efficiency. These trends, although evident in a limited data set, are consistent with the development of competing social groups during the Middle Archaic and the establishment of well-defined, probably geographical boundaries by the Late Archaic. In essence, the projectile point data seem to indicate a period of declining foraging success during the Middle Archaic and a corresponding need to increase information about the location and relationship of competing groups, followed in the Late Archaic by efforts to control resources through the establishment of boundaries.

Turning from a general consideration of Archaic-period trends, I looked more closely at the Mogollon Highlands to provide a case study for the actual transition from hunting and gathering to cultigen husbandry. The choice of this area was logical from three perspectives. First, it is traditionally thought to be the area where introduction originally occurred as a result of climatic conditions favorable for agriculture. Second, because the timing of introduction in this area has recently become suspect, there is a pressing need to resolve this issue. And third, regardless of the accuracy of the older radiocarbon dates, the Mogollon Highlands offered the best-known evidence of abundant remains of preceramic agricultural systems and thus a potentially good opportunity for addressing new theoretical positions on the introduction process.

As the questions of age surrounding the maize collected in the 1940s and 1950s have been resolved through archival research, new excavations, and new radiocarbon assays, our understanding of the appearance of agriculture in the Mogollon Highlands has changed. An introduction date of approximately 3000 B.P., rather than 6000 to 4000 B.P., places the process squarely in a time frame of elevated levels of precipitation throughout the central and eastern Southwest. Increased regional precipitation during this period has two significant implications. On the one hand, it indicates a favorable combination of available moisture and lengthy growing seasons at intermediate to lower elevations, for example the Rio Grande Valley (below 1800 m). On the other hand, increased moisture at higher elevations was probably concomitant with decreased temperature, resulting in a shortened growing season where it was already shorter than what is normally required by maize. In sum, the Late Archaic appearance of agriculture in uplands actually seems contrary to the environmental explanation, given the frost sensitivity of maize and squash.

The nature of cultivation in the context of expectable hunter-gatherer subsistence and mobility strategies supports a nonenvironmental explanation for upland agriculture. The seasonal differences between uplands and lowlands in resource availability and abundance implies that foragers should be at lower elevations in the spring. The cultivation of domesticates at higher elevations, however, absolutely requires that people be present in the spring months to plant. Not only does spring cultivation in montane areas mean foregoing available resources at lower elevations, it also puts the cultivators where they do not have access to many wild resources until late summer, except game animals, which are in poor condition following winter. It seems probable, therefore, that cultigens stored from previous years would have constituted the primary resource sustaining cultivators in uplands during planting season. But to anticipate a conclusion I will make in a moment, it is highly unlikely that agriculture was practiced in the Mogollon Highlands for its own sake, that is, because it was an inherently obvious thing to do in that environmental context.

How then do we resolve the apparent paradox of finding early agriculture in an area ill suited to cultivation and with seasonal mobility constraints incongruous with expectable hunter-gatherer subsistence tactics? To begin, I think we have to look at the nature of regional hunter-gatherer populations, not at grossly defined environmental characterizations such as "favorable" or "unfavorable," which presume that plant distribution is controlled by their ability to tolerate various habitats. This position disregards the far more fundamental fact that domesticated plants only go where people take them.

In an earlier version of this study (Wills 1985), I suggested that because the cultivation of maize and squash in the Mogollon Highlands would require a shift from occupation of lowlands in the spring to far less attractive upland localities, we might be seeing the emplacement of a fully residential population in this region. This would have been accomplished by small groups budding off from parent populations, an expectable emigration process when populations reach stable or homeostatic levels. This budding would have been made possible by the ability to use stored cultigens as a winter and spring food source. In this construct, agriculture would not have been introduced into upland areas before it was introduced into the lowlands, but *transferred* to montane environments as a mechanism for accommodating increasing regional population density. In my interpretation, the parent population continued to maintain a seasonal pattern of movement, linking up with daughter groups in later summer and early fall.

This interpretation neglects a perspective that had originally been one of my primary concerns in studying the acquisition process. Namely, I had assumed that because the inherent value in domesticates for hunter-gatherers was in enhancing predictability, they should probably be seen as a supplement intended to increase foraging success by contributing to the reliability of hunting and gathering. In this model, incipient cultivators who cached cultigens in specific locations could be assured of finding adequate resources in those places later on, regardless of local productivity in wild resources. This strategy would allow them to search an area more thoroughly and perhaps collect low-return items more intensively than if they depended wholly upon finding enough wild food for prolonged encampments. The need to forage intensively is a logical outcome of increasing competition for resources in a given area.

Although this position seemed logical enough, it did not seem to account for the decision to ignore spring resources at lower elevations, unless cultivation at higher altitudes could produce enough surplus to exceed whatever might be expected in the lowlands. Given the demonstrable increase in carrying capacity in lower areas during the Late Archaic and the high risk of cultivation failure in the mountains, I was inclined to view the possibility of excessive surplus as very unlikely. Instead, in light of the difficulties of practicing agriculture in mountain areas, I decided that any groups electing such a strategy must have been, in some sense, forced to it.

Now, having had the luxury of considering both interpretations, I believe the available evidence points to a combination of the two. Since there are few, if any, significant resources in the uplands during the spring, cultivation must serve some future purpose—that is, some other reason than allowing hunter-gatherers to forage for meager or nonexistent spring resources in mountain areas. The obvious conclusion is that it contributes to foraging at other times.

But how? Most likely in two ways: by allowing intensive collecting in areas as described above, but also by giving cultivators an opportunity to "preview" coming attractions. The critical resources in upland areas are basically nuts and animals, and their probable location, condition, and availability the following fall can be ascertained with varying degrees of reliability during spring and summer. If stored cultigens permit the cultivators to monitor these resources and resource areas in the spring, the probability—and hence certainty—of successful foraging during the important autumnal months will be enhanced.

I suggest that it is the capacity for long-term environmental monitoring that underlies the establishment of cultigens in uplands, consistent with increasing competition for upland areas during the fall by regional populations. Such monitoring, however, still requires the presence and relative immobility of cultivators in the area during the spring. It may be that small groups were dispatched to upland localities in advance of the bulk of the population. As noted, the age and sex structures of homeostatic populations encourage emigration and periodic but temporary removal of certain units. In this case, I suspect that young males—those without familial responsibilities and competent in hunting—would have been sent ahead.

This interpretation is also consistent with the obvious implication that cultigens were transferred to uplands from lowland economic systems. Stable populations tend to be "top heavy" with older, infirm, and injured individuals. A system involving annual movement between widely separated areas would be amenable to the incorporation of cultigens only if a portion of the population could be left behind to tend the crops. In the case of the Southwest, the adoption of cultigens may have dramatically increased the productivity of young and old people who were formerly peripheral to most economic activities.

Thus, the process of introducing domesticated plants to the prehistoric Southwest is likely to have depended first on the promotion by regional hunter-gatherer population densities of fairly regular and geographically constrained patterns of movement between upland and lowland areas. The actual acceptance of cultigens would then be predicated on the development of an age structure that freed some people for seasonal sedentism while most of the population pursued wild resources. The decision to accommodate cultigens to the *potential* for cultivation within this socioeconomic system would finally be based on a desire to enhance the predictability of some aspects of the economy.

To put this scenario into a specific geographical context, maize, squash, and beans were probably introduced first to areas such as the Rio Grande Valley or southeastern Arizona as a means of enhancing the security of winter-spring resource availability. The appearance of cultigens in uplands, in contrast, took place later as a strategy for monitoring fall resources, thus responding to competition for montane resources brought on by the convergence in higher elevations of increasing numbers of foraging groups in autumn months.

If these relationships are being accurately represented, the initial acquisition of cultigens in the lowlands may have contributed to the subsequent density-dependent transfer of these plants to upland areas. I would decline to argue that a transfer was caused by lowland cultivation systems supporting growing populations, but it seems clear that such a situation might have developed. It also seems likely that an ongoing agricultural component within a basically hunter-gatherer economy could have given some groups a competitive advantage over nonagricultural groups in foraging success.

I offer these possibilities to show that the acquisition of cultigens in the Southwest may not be easily explained by saying that plants were simply passed along between different local groups. Although marriage networks probably controlled the mechanism of intergroup movement, as Ford (1981) posits, the conditions controlling local movements may have been quite variable. In the construct I have just sketched, the general motivation for the appearance of agriculture in uplands and lowlands was probably the same—increasing predictability—but the specific objectives could have been very different.

Having based the preceding argument on evidence from the Mogollon Highlands, it seems appropriate to examine chronological evidence of cultigens in the lowlands. Recent direct accelerator dates on maize from the Tucson

Basin range between ca. 2800 and 2500 B.P. (Long et al. 1986; Fish et al. 1986); a direct date for maize in the Jemez Mountains of New Mexico was put at approximately 2800 B.P. (Ford 1981); and direct dates on squash and maize from the central San Juan Basin in northwestern New Mexico fall between ca. 3000 and 2700 B.P. (Simmons 1986). In addition, maize from Tornillo Shelter, near Las Cruces in the southern Rio Grande Valley, has produced a new direct date of 3175 ± 240 B.P. (GX-12720) (Upham et al. 1987). This determination was made on a combined sample of cob fragments, meaning that some of the specimens might have been older or younger than the derived date.

The widespread occurrence of maize and squash dated between approximately 3000 and 2800 B.P. may reflect a rapid introduction process. I would argue that because we undoubtedly have not yet found the first sites involved in this process, an introduction period from 3500 to 3000 B.P. may be accurate. I do not think that an introductory period of several hundred years indicates any great rapidity.

Although population density has been named as a variable in the introduction of agriculture, theirs is only a relative relationship. Hunter-gatherers, even if moving within regular annual territories, were still covering lots of ground. For instance, I have posited annual movement between Bat Cave and the Rio Grande Valley, a linear distance of 241 km. It does not seem unlikely that hunter-gatherer groups operating primarily in the central Rio Grande Valley of New Mexico might also, during the course of a year, find themselves in the modern states of Arizona and Texas and still experience declining foraging success from competition. In fact, one possible initial response to declining foraging returns might be an expansion of foraging areas.

If hunter-gatherer groups were indeed moving within relatively regular areas, it probably would not take long for introduced domesticated resources to move large distances. Because localities appropriate for cultivation are not spread homogeneously across the southwestern landscape, the spread of cultigens should probably be seen in terms of ecological nodes within areas, not in terms of whole areas. In this context, an estimate of several hundred years for the wide dispersal of cultigens from one group to another might even be too long. Southwestern archaeologists do not seem impressed by the similar geographic spread of pottery during the following millennium, even though ceramics may have traveled farther in a shorter time.

I assume that the actual timing of the acceptance by any particular social unit or group depended upon the ability of regional populations to achieve an organizational state in which cultigens could be accommodated with very little cost and no real disruption of the existing economic system. I do not mean to ignore the potential role of environmental constraints on production, and much of my argument so far acknowledges the difficulty of practicing agriculture in an inhospitable environment. Furthermore, I would like to suggest at this point that the rather sudden appearance of agriculture in widely separated areas and different habitats in the Southwest might be partially attributable to environmental change.

I noted that the earliest dated maize and squash appear in the Southwest during a period of increased regional precipitation, at least in the eastern portion. A rise in carrying capacity is evident in the Rio Grande Valley with the development of grasslands capable of supporting bison herds. These conditions may have created something of an ecological bridge across the arid northern Chihuahuan Desert, permitting cultivators to move domesticates into the Southwest at that time. If hunter-gatherer groups in the Southwest had evolved an organizational framework suitable for the adoption of agriculture before this bridge developed, then when it did, the subsequent transferal of domesticates might have been very rapid indeed.

It is worth asking if the rapid appearance of a suite of domesticated resources in the Southwest reflects a migration of farmers. Berry (1982) explicitly argues that migration was the medium for dispersal, referring to it as "colonization." Although archaeologists have not developed unambiguous markers for population movement among nonindustrial peoples, there are no obvious discontinuities in the material record or settlement patterns in the Southwest that would indicate this kind of population intrusion. Indeed, he cites projectile point form as the major indicator of migration in the late Archaic (Berry 1982:31), a time of widespread homogeneity in shape. Moreover, his argument is predicated on the culture-historical assumption that projectile points covary with ethnic groups, an untenable position when offered, as it seems to be in this case, as a universal generalization.

The routes of agricultural introduction probably followed the foothills of mountain ranges and the terraces of major river valleys such as the Rio Grande, the Gila, and the Mimbres. These are intermediate locations in elevation, temperature, and precipitation, and the likely site of winter and spring camps throughout the Archaic period.

Archaeologists in the Southwest have not looked for evidence of early agriculture in these areas, having been guided by the assumption that domesticates were first introduced by way of mountain chains to avoid lower elevations. In order to substantiate the construct I have offered, it will be necessary to look for agriculture where we have not expected to find it. Any other strategy can only reify the hypothesis that initial food production occurred in upland areas.

The "suddenness" of the arrival of agriculture might also be explained by the inaccuracy of the accepted age of early domesticates in Mexico, as in the Southwest. If Mesoamerican agriculture is not as old as we think, then the apparent rapidity of introduction to the Southwest, a perception based on the difference between oldest dates in the two regions, might not appear so rapid after all.

Consider, for a moment, the archaeological record of early agriculture in northern Mexico. As the transmission route for agriculture from Mesoamerica to the Southwest, this area is essentially an unknown factor in the diffusion process. Evidence of preceramic or Archaic agriculture in the region consists of extremely limited data collected in the early 1950s.

The single archaeological site supporting a Sierra Madre corridor is Swallow Cave, a rockshelter in Chihuahua which contained the only preceramic maize yet reported from the Sierra Madre (Mangelsdorf and Lister 1956; Lister 1958). Sixteen arbitrary 6-inch excavation levels were removed from the site, and levels 8–16 were considered preceramic. The entire preceramic assemblage of maize specimens consisted of a single chapalote-type cob from level 13 and one cob fragment each from levels 13 and 14. No absolute dates were obtained from Swallow Cave, although Mangelsdorf equated the maize with early maize remains from Bat Cave on the basis of morphology (Mangelsdorf and Lister 1956:159).

Everything about the Swallow Cave maize data urges caution in assigning it to *any* time period on the basis of stratigraphic position. The sample is exceptionally small, seven of the nine preceramic levels had no maize, and the overlying ceramic levels were dated to A.D. 900—a combination of factors very suggestive of stratigraphic displacement. Moreover, given what we now know about the chronology of the Bat Cave maize, dating the Swallow Cave specimens by reference to Bat Cave cannot justify an age earlier than 3000 B.P. Although Swallow Cave may have been a preceramic agriculture site, there is also no reason to assume that it was, and therefore it can currently tell us nothing about the transmission of cultigens to the Southwest.

The only other reported preceramic maize sites in northern Mexico lie nearly 1000 km southeast of Swallow Cave in the state of Tamaulipas, where the excavation of numerous dry rockshelters has produced maize specimens dated to 4450 B.P. (Mangelsdorf, MacNeish, and Galinat 1956, 1964, 1967; MacNeish 1958). The latter date came from La Perra Cave, some 200 km south of the Rio Grande. The preceramic maize from this site consisted of fifteen cobs from zone B, a series of ash and refuse lenses separated by silt layers (MacNeish 1958:30). A burial was recovered from zone B, and according to MacNeish (1958:30), "undoubtedly the digging of this burial pit brought earlier material into later layers." No doubt the converse occurred as well. Zone B varied in thickness, and all excavation levels from this zone were combined into a single group for analysis.

The fifteen La Perra preceramic maize specimens (and in fact, all the maize from La Perra, preceramic and ceramic) were a variety called nal-tel, a primitive form related to chapalote and still grown in Mexico today. Since all the reliably dated preceramic maize in the Southwest is chapalote, and chapalote is not evolved from nal-tel, the La Perra specimens cannot have been an ancestral population for southwestern preceramic maize.

The age estimate of 4450 B.P. for the earliest La Perra maize was taken from a radiocarbon assay of 4455 ± 280 B.P. (C-687) on a mixture of vegetative material found at the base of zone B. MacNeish apparently assumes that all of zone B belongs to this period, but his own description indicates that most of zone B postdates 4450 B.P., and the specimens in zone B are almost certainly younger than 4450 B.P. Furthermore, there is no reliable connection between the sample which produced that date and any maize specimen. Since all the site maize is nal-tel, the possibility of displacement of ceramic-age maize into preceramic deposits is easily apparent. These issues show that the La Perra data have little or no direct bearing on early southwestern agriculture.

MacNeish (1958:167–70) also excavated a series of rockshelters containing preceramic maize in southern Tamaulipas. The maize from these sites was chapalote, and the earliest specimen, a single cob from level 3 in Valenzuela's Cave, dated to the Flaco phase (ca. 4350–3850 B.P.). An assemblage of 187 cobs and 55 cob fragments from Romero's Cave was assigned to the Guerra phase (3850–3200 B.P.), and 412 cobs and 53 cob fragments were placed in the Mesa de Guaje phase (3200–2400 B.P.). The single specimen from the Flaco phase is hardly convincing evidence of agriculture during that period, so we will concentrate on the Guerra and Mesa de Guaje phases.

The dates for MacNeish's southern Tamaulipas phases were obtained by comparing material culture from the rockshelters with diagnostic phase artifacts from northern Tamaulipas (Mangelsdorf, MacNeish, and Galinat 1967:35). The radiocarbon dates used to establish the temporal phases included only two assays for the period after 5000 B.P. and none for the period after 4580 B.P. Apparently, the northern Tamaulipas sequence from about 4500 B.P. onward was based on correlations with material culture from Oaxaca, Mexico, not on absolute dates from the Tamaulipas area (MacNeish 1958:194, 198). In fact, none of the dates assigned to any of the maize from Tamaulipas seems to have come from the archaeological record of Tamaulipas.

Therefore, although there seems little doubt that the southern Tamaulipas maize is preceramic in age, its absolute age is highly uncertain. A conservative estimate, based strictly on published excavation data, suggests a range of 2800 to 2400 B.P. (see MacNeish 1958:table 31)—coeval with or even later than the time of cultigen introduction in the Southwest.

It is not necessary to belabor this point further: the archaeological record of preceramic maize in northern Mexico provides no compelling evidence for a temporal gap between it and preceramic maize in the Southwest. In fact, the data from northern Mexico do not provide much evidence of preceramic agriculture at all, at least not in terms of absolute dates. This is not to say that there was none. Maize cultivation must have been practiced in northern Mexico prior to 3000 B.P., if that date is taken as the earliest estimate of its arrival in the Southwest.

On the other hand, if there is no temporal gap in northern Mexico, and maize was first domesticated in central Mexico around 7000 B.P. (Flannery 1986:8), then the issue of rapid dispersal becomes even more pronounced because it would include the additional area of northern Mexico. My reaction to this is twofold. First, we just do not know enough about northern Mexico to make these sorts of observations. Second, because the maize from central Mexico was dated in the same manner as that from Tamaulipas—by arbitrary excavation levels grouped by zones—perhaps its age has likewise been more assumed than demonstrated. Neither possibility is really an issue here, except in as much as it seems premature to conclude how rapidly the introduction of domesticates to the Southwest from Mesoamerica took place when we do not even know the age of agriculture in the donor area.

Rockshelters, and thus "classic" early agricultural sites consisting of stratified layers of perishable debris in caves, are uncommon along the probable route of introduction through Mexico and into the Southwest. In some rockshelters at lower elevations, there may be evidence of earlier agriculture than that found at Bat Cave or Tularosa Cave, and sites such as Fresnal Shelter (Human Systems Research 1972), caves in the Las Cruces area (Upham et al. 1987), Lemitar Shelter (Anzalone 1972), or Armijo Shelter (Irwin-Williams 1973), which are ambiguous in chronology, may have been part of early lowland agricultural systems.

Although we yet lack empirical evidence of the geography of transmission, there are some important implications in the emerging pattern of initial appearance. For example, it appears that the three basic aboriginal cultigens—maize, beans, and squash—were introduced at the same time. The situation was different in the southeastern United States, for instance, where each species was adopted at different times. Squash arrived between 5000 and 4000 B.P., perhaps three thousand years before maize (Smith 1985). The adoption context in the East consisted of sedentary social systems practicing indigenous plant husbandry in which new cultigens from Mexico were assimilated into existing crop or garden strategies. In the Southwest, by contrast, adoption appears to have taken place in small, mobile social groups in which cultivation departed from ongoing production activities.

This difference suggests that the factors conditioning acceptance were closely tied to characteristics of the specific cultigens. Squash was adopted around 5000 B.P. in the East, but it does not show up until 3000 B.P. in the Southwest; maize occurs at 3000 B.P. in the Southwest, and its appearance in the East is now placed at about 1700–1500 B.P. These patterns imply that the decision to adopt a cultigen was predicated on an assessment of its potential contribution and expected role within the recipient economy; its suitability conditioned the decision to adopt it or not. This in turn validates the assumption made in chapter 1 that adoption would be based on a conscious consideration of the value of a new resource according to its structural role in the economic system.

In other words, the dispersal of domesticated plants into North America from Mesoamerica was not simply a matter of availability. These resources were adopted when the recipient systems made a decision to incorporate them, not necessarily when they became available for the first time. Therefore we should not presume the diffusion process occurred at uniform rates across broad regions.

With these conclusions in mind, we find that the model of early agriculture in the Southwest proposed by Haury in 1962 and still widely accepted today fails to account for the empirical evidence of that process. Instead of a passive transfer of unimportant resources through montane regions sometime between 6000 and 4000 B.P., it seems more likely that agriculture was introduced at lower elevations in a deliberate effort to enhance winter and spring procurement tactics. The subsequent transfer of cultigens to upland zones may reflect a shift to a critical function for agriculture in monitoring wild resource availability in the fall.

This construct is intended not as a criticism of Haury's model but as a revision of it on the basis of new data. It seems important, however, that his model assumed that cultivation was primarily constrained by climate, when logically it is also a matter of social organization. As Cordell (1984:186) notes, maize, squash, and beans can be grown successfully in nearly any part of the Southwest with the appropriate effort. To place the explanatory emphasis within the socioeconomic system rather than the ecological system suggests relationships not evident in a strictly environmental perspective.

It is apparent that the study of early southwestern agriculture requires some reorientation in our thinking. For decades we have used models of culture histories to guide our perceptions of the "logic" of the transition to food production, allowing similarities in artifacts to dictate assumptions about the timing, direction, and motivation (or lack thereof) of introduction. We have not adequately employed our understanding of hunter-gatherers, farmers, the ecology of specific domesticates, or even the historical dynamics of environmental change. As a consequence, we have interpreted the adoption of domesticates by southwestern hunter-gatherers from data generated by arbitrary excavation levels in complexly stratified rockshelters. Individual sites have been taken as typical of economic systems when in fact they are past components within such systems. Having used single sites as models, we have then attempted to accommodate their data to existing frameworks of culture history; it is as common in the 1980s as it was in the 1950s to explain the appearance of cultigens within an area by placing that event within a cultural phase and describing the correlative climatic conditions that existed during that phase.

This approach will not do anymore. Rather than helping to understand the conditions that may have favored the acquisition of domesticated plants by hunter-gatherers, analysis at the level of a cultural phase only obscures relevant variables. It unintentionally conditions us to seek evidence for early agriculture where we already expect to find it, and the form of analysis forces us to conceptualize an economic change in terms of artifact similarities presumed to reflect long-term continuity. From an anthropological vantage, it is as clear that ethnicity is not a unidimensional phenomenon bound to patterns in material culture as it is that economic change cannot be well understood through patterns of continuity.

In this study of early agriculture in the Mogollon Highlands, I have argued that we must drop simplistic culture-historical outlines as the arbiters of agricultural origins. I have also argued that we should treat environmental change as a potential inducement to cultural change, with effects to be ascertained independently of temporal correlations, rather than treat it as a presumed cause.

I am the first to point out that the alternative interpretations I have offered here are based on weak empirical evidence, and to some extent I have worked with material grouped by blocks of time. I do not apologize for this because I am largely handling data collected without the orientation that I brought to the analysis. Instead, I wish to emphasize that to build a better understanding of the agricultural transition in the Southwest we need to begin considering the issue as a process of change, not as an event to be plotted against space-time coordinates. We need to consider individual sites and artifacts as participants in and products of socioeconomic systems, not models for such systems. We are not limited in the study of this extremely important development by dating techniques or methods of collecting information, but we can be limited by our reluctance to broaden the scale of our study and the complexity of the variables we consider.

References

Agogino, George
    1960   The Santa Ana pre-ceramic sites: An Archaic seed-gathering culture in Sandoval County, New Mexico. *Southwest Lore* 25:17–21.

Agogino, George, and Jim Hester
    1953   The Santa Ana pre-ceramic sites. *El Palacio* 60:133–40.
    1956   A re-evaluation of the San Jose non-ceramic cultures. *El Palacio* 63:6–21.

Agogino, George, and Frank C. Hibben
    1957   Central New Mexico Paleo-Indian cultures. *American Antiquity* 23:422–25.

Akazawa, Takeru
    1982   Cultural change in prehistoric Japan: Receptivity to rice agriculture in the Japanese archipelago. In *Advances in World Archaeology*, vol. 1, edited by Fred Wendorf and Angela E. Close, pp. 151–205. Academic Press, New York.

Anderson, Edgar
    1947   *Corn Before Columbus*. Pioneer Hi-Bred Corn Company, Des Moines, Iowa.

Antevs, Ernst
    1949   Age of Cochise artifacts on the Wet Legget. In *Cochise and Mogollon Sites*, by Paul S. Martin, John B. Rinaldo, and Ernst Antevs, pp. 34–78. Fieldiana: Anthropology 38(1). Field Museum of Natural History, Chicago.
    1955   Geologic-climatic dating in the West. *American Antiquity* 20:317–35.

Anzalone, R. D.
    1973   Archaeological investigations in San Lorenzo Canyon, Socorro County, New Mexico. M.A. thesis, Eastern New Mexico University, Portales.

Asch, C. M.
    1960   Post-Pueblo occupation at the Willow Creek Ruin, Point of Pines. *The Kiva* 26:31–42.

Athens, Steven J.
    1977   Theory building and the study of evolutionary process in complex societies. In *For theory building in archaeology*, edited by Lewis R. Binford, pp. 353–84. Academic Press, New York.

Bachhuber, F. W.
    1982   Quaternary history of the Estancia Valley, Central New Mexico. In *Albuquerque country*, edited by Jeffrey A. Grambling and Steven G. Wells, pp. 343–46. New Mexico Geological Society, Socorro.

Baker, Craig

    1981   Archaic culture phenomena. In *High altitude adaptations along Redondo Creek: The Baca Geothermal Anthropological Project*, edited by Craig Baker and Joseph C. Winter, pp. 163–72. Office of Contract Archaeology, University of New Mexico, Albuquerque.

Bayham, Frank E.

    1979   Factors influencing the Archaic pattern of animal exploitation. *The Kiva* 44:219–36.

    1982   A diachronic analysis of prehistoric animal exploitation at Ventana Cave. Ph.D. dissertation, Arizona State University, Tempe.

Beal, John D. (compiler)

    1984   *The Lee Ranch Project: Dimensions of occupational persistence.* Archaeology Program Report no. 84. School of American Research, Santa Fe.

Beckett, Patrick H.

    1973   Cochise culture sites in south central and north central New Mexico. M.A. thesis, Eastern New Mexico University, Portales.

    1980   *The AKE site: Collection and excavation of LA 13423, Catron County, New Mexico.* New Mexico State University Cultural Resource Management Division Report 357. Las Cruces.

    1983   The Archaic prehistory of the Tularosa Basin. In *The prehistory of Rhodes Canyon: Survey and mitigation*, edited by Peter L. Eidenbach, pp. 105–10. Human Systems Research, Tularosa, New Mexico.

Bender, Barbara

    1978   Gatherer-hunter to farmer: A social perspective. *World Archaeology* 10:204–22.

    1981   Gatherer-hunter intensification. In *Economic archaeology: Towards an integration of ecological and social approaches*, edited by Alison Sheridan and Geoff Bailey, pp. 149–57. British Archaeological Reports, International Series no. 96.

Bennet, John W.

    1976   *The ecological transition: Cultural anthropology and human adaptation.* Pergamon Press, New York.

Berry, Claudia F., and Michael S. Berry

    1986   Chronological and conceptual models of the Southwest Archaic. In *Anthropology of the desert West: Essays in honor of Jesse D. Jennings*, edited by Carol J. Condie and Don D. Fowler, pp. 253–327. University of Utah Anthropological Papers, no. 110. Salt Lake City.

Berry, Claudia F., and William Marmaduke

    1982   *Cultural resources overview: The middle Gila Basin, an archaeological and historical overview.* Northland Research, Flagstaff.

Berry, Michael S.

    1982   *Time, space and transition in Anazasi prehistory.* University of Utah Press, Salt Lake City.

Betancourt, Julio L., and Thomas R. Van Devender

    1981   Holocene vegetation in Chaco Canyon, New Mexico. *Science* 214:656–58.

Binford, Lewis R.

    1962   Archaeology as anthropology. *American Antiquity* 28:217–25.

1972   Directionality in archaeological sequences. In *An archaeological perspective,* by Lewis R. Binford, pp. 214-26. Academic Press, New York.

1978   *Nunamiut ethnoarchaeology.* Academic Press, New York.

1980   Willow smoke and dogs' tails: Hunter-gatherer settlement systems and archaeological site formation. *American Antiquity* 45:4-20.

1982   The archaeology of place. *Journal of Anthropological Archaeology* 1:5-31.

1983a   *In pursuit of the past.* Thames and Hudson, New York.

1983b   Long term land use patterns: some implications for archaeology. In *Lulu linear punctated: Essays in honor of George Irving Quimby,* edited by R. C. Dunnell and Donald K. Grayson, pp. 27-53. Papers of the University of Michigan Museum of Anthropology, no. 72. Ann Arbor.

1986   An Alyawara day: Making men's knives and beyond. *American Antiquity* 51:547-62.

Bleed, Peter
1986   The optimal design of hunting weapons: Maintainability or reliability. *American Antiquity* 51:737-47.

Bogucki, Peter
1987   The establishment of agrarian communities on the north European plain. *Current Anthropology* 28:1-24.

Botelio, Eugene
1955   Pinto Basin points in Utah. *American Antiquity* 21:185-86.

Braun, David P., and Stephen Plog
1982   Evolution of "tribal" social networks: Theory and prehistoric North America. *American Antiquity* 47:504-25.

Brew, John O., and E. B. Danson
1948   The 1947 reconnaissance and the proposed Upper Gila Project of the Peabody Museum of Harvard University. *El Palacio* 55:211-22.

Brooks, Alison S., Diane E. Gelburd, and John E. Yellen
1984   Food production and culture change among the !Kung San: Implications for prehistoric research. In *Hunters to farmers: The causes and consequences of food production in Africa,* edited by J. Desmond Clark and Steven A. Brandt, pp. 293-310. University of California Press, Berkeley and Los Angeles.

Broster, John B.
1983   PaleoIndian adaptation to high-altitudes on Cebolleta Mesa. In *High altitude adaptation in the Southwest,* edited by Joseph C. Winter, pp. 108-14. USDA Forest Service, Albuquerque.

Bryan, K., and Joseph H. Toulouse, Jr.
1943   The San Jose non-ceramic culture and its relation to a Puebloan culture in New Mexico. *American Antiquity* 8:269-80.

Bryant, Vaughn M., Jr.
1974   Prehistoric diet in southwest Texas: The coprolite evidence. *American Antiquity* 39:407-19.

1977   Late quaternary pollen records from the east-central periphery of the Chihuahuan Desert. In *Transactions of the symposium on the biological resources of the Chihuahuan Desert region,* edited by Roland H. Wauer and David H. Riskind, pp. 3-22. National Park Service, Washington, D.C.

Bryant, Vaughn M., and Harry J. Shafer
1977   The late quaternary paleoenvironment of Texas: A model for the archaeologist. *Bulletin of the Texas Archaeological Society* 48:1–25.

Bryson, R. A., D. A. Bareis, and W. M. Wendland
1970   The character of late-glacial and post-glacial climatic changes. In *Pleistocene and recent environments of the central Great Plains*, edited by W. Dort and J. K. Jones, pp. 53–74. University of Kansas Press, Lawrence.

Bullard, William R.
1962   *The Cerro Colorado site and pithouse architecture in the southwestern United States prior to A.D. 900*. Papers of the Peabody Museum of Archaeology and Ethnology 74(2). Harvard University, Cambridge, Massachusetts.

Bureau of Land Management
1981   *Final environmental statement on grazing management in the east Socorro ES area.* Department of the Interior, Washington, D.C.
1983   *Draft environmental impact statement for the proposed west Socorro rangeland management program.* Department of the Interior, Washington, D.C.

Campbell, Elizabeth W., William H. Campbell, Ernst Antevs,
Charles A. Amsden, Joseph A. Barbieri, and Francis D. Bode
1937   *The archaeology of Pleistocene Lake Mohave.* Southwest Museum Papers, no. 11. Los Angeles.

Campbell, John M., and Florence H. Ellis
1952   The Atrisco sites: Cochise manifestations in the middle Rio Grande Valley. *American Antiquity* 18:211–21.

Carter, George F.
1945   *Plant geography and culture history in the American Southwest.* Viking Fund Publication in Anthropology no. 5. New York.

Cashdan, Elizabeth
1983   Territoriality among human foragers: Ecological models and an application to four Bushman groups. *Current Anthropology* 24:47–66.

Castetter, Edward F., and M. E. Opler
1936   *The ethnobiology of the Chiricahua and Mescalero Apache. A. The use of plants for food, beverages and narcotics.* University of New Mexico Bulletin no. 297. Albuquerque.

Cattanach, George S., Jr.
1966   A San Pedro stage site near Fairbank, Arizona. *The Kiva* 32:1–24.

Chapman, Richard C.
1977   Analysis of the lithic assemblages. In *Settlement and subsistence along the lower Chaco River: The CGP Survey*, edited by C. A. Reher, pp. 371–452. University of New Mexico Press, Albuquerque.
1980   The Archaic period in the American Southwest: Facts and fantasy. Ph.D. dissertation, University of New Mexico, Albuquerque.

Chapman, Richard C., and Jan V. Biella
1977   Survey of Cochiti Reservoir: Presentation of data. In *Archeological investigations in Cochiti Reservoir, New Mexico*, vol. 1, *A survey of regional variability*, edited by Jan V. Biella and Richard C. Chapman, pp. 201–94. University of New Mexico Press, Albuquerque.

Christenson, Andrew L.
1980   Change in the human food niche in response to population growth. In *Modeling change in prehistoric subsistence economies*, edited by Timothy K. Earle and Andrew L. Christenson, pp. 31–73. Academic Press, New York.

Classen, M. M., and R. H. Shaw
1970   Water deficit effects on corn, pt. 2, Grain component. *Agronomy Journal* 62:652–55.

Cohen, Mark Nathan
1977   *The food crisis in prehistory*. Yale University Press, New Haven.

Conkey, Margaret W.
1978   Style and information in cultural evolution: Toward a predictive model for the Paleolithic. In *Social archaeology: Beyond subsistence and dating*, edited by Charles L. Redman, William T. Langhorne, Mary Jane Berman, Nina M. Versagg, Edward V. Curtin, and Jeffry C. Wanser, pp. 61–85. Academic Press, New York.

Conrad, Michael
1976   Biological adaptability: The statistical state model. *Bioscience* 26:319–24.

Cordell, Linda S.
1979   *Cultural resources overview: Middle Rio Grande Valley*. Bureau of Land Management, Albuquerque.
1984   *Prehistory of the Southwest*. Academic Press, New York.

Cordell, Linda S., and Steadman Upham
1984   Agriculture in the Southwest. In *Stage I site locational modeling in the southwestern region*, edited by Linda S. Cordell and Dee F. Green, pp. 29–44. U.S. Forest Service, Albuquerque.

Crane, H. R., and James B. Griffin
1958   University of Michigan radiocarbon dates, pt. 3. *Science* 128:1117–22.
1960   University of Michigan radiocarbon dates, pt. 5. *Radiocarbon* 2:31–48.

Crawford, Gary W., and Masakazu Yoshizaki
1987   Ainu ancestors and prehistoric Asian agriculture. *Journal of Archaeological Science* 14:201–13.

Cushing, Frank H.
1974   *Zuni Breadstuff*. 2d ed. Museum of the American Indian, Heye Foundation, New York.

Cutler, Hugh C.
1952   A survey of the plant remains of Tularosa Cave. In *Mogollon change and cultural continuity: The stratigraphic analysis of Tularosa and Cordova Caves*, by Paul S. Martin, John B. Rinaldo, Elaine Bluhm, H. Cutler, and R. Grange, pp. 446–80. Fieldiana: Anthropology 40. Field Museum of Natural History, Chicago.
1968   Origins of agriculture in the Americas. *Latin America Research Review* 3:3–21.

Cutler, Hugh C., and Thomas W. Whitaker
1961   History and distribution of the cultivated cucurbits in the Americas. *American Antiquity* 26:469–85.

Damon, P. E., and A. Long
1962   University of Arizona radiocarbon dates, pt. 3. *Radiocarbon* 4:239–49.

Dering, James Philip
1979   *Pollen and plant macrofossil vegetation recovered from Hinds Cave, Val Verde County, Texas.* Texas A&M University, College Station.

Dibble, David S.
1968   *Bonfire shelter: A stratified bison kill site, Val Verde County, Texas.* Texas Memorial Museum Miscellaneous Papers, no. 1. Austin.

Dick, Herbert W.
1943   Alluvial sites of central New Mexico. *New Mexico Anthropologist* 25:19–22.
1951   Evidences of early man in Bat Cave and on the Plains of San Augustin, New Mexico. In *Indian tribes of aboriginal America,* edited by Sol Tax, pp. 158–63. University of Chicago Press, Chicago.
1954   The Bat Cave corn complex: A note on its distribution and archaeological significance. *El Palacio* 61:139–44.
1965   *Bat Cave.* School of American Research Monograph no. 27. Santa Fe.

Dillehay, Tom D.
1974   Late Quaternary bison population changes on the southern plains. *Plains Anthropologist* 19:180–96.

Dobzhansky, Theodosius
1972   On the evolutionary uniqueness of man. *Evolutionary Biology* 6:415–30.

Duncan, Rosalind L.
1971   The Cochise Culture: An explanation of archaeological remains. M.A. thesis, University of California, Los Angeles.

Dunnell, Robert C.
1978   Style and function: a fundamental dichotomy. *American Antiquity* 43:192–202.
1980   Evolutionary theory and archaeology. In *Advances in Archaeological Method and Theory,* vol. 3, edited by Michael Schiffer, pp. 35–99. Academic Press, New York.

Dyson-Hudson, Rada, and Eric Alden Smith
1978   Human territoriality: An ecological assessment. *American Anthropologist* 80:21–41.

Eder, James F.
1984   The impact of subsistence change on mobility and settlement patterns in a tropical forest foraging economy: Some implications for archaeology. *American Anthropologist* 86:837–53.

Edmonson, M. S.
1961   Neolithic diffusion rates. *Current Anthropology* 2:71–102.

Eggan, Fred
1961   Comment. *Current Anthropology* 2:87.

Eisenhood, Bill
1979   Temperature. In *New Mexico in maps,* edited by J. L. Williams and Paul E. McAllister, pp. 8–9. University of New Mexico Press, Albuquerque.

Eldridge, N., and Stephen J. Gould
  1972   Punctuated equilibria: An alternative to phyletic gradualism. In *Models in paleobiology*, edited by T. J. M. Schopf, pp. 82–115. Freeman, Cooper, San Francisco.

Epstein, Jeremiah F.
  1960   *Centipede and Damp caves: Excavations in Val Verde County, Texas, 1958.* Report submitted to the National Park Service by the Texas Archeological Salvage Project, University of Texas, Austin.

Evans, Oren F.
  1957   Probable use of stone projectile points. *American Antiquity* 23:83–84.

Fay, George E.
  1955   Prepottery, lithic complex from Sonora, Mexico. *Science* 121:777–78.
  1956   Peralta complex: A Sonoran variant of the Cochise Culture. *Science* 124:1029.
  1967   *An archaeological study of the Peralta complex.* Occasional Publications in Anthropology, no. 1. Colorado State College Museum of Anthropology, Greeley.
  1968   *A preliminary archaeological survey of Guaymas, Sonora, Mexico.* Occasional Publications in Anthropology, no. 3. Colorado State College Museum of Anthropology, Greeley.

Ferguson, G. J., and W. F. Libby
  1963   UCLA radiocarbon dates, pt 2. *Radiocarbon* 5:1–22.

Fields, Ross C., and Jeffrey S. Girard
  1983   *Investigations at Site 32 (41EP325), Keystone Dam Project.* Reports of Investigations, no. 21. Prewitt and Associates, Austin, Texas.

Findlow, Frank J., and Marisa Bolognese
  1982   Regional modeling of obsidian procurement in the American Southwest. In *Contexts for prehistoric exchange*, edited by T. K. Earle and J. G. Ericson, pp. 53–81. Academic Press, New York.

Fish, Paul R., Suzanne K. Fish, Austin Long, and Charles Miksicek
  1986   Early corn remains from Tumamoc Hill, southern Arizona. *American Antiquity* 51:567–71.

Flannery, Kent V.
  1968   Archaeological systems theory and early Mesoamerica. In *Anthropological archaeology in the Americas*, edited by Betty J. Meggars, pp. 67–87. Anthropological Society of Washington, Washington, D. C.
  1973   The origins of agriculture. *Annual Review of Anthropology* 2:271–309.
  1986   *Guila Naquitz: Archaic foraging and early agriculture in Oaxaca Mexico.* Academic Press, New York.

Ford, Richard I.
  1968   An ecological analysis involving the population of San Juan Pueblo, New Mexico. Ph.D. dissertation, University of Michigan, Ann Arbor.
  1977   Evolutionary ecology and the evolution of human ecosystems: A case study from the midwestern U.S.A. In *Explanation of prehistoric change*, edited by James N. Hill, pp. 153–84. University of New Mexico Press, Albuquerque.

1981   Gardening and farming before A.D. 1000: Patterns of prehistoric cultiva-
        tion north of Mexico. *Journal of Ethnobiology* 1:6–27.
1984   Ecological consequences of early agriculture in the Southwest. In *Selected
        papers on the archaeology of Black Mesa*, vol. 2, edited by Stephen Plog and
        Shirley Powell, pp. 127–38. Southern Illinois University Press,
        Carbondale and Edwardsville.

Forde, C. Daryll
1931   Hopi agriculture and land ownership. *Journal of the Royal Anthropological
        Society* 61:357–412.

Fredlund, Glen
1984   Palynological analysis of sediments from Sheep Camp and Ashislepah
        shelters. In *Archaic prehistory and paleoenvironments in the San Juan Basin, New
        Mexico: The Chaco shelters project*, edited by Alan H. Simmons, pp. 186–211.
        Project Report Series no. 53. University of Kansas Museum of Anthro-
        pology, Lawrence.

Freeman, C. E.
1972   Pollen study of some alluvial deposits in Dona Ana County, southern
        New Mexico. *Texas Journal of Science* 24:203–20.

Frison, George C.
1976   *The Casper site*. Academic Press, New York.

Fritz, John M.
1974   The Hay Hollow site subsistence system: east-central Arizona. Ph.D. dis-
        sertation, University of Chicago.

Fromby, D. E.
1986   Pinto-Gypsum complex projectile points from Arizona and New Mexico.
        The Kiva 51:99–127.

Fulgam, Thomas, and Frank C. Hibben
1980   An Archaic hunting culture. Ms. on file at the University of New Mex-
        ico, Albuquerque.

Galinat, Walton C.
1979   Botany and origin of maize. CIBA-GEIGY Technical Monograph. Basle,
        Switzerland.
1985   Domestication and diffusion of maize. In *Prehistoric food production in North
        America*, edited by Richard I. Ford, pp. 245–78. Anthropological Paper
        no. 75. Museum of Anthropology, University of Michigan, Ann Arbor.

Galinat, Walton C., and Robert G. Campbell
1967   The diffusion of eight-rowed maize from the Southwest to the central
        plains. Monograph Series no. 1. Massachusetts Agricultural Experiment
        Station, Amherst.

Gatewood, John B.
1984   Cooperation, competition, and synergy: Information sharing groups
        among southeast Alaskan salmon seiners. *American Ethnologist* 11:350–70.

Gentry, H. S.
1969   The origin of the common bean, *Phaseolus vulgaris*. *Economic Botany*
        23:55–69.

Gifford, Diane
  1981   Taphonomy and paleoecology: a critical review of archaeology's sister dis-
          ciplines. In *Advances in archaeological method and theory*, vol. 4, edited by M.
          B. Schiffer, pp. 365–438. Academic Press, New York.

Gillespie, William B.
  1985   Holocene climate and environment of Chaco Canyon. In *Environment and
          subsistence of Chaco Canyon*, edited by F. Joan Mathien, pp. 13–16. Publica-
          tions in Archeology 18E. National Park Service, Albuquerque.

Glassow, Michael A.
  1980   *Prehistoric agricultural development in the northern Southwest*. Ballena Press
          Anthropology Papers no. 16. Socorro, New Mexico.

Goodwin, Grenville
  1971   *Western Apache raiding and warfare*. University of Arizona Press, Tucson.

Gould, Richard A.
  1980   *Living archaeology*. Cambridge University Press, Cambridge.

Gould, Richard A., Dorothy A. Koster, and Ann H. L. Sontz
  1971   The lithic assemblage of the Western Desert Aborigines of Australia.
          American Antiquity 36:149–69.

Green, Stanton W.
  1980   Toward a general model of agricultural systems. In *Advances in archaeologi-
          cal method and theory*, vol. 3, edited by Michael Schiffer, pp. 311–55.
          Academic Press, New York.

Gumerman, George
  1966   Two Basket Maker II pithouse villages in eastern Arizona: A preliminary
          report. *Plateau* 39:80–87.

Hadlock, Harry L.
  1962   Surface surveys of lithic sites on the Gallegos Wash. *El Palacio* 69:178–86.

Hall, Stephen A.
  1977   Late Quaternary sedimentation and paleoecologic history of Chaco
          Canyon, New Mexico. *Geologic Society of America Bulletin* 88:1593–1618.
  1985   Quaternary pollen analysis and vegetational history of the Southwest. In
          Pollen records of late-Quaternary North American sediments, edited by Vaughn
          Bryant and R. G. Holloway, pp. 95–123. American Association of Strati-
          graphic Palynologists, Dallas.

Harlan, J. R., and J. M. M. de Wet
  1973   On the quality of evidence for origin and dispersal of cultivated plants.
          Current Anthropology 14:51–65.

Harlan, J. R., J. M. M. de Wet, and E. G. Price
  1973   Comparative evolution of cereals. *Evolution* 27:311–325.

Harrington, Mark R.
  1933   *Gypsum Cave, Nevada*. Southwest Museum Papers no. 8. Los Angeles.

Harris, Arthur H.
  1970   The dry cave mammalian fauna and late pluvial conditions in southeast-
          ern New Mexico. *Texas Journal of Science* 22:3–27.

Harris, Arthur H., and James S. Findley
   1964   Pleistocene-recent fauna of the Isleta caves, Bernalillo County, New
           Mexico. *American Journal of Science* 262:114-20.

Harrison, Gary W.
   1979   Stability under environmental stress: Resistance, resilience, persistence
           and variability. *American Naturalist* 113:659-69.

Hassan, Fekri
   1981   *Demographic archaeology.* Academic Press, New York.

Haury, Emil W.
   1950   *The stratigraphy and archaeology of Ventana Cave.* The University of New Mex-
           ico Press and the University of Arizona Press, Albuquerque and Tucson.
   1957   An alluvial site on the San Carlos Indian reservation. *American Antiquity*
           23:2-27.
   1962   The greater American Southwest. In *Courses toward urban life: Some archaeo-
           logical considerations of cultural alternates,* edited by Robert J. Braidwood and
           Gordon R. Willey, pp. 106-31. Viking Fund Publications in Anthropol-
           ogy no. 32. New York.

Hayden, Brian
   1981   Research and development in the Stone Age: Technological transitions
           among hunter-gatherers. *Current Anthropology* 22:519-48.
   1982   Interaction parameters and the demise of PaleoIndian craftsmanship.
           Plains Anthropologist 27:109-23.

Haynes, C. Vance
   1968   Geochronology of late-Quaternary alluvium. In *Means of correlating Quater-
           nary successions,* edited by Roger B. Morrison and Herbert E. Wright, pp.
           591-631. University of Utah Press, Salt Lake City.

Haynes, C. Vance, Jr., Donald C. Grey, and Austin Long
   1971   Arizona radiocarbon dates VIII. *Radiocarbon* 13:1-18.

Haynes, C. Vance, and Herbert Haas
   1974   Southern Methodist University radiocarbon date list I. *Radiocarbon*
           16:368-80.

Heiser, Charles B.
   1973   *Seed to civilization: The story of man's food.* W. H. Freeman, San Fransico.

Heller, Maurice
   1976   Zooarchaeology of Tularosa Cave, Catron County, New Mexico. M.A.
           thesis, University of Texas, El Paso.

Hevly, Richard H.
   1964   Paleoecology of Laguna Salada. In *Chapters in the prehistory of eastern
           Arizona,* vol. 2, by Paul S. Martin, John B. Rinaldo, William A.
           Longacre, Leslie G. Freeman, James A. Brown, Richard H. Hevly, and
           M. E. Cooley, pp. 171-87. Fieldiana: Anthropology 55. Field Museum of
           Natural History, Chicago.
   1980   Pollen analysis of the Ake site. In *The Ake site: collection and excavation of LA
           13423, Catron County, New Mexico,* edited by Patrick H. Beckett, pp. 257-
           66. Cultural Resources Mangement Division, Report no. 357. New
           Mexico State University, Department of Sociology and Anthropology,
           Las Cruces.

1983   High-altitude biotic resources, paleoenvironments, and demographic patterns: Southern Colorado plateaus, A.D. 500–1400. In *High altitude adaptations in the Southwest*, edited by Joseph C. Winter, pp. 22–40. Cultural Resources Management Report no. 2. USDA Forest Service, Albuquerque.

Hibben, Frank C.
1941   *Evidences of early occupations in Sandia Cave, New Mexico and other sites in the Sandia-Manzano region*. Smithsonian Institution Misc. Collections 99 (23). Washington, D. C.
1951   Sites of the Paleo-Indian in the middle Rio Grande Valley. *American Antiquity* 17:41–46.

Hicks, Patricia A.
1984   Bajada phase projectile points: Inter-regional comparisons. Paper presented at the 49th annual meeting of the Society for American Archaeology, Portland, Oregon.

Hill, Jane H.
1978   Language contact systems and human adaptations. *Journal of Anthropological Research* 34:1–26.

Hockett, Charles F., and Robert Ascher
1964   The human revolution. *Current Anthropology* 3:135–68.

Hodder, Ian
1979   Economic and social stress and material culture patterning. *American Antiquity* 44:446–54.
1982   *Symbols in action*. Cambridge University Press.

Honea, Kenneth
1969   The Rio Grande complex and the northern Plains. *Plains Anthropologist* 14:57–70.

Hough, Walter
1907   *Antiquities of the Upper Gila and Salt River valleys in New Mexico and Arizona*. Bureau of American Ethnology Bulletin no. 35. Washington, D. C.

Huckell, Bruce B.
1973a   The Gold Gulch site: A specialized Cochise site near Bowie, Arizona. *The Kiva* 39:105–29.
1973b   The Hardt Creek Site. *The Kiva* 39:171–97.

Huckell, Bruce B., and Lisa W. Huckell
1985   New light on the Late Archaic period of the southern Southwest. Paper presented at the 50th annual meeting of the Society for American Archaeology, Denver.

Human Systems Research
1972   *Training bulletin*. Tularosa, New Mexico.

Hunt, Alice P., and Dallas Tanner
1960   Early man sites near Moab, Utah. *American Antiquity* 26:110–17.

Hunter-Anderson, Rosalind L.
1986   *Prehistoric adaptation in the American Southwest*. Cambridge University Press.

Hurt, Wesley R., and Daniel McKnight
    1949   Archaeology of the San Augustine Plains: A preliminary report. *American Antiquity* 3:172–94.

Iltis, Hugh H.
    1983   From teosinte to maize: The catastrophic sexual transmutation. *Science* 222:886–94.

Irwin-Williams, Cynthia
    1967   Picosa: The elementary Southwestern culture. *American Antiquity* 32:441–57.
    1968   Archaic culture history in the southwestern United States. *Eastern New Mexico University Contributions in Anthropology* 1:48–54.
    1973   The Oshara Tradition: Origins of Anasazi culture. *Eastern New Mexico Contributions in Anthropology* 5(1):1–30.
    1979   Post-Pleistocene archeology, 7000–2000 B.C. In *Handbook of North American Indians*, vol. 9, *Southwest*, edited by Alfonso Ortiz, pp. 31–42. Smithsonian Institution, Washington, D. C.

Irwin-Williams, Cynthia, and C. Vance Haynes
    1970   Climatic change and early population dynamics in the southwestern United States. *Quaternary Research* 1:59–71.

Jennings, Jesse D.
    1967   Review of *Bat Cave*. *American Antiquity* 32:123.
    1978   *Prehistory of Utah and the eastern Great Basin*. University of Utah Anthropology Papers no. 98. Salt Lake City.

Jennings, Jesse D. (editor)
    1955   The American Southwest: A problem in cultural isolation. In *Seminars in archaeology: 1955*, edited by Robert Wauchope, pp. 59–128. *American Antiquity* 22(2).

Johnson, Frederick
    1955   Reflections upon the significance of radiocarbon dates. In *Radiocarbon dating*, by Willard F. Libby, pp. 141–62. University of Chicago Press.

Johnson, Gregory A.
    1978   Information sources and the development of decision-making organizations. In *Social archeology: Beyond subsistence and dating*, edited by Charles L. Redman, William T. Langhorne, Mary Jane Berman, Nina M. Versagg, Edward V. Curtin, and Jeffry C. Wanser, pp. 87–112. Academic Press, New York.
    1983   Decision-making organization and pastoral nomad camp size. *Human Ecology* 11:175–99.

Johnson, LeRoy, Jr.
    1964   *The Devil's Mouth site: A stratified campsite at Amistad Reservoir, Val Verde County, Texas*. Department of Anthropology, Archaeology Series no. 6. University of Texas, Austin.

Judge, W. James
    1973   *PaleoIndian occupation of the Rio Grande Valley in New Mexico*. University of New Mexico Press, Albuquerque.
    1981   The Paleo-Indian and Basketmaker periods: An overview and some

research problems. In *The San Juan tomorrow*, edited by Fred Plog and Walter Wait, pp. 5–58. National Park Service, Southwest Region, Santa Fe.

Kaplan, Lawrence
1956   The cultivated bean of the prehistoric Southwest. *Annals of the Missouri Botanical Garden* 43:189–251.
1963   Archaeobotany of Cordova Cave, New Mexico. *Economic Botany* 18:350–59.
1965   Archaeology and domestication in American *Phaseolus. Economic Botany* 19:358–68.
1981   What is the origin of the common bean? *Economic Botany* 35:240–54.

Kelley, J. Charles, T. N. Campbell, and Donald J. Lehmer
1940   *The association of archaeological materials with geological deposits in the Big Bend region of Texas.* West Texas Historical and Scientific Society Publication no. 10. Alpine, Texas.

Kelly, Robert L.
1983   Hunter-gatherer mobility strategies. *Journal of Anthropological Research* 39:277–306.

Kelly, Thomas C.
1963   Archaeological investigations at Roark Cave, Brewster County, Texas. *Bulletin of the Texas Archaeological Society* 33:191–227.

Kelly, Thomas C., and Harvey P. Smith, Jr.
1963   An investigation of archaeological sites in Reagan Canyon, Brewster County, Texas. *Bulletin of the Texas Archaeological Society* 33:167–90.

Kidder, A. V.
1954   Review of *Mogollon cultural change and continuity, the stratigraphic analysis of Tularosa and Cordova caves. American Antiquity* 19:298–300.

King, Frances B.
1987   The evolutionary effects of plant cultivation. In *Emergent horticultural economies of the eastern woodlands*, edited by W. F. Keegan, pp. 51–65. Occasional Paper no. 7. Center for Archaeological Investigations, Southern Illinois University, Carbondale.

Kirch, Patrick V.
1980   The archaeological study of adaptation: theoretical and methodological issues. In *Advances in archaeological method and theory*, vol. 3, edited by Michael B. Schiffer, pp. 101–55. Academic Press, New York.

Kirkby, Anne V. T.
1973   The use of land and water resources in the past and present Valley of Oaxaca, Mexico. Memoirs of the University of Michigan Museum of Anthropology, no. 5. Ann Arbor.

Klein, Jeffrey, J. C. Lerman, P. E. Damon, and E. K. Ralph
1982   Calibration of radiocarbon dates: Tables based on the concensus data of the workshop on calibrating the radiocarbon time scale. *Radiocarbon* 24:103–50.

Knox, J. C.
1983   Responses of river systems to Holocene climates. In *Late Quaternary*

environments of the United States, vol. 2, *The Holocene*, edited by H. E. Wright, pp. 26-41. University of Minnesota Press, Minneapolis.

Lang, Richard W.
1977   *Archaeological survey of the Upper San Cristobal Arroyo drainage, Galisteo Basin, Santa Fe County, New Mexico.* School of American Research, Contract Archaeology Program. Santa Fe.
1980   *Archaeological investigations at a Pueblo agricultural site, and Archaic and Puebloan encampments on the Rio Ojo Caliente, Rio Arriba County, New Mexico.* School of American Research, Contract Archaeology Program. Santa Fe.

Lanner, Ronald M.
1981   *The Piñon: A Natural and Cultural History.* University of Nevada Press, Reno.

Larick, Roy
1985   Spears, style and time among Maa-speaking pastoralists. *Journal of Anthropological Archaeology* 4:206-20.

LeBlanc, Steven A.
1982   The advent of pottery in the Southwest. In *Southwest ceramics: A comparative review*, edited by Albert H. Schroeder, pp. 27-52. Arizona Archaeologist, Phoenix.

Lechtman, Heather
1976   Style in technology: some early thoughts. In *Style, organization and dynamics of technology*, edited by Heather Lechtman and Robert Merrill, pp. 3-20. 1975 Proceedings of the American Ethnological Society. Seattle.

Lee, Richard B.
1979   *The !Kung San: Men, women and work in a foraging society.* Cambridge University Press.

Levine, H. B.
1984   Controlling access: Forms of "territoriality" in three New Zealand crayfishing villages. *Ethnology* 23:89-100.

Libby, Arnold
1955   *Radiocarbon dating.* University of Chicago Press.

Linskey, Patricia K.
1975   Cochise and Mogollon hunting patterns in west-central New Mexico. In *Collected papers in honor of Florence Hawley Ellis*, edited by Theodore R. Frisbie, pp. 246-71. Papers of the Archaeological Society of New Mexico, no. 2. Albuquerque.

Lister, Robert H.
1951a   Two projectile point types from Dinosaur National Monument, Colorado. *Southwest Lore* 17:19-20.
1951b   *Excavations at Hells Midden, Dinosaur National Monument.* University of Colorado Studies, Series in Anthropology no. 3. Boulder.
1953   The stemmed, indented base point, a possible horizon marker. *American Antiquity* 18:265.
1958   *Archaeological excavations in the northern Sierra Madre Occidental, Chihuahua and Sonora, Mexico.* University of Colorado Studies, Series in Anthropology no. 7. Boulder.

Long, Austin, R. I. Ford, D. J. Donahue, A. J. T. Jull, T. W. Linick, L. F. Warneke, and L. J. Toolin
  1986   Age of first cultigens in southwestern U.S. inferred from accelerator mass spectrometric analysis of C-14 on corn, beans and squash. Paper presented at the 51st annual meeting of the Society for American Archaeology, New Orleans.

Long, Austin, and Bruce Rippeteau
  1974   Testing contemporaneity and averaging radiocarbon dates. *American Antiquity* 39:205–15.

Longacre, William A.
  1962   Archaeological reconnaissance in eastern Arizona. In *Chapters in the prehistory of Eastern Arizona*, vol. 1, edited by Paul S. Martin, pp. 148–62. Fieldiana: Anthropology 53. Field Museum of Natural History, Chicago.

Lourandos, Harry
  1980   Change or stability? Hydraulics, hunter-gatherers and population in temperate Australia. *World Archaeology* 11:245–64.

Lowe, John W. G.
  1985   Qualitative systems theory: Its utility and limitations. *Journal of Anthropological Research* 41:42–61.

Lyon, M. W., Jr.
  1907   Mammal remains from two prehistoric village sites in New Mexico and Arizona. *Proceedings of the U.S. National Museum* 21:647–49.

Lyons, Thomas R.
  1969   A study of the Paleo-Indian and Desert Culture complexes of the Estancia Valley area, New Mexico. Ph.D. dissertation, University of New Mexico, Albuquerque.

Mackey, James C.
  1983   The documentation of environmental control of morphological variability in archaeological maize: A paleoenvironmental reconstruction technique. *Plains Anthropologist* 28:209–17.

MacNeish, Richard S.
  1958   *Preliminary archaeological investigations in the Sierra de Tamaulipas, Mexico.* Transactions of the American Philosophical Society 48 (6). Philadephia.
  1964   The food gathering and incipient agriculture stage of prehistoric Middle America. In *Natural environments and early cultures*, edited by R. C. West, pp. 413–26. University of Texas Press, Austin.

Mangelsdorf, Paul C.
  1950   The mystery of corn. *Scientific American* 183:20–29.
  1958   Ancestor of corn. *Science* 128:1313–20.
  1974   *Corn.* Belknap Press, Cambridge, Massachusetts.

Mangelsdorf, Paul C., Herbert W. Dick, and Julian Camara-Hernandez
  1967   Bat Cave revisited. *Botanical Museum Leaflets, Harvard University* 22:1–31.

Mangelsdorf, Paul C., and Robert H. Lister
  1956   Archaeological evidence on the evolution of maize in northwestern Mexico. *Botanical Museum Leaflets, Harvard University* 17:151–78.

Mangelsdorf, Paul C., Richard S. MacNeish, and Walton G. Galinat
1956   Archaeological evidence on the diffusion and evolution of maize in northeastern Mexico. *Botanical Museum Leaflets, Harvard University* 17:125–50.
1964   Domestication of corn. *Science* 143:538–45.
1967   Prehistoric maize, teosinte, and tripsacum from Tamaulipas, Mexico. *Botanical Museum Leaflets, Harvard University* 22:33–52.

Mangelsdorf, Paul C., and C. Earle Smith
1949   New archaeological evidence on evolution in maize. *Botanical Museum Leaflets, Harvard University* 13:213–47.

Markgraf, Vera, J. Platt Bradbury, R. M. Forester, G. Singh, and R. S. Sternberg
1984   San Agustin Plains, New Mexico: Age and paleoenvironmental potential reassessed. *Quaternary Research* 22:336–43.

Marmaduke, William S.
1978   Prehistoric culture in Trans-Pecos Texas: An ecological explanation. Ph.D. dissertation, University of Texas, Austin.

Marroquin, Jorge S.
1977   A physiognomic analysis of the types of transitional vegetation on the eastern parts of the Chihuahuan Desert in Coahuila, Mexico. In *Transactions of the symposium on the biological resources of the Chihuahuan Desert region, United States and Mexico*, edited by Roland H. Wauer and David H. Riskind, pp. 249–72. National Park Service, Washington, D. C.

Martin, Paul S., and Fred Plog
1973   *The archaeology of Arizona.* Natural History Press, New York.

Martin, Paul S., John B. Rinaldo, and Ernst Antevs
1949   *Cochise and Mogollon sites.* Fieldiana: Anthropology 38(1). Field Museum of Natural History, Chicago.

Martin, Paul S., John B. Rinaldo, and Elaine Bluhm
1954   *Caves of the Reserve area.* Fieldiana: Anthropology 42. Field Museum of Natural History, Chicago.

Martin, Paul S., John B. Rinaldo, Elaine Bluhm, H. Cutler, and R. Grange
1952   *Mogollon cultural continuity and change: The stratigraphic analysis of Tularosa and Cordova caves.* Fieldiana: Anthropology 40. Field Museum of Natural History, Chicago.

Martin, Paul S., and James Schoenwetter
1960   Arizona's oldest cornfield. *Science* 132:33–34.

McGuire, Randall H., and Michael B. Schiffer
1983   A theory of architectural design. *Journal of Anthropological Archaeology* 3:277–303.

Minnis, Paul
1985   Domesticating plants and people in the Greater American Southwest. In *Prehistoric food production in North America*, edited by Richard I. Ford, pp. 309–40. Anthropological Papers, no. 75. Museum of Anthropology, University of Michigan, Ann Arbor.

Mohr, Albert, and L. L. Sample
1959   San Jose sites in southeastern Utah. *El Palacio* 66:109–19.

Moore, James A.

1981   The effects of information networks in hunter-gatherer societies. In *Hunter-gatherer foraging strategies*, edited by Bruce Winterhalder and Eric Alden Smith, pp. 194–217. University of Chicago Press.

Moore, James L., and Joseph C. Winter (editors)

1980   *Human adaptations in a marginal environment: The UII Mitigation Project.* Office of Contract Archaeology, University of New Mexico, Albuquerque.

Morris, Earl H., and Robert F. Burgh

1954   *Basketmaker II Sites Near Durango, Colorado.* Publication no. 604. Carnegie Institution of Washington, D. C.

Nance, Roger G.

1972   Cultural evidence for the Altithermal in Texas and Mexico. *Southwest Journal of Anthropology* 28:179–92.

Nelson, Fred

1984   Results of analysis of obsidian artifacts from Bat Cave, Catron County, New Mexico. Report submitted to Musuem of Anthropology, University of Michigan, Ann Arbor.

Nichols, Deborah L., and F. E. Smiley

1984   A summary of prehistoric research on northern Black Mesa. In *Excavations on Black Mesa, 1982: A descriptive report*, edited by Deborah L. Nichols and F. E. Smiley, pp. 87–108. Research Paper no. 39. Center for Archaeological Investigations, Southern Illinois University, Carbondale.

O'Laughlin, Thomas C.

1980   *The Keystone Dam site and other Archaic and Formative sites in northwest El Paso, Texas.* Publications in Anthropology, no. 8. El Paso Centennial Museum, University of Texas, El Paso.

Opler, Morris Edward

1941   *An Apache Life-way.* University of Chicago Press.

Osborn, Alan J.

1977   Strandloopers, mermaids, and other fairy tales: Ecological determinants of marine resource utilization—the Peruvian case. In *For theory building in archaeology*, edited by Lewis R. Binford, pp. 157–206. Academic Press, New York.

Page, Gordon B.

1940   *Hopi agricultural notes.* USDA Soil Conservation Service. Washington, D. C.

Parry, William J.

1980   The use of edge morphology and other attributes in functional classification of chipped stone tools. Paper presented at the 45th annual meeting of the Society for American Archaeology, Philadelphia.

Parry, William J., Galen R. Burgett, and F. E. Smiley

1985   The Archaic occupation of Black Mesa, Arizona. Paper presented at the 50th annual meeting of the Society for American Archaeology, Denver.

Pianka, Eric R.
  1978   *Evolutionary ecology*. Harper and Row, New York.

Plog, Stephen
  1980   *Stylistic variation in prehistoric ceramics*. Cambridge University Press.
  1983   Analysis of style in artifacts. *Annual Review of Anthropology* 12:125–42.

Powers, William E.
  1939   Basin and shore features of extinct Lake San Augustin, New Mexico. *Journal of Geomorphology* 2:207–17.

Pryor, Frederic L.
  1986   The adoption of agriculture: Some theoretical and empirical evidence. *American Anthropologist* 88:879–97.

Quimby, George I.
  1949   Excavations. In *Cochise and Mogollon Sites: Pine Lawn Valley, Western New Mexico*, edited by Paul S. Martin, John B. Rinaldo, and Ernst Antevs, pp. 26–33. Fieldiana: Anthropology 38(1). Field Museum of Natural History, Chicago.

Ralph, E. K., H. N. Michael, and M. C. Han
  1973   Radiocarbon dates and reality. *MASCA Newsletter* 9:1–20.

Reher, Charles A., and Daniel C. Witter
  1977   Archaic settlement and vegetative diversity. In *Settlement and subsistence along the lower Chaco River*, edited by Charles A. Reher, pp. 113–26. University of New Mexico Press, Albuquerque.

Reinhart, Theodore R.
  1967   The Rio Rancho Phase: A preliminary report on early Basketmaker culture in the middle Rio Grande Valley, New Mexico. *American Antiquity* 32:458–70.
  1968   Late Archaic cultures of the middle Rio Grande Valley, New Mexico. Ph.D. dissertation, University of New Mexico.

Renaud, E. B.
  1942   *Reconnaissance work in the upper Rio Grande Valley, Colorado and New Mexico*. University of Denver Archaeological Series, no. 3.

Reynolds, Robert G.
  1981   An adaptive computer simulation model of the acquisition of incipient agriculture in prehistoric Oaxaca, Mexico. Paper presented at the tenth Congress of the IUPPS, Mexico City.
  1986   An adaptive computer model for the evolution of plant collecting and early agriculture in the eastern Valley of Oaxaca. In *Guila Naquitz: Archaic foraging and early agriculture in Oaxaca, Mexico*, edited by Kent V. Flannery, pp. 439–500. Academic Press, New York.

Reynolds, Robert G., and B. P. Zeigler
  1979   A formal mathematical model for the operation of consensus-based hunting and gathering bands. In *Transformations: Mathematical approaches to culture change*, edited by Colin C. Renfrew and K. Cooke, pp. 405–18. Academic Press, New York.

Rick, John W.
1987   Dates as data: An examination of the Peruvian preceramic radiocarbon record. *American Antiquity* 52:55–73.

Riechert, Susan E., and Peter Hammerstein
1983   Game theory in the ecological context. *Annual Review of Ecological Systematics* 14:377–409.

Rindos, David
1980   Symbiosis, instability and the origins and spread of agriculture. *Current Anthropology* 21:751–72.
1984   *The origins of agriculture*. Academic Press, New York.

Roosa, William B.
1956   Preliminary report on the Lucy site. *El Palacio* 63:36–49.
1967   Data on early sites in central New Mexico and Michigan. Ph.D. dissertation, University of Michigan, Ann Arbor.

Rowley-Conwy, Peter
1984   The laziness of the short-distance hunter: The origins of agriculture in western Denmark. *Journal of Anthropological Archaeology* 3:300–324.

Sackett, James
1982   Approaches to style in lithic archaeology. *Journal of Anthropological Archaeology* 1:59–112.
1986   Isochrestism and style: A clarification. *Journal of Anthropological Archaeology* 5:266–77.

Sahlins, Marshall D.
1972   *Stone age economics*. Aldine Press, Chicago.

Salwen, Bert
1960   The introduction of leather footgear in the Pueblo area. *Ethnohistory* 7:206–38.

Sauer, Carl O.
1952   *Agricultural origins and dispersals*. Bowman Memorial Lectures, Series 2. American Geographic Society, New York.

Saxe, Arthur
1970   Social dimensions of mortuary practices. Ph.D. dissertation, University of Michigan, Ann Arbor.

Sayles, E. B.
1945   The San Simon branch. Excavations at Cave Creek and in the San Simon Valley. *Medallion Papers* 34. Gila Pueblo, Globe, Arizona.
1983   *The Cochise cultural sequence in southeastern Arizona*. Anthropological Papers of the University of Arizona, no. 42. Tucson.

Sayles, E. B., and Ernst Antevs
1941   *The Cochise Culture*. Medallion Papers no. 29. Gila Pueblo, Globe, Arizona.

Schaafsma, Curtis
1979   Archaeological studies in the Abiquiu Reservoir district. *Discovery* pp. 1–29, School of American Research, Santa Fe.

Schacht, Robert M.
1980   Two models of population growth. *American Anthropologist* 82:782–98.

Schiffer, Michael
1976   *Behavioral archeology.* Academic Press, New York.
1983   Toward the identification of formation processes. *American Antiquity* 48:675–706.
1986   Radiocarbon dates and the "old wood" problem: The case of the Hohokam chronology. *Journal of Archaeological Science* 13:13–30.

Schroeder, Albert H.
1965   Unregulated diffusion from Mexico to the Southwest prior to A.D. 700. *American Antiquity* 30:297–309.

Schuetz, Mardith K.
1956   An analysis of Val Verde County cave material. *Bulletin of the Texas Archaeological Society* 27:129–60.

Scott, Linda
1985   Pollen analysis at Sisyphus Shelter. In *Sisyphus Shelter,* edited by John Gooding and William L. Shields, pp. 165–188. Cultural Resources Series, no. 18. Bureau of Land Management, Denver.

Shafer, Harry J.
1977   Art and territoriality in the lower Pecos Archaic. *Plains Anthropologist* 22:13–22.

Simmons, Alan H.
1984   *Archaic prehistory and paleoenvironments in the San Juan Basin, New Mexico: The Chaco Shelters Project.* University of Kansas Museum of Anthropology Project Report Series, no. 53. Lawrence.
1986   New evidence for the early use of cultigens in the American Southwest. *American Antiquity* 51:73–88.

Sinopoli, Carla M.
1985   Style in arrows: A study of an ethnographic collection from the western United States. Ms. on file at the Museum of Anthropology, University of Michigan, Ann Arbor.

Slobodkin, L. B.
1968   Toward a predictive theory of evolution. In *Population biology and evolution,* edited by Richard C. Lewontin, pp. 187–205. Syracuse University Press.
1977   Evolution is no help. *World Archaeology* 8:332–43.

Smiley, F. E.
1985   Chronometrics and early agricultural adaptations in northeastern Arizona: Approaches to the interpretations of radiocarbon dates. Ph.D. dissertation, University of Michigan, Ann Arbor.

Smith, Bruce D.
1985   The role of *Chenopodium* as a domesticate in pre-maize garden systems of the eastern United States. *Southeastern Archaeology* 4:51–72.
1987   The independent domestication of indigenous seed-bearing plants in eastern North America. In *Emergent horticultural economies of the eastern woodlands,* edited by W. F. Keegan, pp. 3–48. Occasional Paper no. 7. Center for Archaeological Investigations, Southern Illinois University, Carbondale.

Smith, C. Earle
　1950　Prehistoric plant remains from Bat Cave. *Botanical Museum Leaflets, Harvard University* 14:157–80.

Smith, Eric A.
　1983　Optimal foraging theory in anthropology: A critical review. *Current Anthropology* 24:625–652.

Speth, John D., and Gregory A. Johnson
　1977　Problems in the use of correlation for the investigation of tool kits and activity areas. In *For the director: Essays in honor of James B. Griffin*, edited by G. B. Quimby, pp. 35–57. Academic Press, New York.

Speth, John D., and Katherine A. Spielmann
　1982　Energy source, protein metabolism and hunter-gatherer subsistence strategies. *Journal of Anthropological Archaeology* 2:1–31.

Stearns, Thomas B.
　1981　Palynological evidence of the prehistoric effective environment. In *High altitude adaptations along Redondo Creek: The Baca Geothermal Project*, edited by Craig Baker and Joseph C. Winter, pp. 25–40. Office of Contract Archaeology, University of New Mexico. Albuquerque.

Steward, Julian
　1938　*Basin-plateau aboriginal sociopolitical groups*. Bureau of American Ethnology Bulletin no. 120. Washington, D. C.

Stuiver, Minze, and Gordon W. Pearson
　1986　High precision calibration of the radiocarbon time scale, A.D. 1950–5000 B.C. *Radiocarbon* 28:805–38.

Stuiver, Minze, and Henry A. Polach
　1977　Reporting of C-14 data. *Radiocarbon* 19:355–63.

Stuiver, Minze, and Paula J. Reimer
　1986　A computer program for radiocarbon age calibration. *Radiocarbon* 28:1022–30.

Suess, Hans E.
　1980　The radiocarbon record in tree rings of the last 8000 years. *Radiocarbon* 22:200–209.

Suhm, Dee Ann, and Edward B. Jelks
　1962　*Handbook of Texas archeology: Type descriptions*. Texas Archeological Society and Texas Memorial Museum, Austin.

Taylor, Walter W.
　1956　Some implications of the carbon-14 dates from a cave in Coahuila, Mexico. *Bulletin of the Texas Archaeological Society* 27:215–34.

Thomas, David Hurst
　1973　An empirical test for Steward's model of Great Basin settlement patterns. *American Antiquity* 38:155–76.
　1978　Arrowheads and atlatl darts: How the stones got the shaft. *American Antiquity* 43:461–72.
　1981　How to classify the projectile points from Monitor Valley, Nevada. *Journal of California and Great Basin Anthropology* 3:7–43.

Thoms, Alston Vern
    1977   A preliminary projectile point typology for the southern portion of the northern Rio Grande. M.A. thesis, Texas Tech University, Lubbock.

Toll, H. Wolcott, Mollie S. Toll, Marcia L. Newren, and William B. Gillespie
    1986   Experimental corn plots in Chaco Canyon: The life and hard time of *Zea mays L*. In *Environment and subsistence of Chaco Canyon*, edited by F. Joan Mathien, pp. 79–134. Publications in Archaeology 18E. National Park Service, Albuquerque.

Upham, Steadman, Richard S. MacNeish, Walton Galinat, and Christopher M. Stevenson
    1987   Evidence concerning the origin of maiz de ocho. *American Anthropologist* 89:410–19.

van der Leeuw, S. E.
    1981   Information flows, flow structures and the explanation of change in human institutions. In *Archaeological approaches to the study of complexity*, edited by S. E. van der Leeuw, pp. 229–312. Universiteit van Amsterdam.

Van Devender, Thomas R.
    1977   Holocene woodlands in the southwestern deserts. *Science* 198:189–92.

Van Devender, Thomas R., Julio Betancourt, and Mark Wimberly
    1984   Biogeographic implications of a packrat midden sequence from the Sacramento Mountains, south-central New Mexico. *Quaternary Research* 22:344–60.

Van Devender, Thomas R., and W. Geoffrey Spaulding
    1979   Development of vegetation and climate in the southwestern United States. *Science* 204:701–10.

Vierra, Bradley J.
    1980   A summary and comparison of excavated Archaic and Anasazi sites. In *Human adaptations in a marginal environment: The UII Mitigation Project*, edited by James L. Moore and Joseph C. Winter, pp. 382–86. Office of Contract Archaeology, University of New Mexico, Albuquerque.

Vivian, R. Gwinn
    1970   An Apache site on Ranch Creek, southeast Arizona. *The Kiva* 35:125–30.

Vogler, Lawrence E., Dennis Gilpin, and Joseph K. Anderson
    1983   *Cultural resource investigations on Gallegos Mesa: Excavations in Blocks VIII and IX, and testing operations in Blocks X and XI, Navajo Indian Irrigation Project, San Juan County, New Mexico*. Navajo Nation Papers in Anthropology, no. 24. Window Rock, Arizona.

Waber, Sue B., Lyndi A. Hubbell, and Nancy E. Wood
    1982   LA 12566, an Archaic site. In *Bandelier: Excavations in the flood pool of Cochiti Lake, New Mexico*, edited by Lyndi Hubbell and Diane Traylor, pp. 313–55. National Park Service, Santa Fe.

Wait, Walter K.
    1983   A preliminary model for the preceramic at Star Lake. In *The Star Lake Archaeological Project: Anthropology of a headwaters area of Chaco Wash, New*

Mexico, edited by Walter K. Wait and Ben A. Nelson, pp. 131–52. Southern Illinois University Press, Carbondale and Edwardsville.

Waltz, Edward C.
1982   Resource characteristics and the evolution of information centers. *American Naturalist* 119:73–90.

Waterbolk, H. T.
1971   Working with radiocarbon dates. *Proceedings of the Prehistoric Society* 37:15–33.

Weatherwax, Paul
1950   The history of corn. *Scientific Monthly* 71:50–60.

Weber, Robert
1980   Geology of the Ake site. In *The Ake site: Collection and excavation of LA13423, Catron County, New Mexico*, edited by Patrick H. Beckett, pp. 223–38. Cultural Resources Management Division Report 357. New Mexico State University, Las Cruces.

Weltfish, Gene
1965   *The Lost Universe*. University of Nebraska Press, Lincoln.

Wendorf, Fred
1953   Archaeological studies in the Petrified Forest National Monument. Museum of Northern Arizona Bulletin no. 27. Flagstaff.

Wendorf, Fred, and Tully H. Thomas
1951   Early man sites near Concho, Arizona. *American Antiquity* 17:107–14.

Whalen, Norman M.
1973   Agriculture and the Cochise. *The Kiva* 39:89–96.

White, Theodore E.
1953   Observations on the butchering technique of some aboriginal peoples, no. 2. *American Antiquity* 19:396–98.

Wiessner, Polly
1982a   Beyond willow smoke and dogs' tails: A comment on Binford's analysis of hunter-gatherer settlement systems. *American Antiquity* 47:171–77.
1982b   Risk, reciprocity and social influences on !Kung San economics. In *Politics and history in band societies*, edited by Eleanor Leacock and Richard Lee, pp. 61–84. Cambridge University Press.
1984   Reconsidering the behavioral basis for style: A case study among the Kalahari San. *Journal of Anthropological Archaeology* 3:190–234.

Wills, Wirt H.
1985   Early agriculture in the Mogollon Highlands of New Mexico. Ph.D. dissertation, University of Michigan, Ann Arbor.

Wills, Wirt H., Richard I. Ford, and John D. Speth
1984   Preliminary report of the University of Michigan investigations at Bat Cave (LA 4935). Ms. on file at the Bureau of Land Management, Socorro, New Mexico.

Wills, Wirt H., and Oliver M. Lee
1984   The Lee site. Manuscript on file at the University of New Mexico, Albuquerque.

Wilmsen, Edwin N.
1973   Interaction, spacing and the organization of hunting bands. *Journal of Anthropological Research* 29:1–31.

Windmiller, Ric
1973   The late Cochise Culture in the Sulphur Spring Valley, southeastern Arizona: Archaeology of the Fairchild site. *The Kiva* 39:131–69.

Winterhalder, Bruce, and Eric Alden Smith
1982   *Hunter-gatherer foraging strategies: Ethnographic and archeological analyses.* University of Chicago Press.

Wobst, H. Martin
1974   Boundary conditions for Paleolithic social systems: A simulation approach. *American Antiquity* 38:147–78.
1976   Locational relationships in Paleolithic society. *Journal of Human Evolution* 5:49–58.
1977   Stylistic behavior and information exchange. In *For the director: Research essays in honor of James B. Griffin*, edited by Charles L. Cleland, pp. 317–47. University of Michigan Museum of Anthropology Papers in Anthropology, no. 61. Ann Arbor.
1981   Paleolithic archaeology: Some problems with form, time and space. In *Hunter-gatherer economy in prehistory*, edited by Geoff Bailey, pp. 220–25. Cambridge University Press.

Woodbury, Richard B., and Ezra B. W. Zubrow
1979   Agricultural beginnings, 2000 B.C.–A.D. 500. In *Handbook of North American Indians*, vol. 9, *Southwest*, edited by Alfonso Ortiz, pp. 43–60. Smithsonian Institution, Washington, D. C.

Worman, Fredrick C. V.
1953   A report on a cache of obsidian artifacts from the Pajarito Plateau. *El Palacio* 60:12–15.

Yellen, John E.
1977   *Archaeological approaches to the present: Models for reconstructing the past.* Academic Press, New York.

Yengoyan, Aram A.
1972   Ritual and exchange in aboriginal Australia: An adaptive interpretation of male initiation rites. In *Social exchange and interaction*, edited by Edwin N. Wilmsen, pp. 5–10. Anthropological Papers no. 46. Museum of Anthropology, University of Michigan, Ann Arbor.
1976   Structure, event and ecology in aboriginal Australia: A comparative viewpoint. In *Tribes and boundaries in Australia*, edited by Nicolas Peterson, pp. 121–32. Social Anthropology Series, no. 10. Australian Institute of Aboriginal Studies, Canberra.

Zukas, Jonas A., T. Nicholas, H. F. Swift, L. G. Greszczuk, and D. R. Curran
1982   *Impact dynamics.* John Wiley & Sons, New York.

Zvelebil, Marek
1981   *From forager to farmer in the boreal zone: Reconstructing economic patterns through catchment analysis in prehistoric Finland.* British Archaeological Reports, International Series 115(i).

Index

Chihuahuan Desert, 51, 54, 150
Chipped stone artifacts, distribution of, 97
Chiricahua–Amargosa II, 13, 26
Chiricahua projectile points, 18, 22, 23; measurement of, 21, 22; outlines of, 19
Chiricahua stage, 14–15, 17, 24, 25, 26; description of, 12–13; grinding stones of, 16
Chronologies. *See* Radiocarbon chronologies
Cienega Creek, 10, 69, 85; agriculture at, 101, 140–41; cremations at, 140–41; description of, 26, 137–38, 140–41; maize at, 12, 138, 140; occupation of, 138; patterning at, 141; schematic profile of, 138, 139
Cienega Creek projectile points, 85
Cloth, fragments of, 134
Cobs, 113, 117, 128, 129, 131, 132, 134, 136, 152; measuring, 126, 127
Cochise Culture, 9, 14–15, 17, 25–29; agriculture of, 10–11; boundaries of, 10; chart about, 9; description of, 8; ground stones of, 17; model of, 27–29; projectile points of, 18; stages of, 12–13
Cochise stage, 13, 16, 24
Cody projectile points, 94
Colonization, agriculture and, 5
Competition, 47, 72, 144; stress and, 74
Cordage, 123, 129
Cordilleran ice mass, 51
Cordova Cave, 10, 27, 85, 87, 136, 137; agriculture at, 101; description of, 26–27, 133–35; lithic artifacts at, 131; plant remains from, 134, 135; pottery at, 133; stone tools at, 134
Cordova Creek, 135
Corn, 125, 135; storage of, 39. *See also* Maize
Corridor model, 3–4, 11; variations on, 4–5
Cremations, 140–41. *See also* Burials
Cultigens, 125–28; adoption of, 101, 121, 143; transfer of, 146–49, 154. *See also* Agriculture; Cultivation; Domesticated plants
Cultivars. *See* Agriculture; Cultigens; Cultivation; Domesticated plants
Cultivation, 38, 40–41, 41n.3; definition of, 32; timing of, 41; tools for, 119–20. *See also* Agriculture; Cultigens; Domesticated plants
Cultural boundaries, 28; perceptions about, 10
Cultural changes, 102; environmental changes and, 155; models of, 9
Culture–historical models: dropping, 155; significance of, 7
Culture–historical periods, projectile points and, 75
Culture history, 7, 154–55

Cumulative frequency distribution, 62, 64
Cutting, tools for, 120

Damp Cave, 24
Dating, 11, 61, 117, 118; chronometric, 58; radiocarbon, 58n.1, 59, 60, 62, 63, 64, 104, 108–11, 119, 125, 129, 138; reliability of, 59
Debitage, 96, 121; lithic, 113
Density. *See* Population density
Density dependence, 5–6, 35–36, 44–45, 47, 71, 72, 74, 144, 147–48
Desert Culture, 8, 15
Devil's Mouth, 24
Distributions, 37, 59, 62, 146–48, 154
Domesticated plants, 5, 6, 31–33, 36–37; adoption of, 2, 3, 10, 31, 36, 47, 49, 50, 154, 155; cultivation of, 1, 40, 45, 146; dating, 7–8; population density and, 148, 149; predictability of, 33, 143; social distance and, 46; storage of, 38–39, 43; transfer of, 150, 154. *See also* Agriculture; Cultigens; Cultivation
Domesticates. *See* Domesticated plants
Dormancy, 38–39
Dust bowl, 56

Early Archaic, 66, 67, 76, 77, 78, 88, 89, 144
Early Holocene, 53, 66, 92, 96
Environmental boundaries, changes in, 57
Environmental changes, 49–50, 51–58, 69, 71; cultural changes and, 155; hunter-gatherer economies and, 54–55; population density and, 34–35; reduction of, 47; structural changes and, 50
Estancia Basin, 52, 54, 66
"Ethnicity," regional, 28

Faunal remains, 123, 131
Field Museum of Natural History, 16, 18, 19, 21, 26, 131, 135
Flaco phase, 152
Folsom projectile points, 94, 96
Food production strategies, dispersal of, 1–2
Food resources, 92–94; stress on, 5. *See also* Density dependence
Foraging, 1, 42, 43, 44, 55, 56, 67, 144, 145, 147, 149
Franklin Mountains, 68
Fresnal Shelter, 153
Fruits, collecting, 92, 94